O9-BTJ-624

$7—
8/23
COOk

To William & Arthur —
I hope this book brings
back wonderful memories of your childhood
and your grandfather. I also hope you learn
about a few new cheesemakers, and that you
smile and say American cheese!

Warm wishes

July 2002

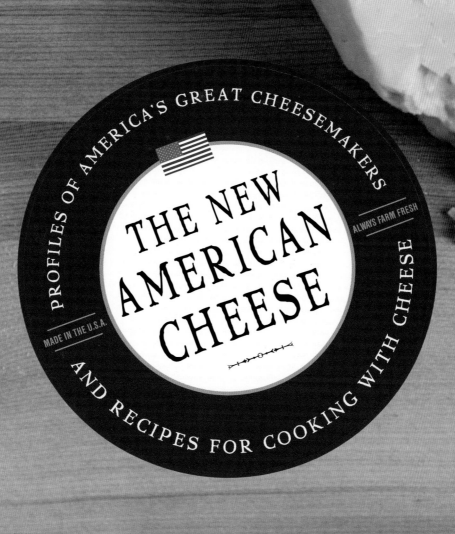

PROFILES OF AMERICA'S GREAT CHEESEMAKERS

ALWAYS FARM FRESH

THE NEW AMERICAN CHEESE

MADE IN THE U.S.A.

AND RECIPES FOR COOKING WITH CHEESE

LAURA WERLIN

PHOTOGRAPHS BY MARTIN JACOBS
FOREWORD BY STEVEN JENKINS

Stewart, Tabori & Chang
New York

To Artie,

whose patience and love soared during
times when both were the most difficult to give.

⊱────◦────⊰

PAGE 1: Cypress Grove Chèvre (California).
FRONTISPIECE: Cheeses from California to Vermont. Clockwise from top:
Old Chatham Sheepherding Company Camembert (New York), Maytag Blue Cheese (Iowa),
Vermont Shepherd (Vermont), Vella Dry Jack (California), and (center), Capriole Wabash
Cannonball (Indiana). Far right: Belgioioso Provolone (Wisconsin)

⊱────◦────⊰

Text and recipes copyright © 2000 Laura Werlin
Photographs copyright © 2000 Martin Jacobs

EDITED BY Julie Stillman
DESIGNED BY Nina Barnett
PRODUCTION BY Kim Tyner

All rights reserved. No portion of this book may be reproduced, stored in a retrieval system,
or transmitted in any form or by any means, mechanical, electronic, photocopying, recording,
or otherwise, without written permission from the publisher.

Published in 2000 by
Stewart, Tabori & Chang
A division of Harry N. Abrams, Inc.
115 West 18th Street
New York, NY 10011

Library of Congress Cataloging-in-Publication Data
Werlin, Laura.
The new American cheese: profiles of America's great cheesemakers and recipes for cooking with cheese/
by Laura Werlin; photographs by Martin Jacobs; foreword by Steven Jenkins.
p. cm.
Includes bibliographical references and index.
ISBN: 1-55670-990-0
1. Cheese—United States. 2. Cheese—Varieties—United States. 3. Cheesemakers—United States.
4. Cookery (Cheese). I. Title.

SF274.U6W47 2000
641.3'73'0973—dc21   99-052588

Printed in Italy

10 9 8 7 6 5 4 3 2

CONTENTS

CHEESE HISTORY, CHEESEMAKERS, RECIPES, AND MORE

FOREWORD

IN 1986 I WROTE A FIVE THOUSAND-WORD ESSAY for the quarterly *Journal of Gastronomy*, the organ of the American Institute of Wine & Food. The piece was about how proud we all should be that there were a few good cheeses being made in America by nice, hard-working people. I wrote furiously, hoping to come off as serious, yet friendly. I don't remember if they paid me anything or not. They should have—it was a damned good article. Nor do I recall getting any congratulatory phone calls for my keen observations on the state of American cheesemaking.

Yet even with the support of the leading lights of the food and wine industries, it took at least another decade for American cheeses and cheesemaking artisans to get some real attention, not to mention some egregiously tardy respect.

There is a palpable difference between the American artisanal cheeses of thirteen years ago and those we celebrate today. Back then, there was a limited selection in terms of the types of cheese available. Washed-rind cheeses, as typified by Munster d'Alsace, simply did not exist here. These excruciatingly delicious cheeses have now begun to emerge. Aged goat cheeses were unheard of then; today Americans can exult in numerous examples of fine aged chèvre. Sheep's milk cheeses? Impossible then, all the rage now. The American artisanal cheeses I sell now are more than a match for any of their closest European counterparts.

The American artisanal cheese collections at the two Fairway markets in Manhattan where I work have tripled or quadrupled since then. What we American cheesemongers worked so hard to accomplish has been realized: American artisanal cheeses have assumed the starring and dominant role in most of America's finest cheese shops. And scads of other specialty stores, supermarkets, and restaurant menus now feature serious American cheeses. Nationally distributed mainstream magazines and big city newspapers have contributed mightily to the interest in and ensuing popularity of American artisanal cheesemaking. And you hold in your hands the first book to take an in-depth look at the art and craft of cheesemaking in America. It's a reference, it's a cookbook, it's a coffee table book—it's all three! We've come a long way. Who would have ever thought that in the land where the vast majority sees cheese as rectangular blocks of solidified floor wax, America's own cheese was destined to become a foodstuff as proud and exalted as any other?

But it bothers me that cheese has suddenly become hip. We Americans lurch from one silly fashion to the next, never pausing long enough to savor the flavor (literally) of the moment. Our attention span is too short. I wish I could figure out how to slow the passage of these days, restrain the magazine editors, chefs, and fashionistas, clap hands on their shoulders and say, "Wait a minute! Cheese is timeless! It has been with us longer than recorded history! It is not something to be trifled with, to be abruptly awarded legitimacy!" We need to realize that cheese is peasant food, the antithesis of the notion of "gourmet." Artisanal cheese is simplicity, rusticity, and straightforwardness incarnate—the purest and most powerful link humanity has to God or the supernatural, whichever you prefer. If neither, then consider the sheer romance of cheese—the silent courtship and constantly renewable issue of weather, soil, herbage, beast, milk, and human. American cheeses have risen, finally taking their rightful place in the realm of gastronomy.

As I ranted on about in that journal article thirteen years ago, what we *don't* need from new American artisanal cheesemakers is bland, boring cheese, cheese with added flavorings and phony, European-sounding names. Nor do we need cheese made from milk that has been pasteurized into a Casper the Friendly Ghost Substance. Nonetheless, Codex Alimentarius, an arm of the World Health Organization, is attempting to ban all raw milk cheeses because of so-called health reasons. This is in spite of the fact that virtually every illness related to the consumption of cheese—not just in America but in Europe as well—has been blamed on raw milk, yet ultimately has been traced directly to cheese made from pasteurized milk. The reality is, there are good bacteria and bad bacteria. The good bacteria help turn milk into cheese and contribute greatly to the complexity and memorability of a cheese's flavor. The bad bacteria rarely survive in raw milk, and can actually thrive in pasteurized milk where there is no other bacterial competition.

The American Cheese society is mounting an effort to confront this lunacy. For good reason. Artisanal cheese is made by people, by hand, using the traditional tools and the old recipes. Artisanal cheesemaking facilities are immaculate. Cheese factories often are not. The world's great cheeses have always been made from raw milk. No one is dying from them. No one is getting sick from them. They are the healthiest, most delicious, and most nearly perfect foodstuff that exists. With the explosion of artisanal cheeses, it would be a travesty to decimate this national treasure, not to mention put talented American cheesemakers out of business.

American cheese is catching on like wildfire. Why stop its progress? Today in America, we have such a wealth to choose from: Judy Schad's astonishing Capriole cheeses from Indiana, Mary Keehn's equally stunning Cypress Grove cheeses from northern California, Franklin Peluso's startlingly unique Teleme, also from California (I put the Teleme away for at least a month), Scott Fletcher's masterly Grafton Vermont Cheddar.

I've been giving cheese tasting lectures for years. These sessions are well attended, there's a lot of give-and-take, and I defy you to describe anything that's more fun. Whenever I suspect that a forthcoming tasting lecture might receive special scrutiny, I make it an American event, and am always amazed at how boffo it turns out. I can easily serve a dozen American artisanal cheeses varying in texture and flavor intensity from pudding-soft to rock-hard, and from a gentle caress to a slap across the face. The hard part is making choices. Alas, the life of a curator.

Now let Laura Werlin be your guide to American cheese. She has sought out an amazing collection of the people and products that are the light of American artisanal cheesemaking today.

Steven Jenkins

ACKNOWLEDGMENTS

IN ITS INFANCY, A BOOK IN ITS FINISHED FORM is barely conceivable. It is raw, undeveloped, a germ of a concept, and it feels as though it will take a large dose of magic to transform that concept into pages that are replete with information, interest, and intrigue. What a task. Yet it is that very challenge and the inherent desire to bring a particular idea forward that propel an author toward completion. But desire is not the only fuel that thrusts an author ahead. It is also other people. Indeed, no author works alone, no matter how it feels at times. For that reason, I wish to thank the following people for giving of themselves in countless ways to help channel the passion behind this idea. They made the telling of this story more valuable, insightful, and interesting than I could ever have done on my own.

First, my sincere thanks to my agent and friend, Carole Bidnick, whose unyielding support, persistence, and sheer exuberance brought this project to life. To my editor, Julie Stillman, who remained a safe port in the middle of the deadline frenzy and whose advice was sound and thoughtful. To Leslie Stoker, president and publisher of Stewart, Tabori & Chang, who believed in this project and who, with all of her own pressures, always had the grace to withhold her worries, focusing instead on mine. And to my photographer, Martin Jacobs, who attacked this project with the enthusiasm of a first-timer but with the wisdom of an experienced artist.

To the cheesemakers who graciously gave of their time and who allowed me to impose on them while they tended to their art, I thank you: the Callahan family—Cindy, Liam, Diana, and Brett—of Bellwether Farms; Jennifer Bice of Redwood Hill Farms; Scott Fletcher of Grafton Village Cheese Company; and Sue Conley, Peggy Smith, and Kate Arding of Cowgirl Creamery and Tomales Bay Foods.

A special note of gratitude for Steven Schack of Redwood Hill Farms, who succumbed to cancer shortly before the completion of this book. He was the very first person to invite me into his cheesemaking world, and I will always be grateful.

My sincere thanks to Laura Jacobs-Welch, who keeps the American Cheese Society together, and former American Cheese Society president Dan Strongin who spent hours systematically illuminating me on all things that are cheese. My heartfelt appreciation goes to Debra Dickerson, Kathleen Shannon Finn, and Andrea London for sharing their expertise, and to Nancy Fletcher of the California Milk Advisory Board and Lisa Henry, Jennifer Plant, and Ann Cheney of Torme and Company, who were integral to this book by offering specific information or guidance toward that information. Thanks also to Patrick Geoghegan and Marilyn Wilkinson of the Wisconsin Milk Marketing Board for their assistance.

My deepest gratitude to Dr. George Haenlein for his patient explanations and feedback on the information in the nutrition chapter as well as to Ann Coulston, research dietitian, Dr. Marcia Pelchat of the Monell Chemical Senses Center in Pennsylvania, and Dr. William Wendorff of the University of Wisconsin.

Several retailers were exceptionally valuable to this process: David Zaft of The Pasta Shop in Oakland, California, Jesse Schwartzburg and Matt Rubiner of Formaggio Kitchen in Cambridge, Massachusetts, and David Levine, cheese and charcûterie manager at Dean & Deluca in the Napa Valley, who allowed me to work with him behind the cheese counter and listen to the customers' questions about cheese. That experience proved critical to answering those questions within these pages. Thanks also to Alison Leber and Karin Collins, owners of Brie & Bordeaux in Seattle, who helped me sort through the many cheese and wine pairing possibilities to eventually come to my own conclusions, and to Ari Weinzweig of Zingerman's Deli in Ann Arbor, Michigan.

My profound appreciation to Antonia Allegra, whose innate compassion and education of fledgling food writers led me beyond my fears and into this book; Roberta Klugman, who gives resourcefulness new meaning and whose willingness to share her information and ideas breaks the bounds of kindness; and Flo Braker who took me by the hand and led me into her food world, even when it meant leaving my world of television news. No longer could I be a source of the news anchor gossip that Flo so enjoyed.

Finally, the love and assistance of friends and family were no less important to this book than the information itself. My deepest thanks go to Lori Lyn Narlock, whose encouragement and belief in this project often surpassed my own; Karen Martin, friend and writer, whose own struggle with words on a page never prevented her from helping me with mine; Cheryl Gould, who took the task of recipe testing to new heights by evaluating the dishes in such detail that I remain incredulous that she could maintain a life aside from cooking; Dana Whitaker, and her son, Jack, who jogged alongside me in the early morning cold and patiently listened to endless accounts of this book's progression; and Suzy Sharp, gardener, chef, and friend, whose feedback and love of food permeate these pages.

The rest of my family could easily be listed as co-authors. My sister, Andrea, was not only helpful with recipe testing but remained a willing contributor and a steady force in shaping this book. Her understated and devoted way sustained me here and everywhere.

I thank my father, who instilled in me a true love of words early in life. His devotion to painstakingly crafting sentences often seemed arduous, but the results were unfailingly impressive. I now appreciate that devotion more than ever, and I strive daily to match his talent as a wordsmith. I also thank him for giving more worthwhile computer help than any manual ever could.

For my mother, whose love and knowledge of history made her a better research assistant than any author—or daughter—could hope for. So, too, did her phone skills and now-stellar Internet abilities, which yielded crucial information. Her enthusiasm for recipe testing was inspirational; her exuberance in sharing many of these finished dishes with her friends was the ultimate in motherly endorsement; and her unconditional love and support allowed me to see that all things are possible.

And to my husband, Artie Berliner, whose gentle encouragement, strength, and love provided the foundation that would transform an idea into this project. He endured dinners that consisted of several courses all containing cheese, refrigerator shelves packed so high that one false move meant a tumble of cheeses on the floor, and living with someone whose conversational skills were suddenly limited to the subject of this book. His ability to be my pillar with no exchange of words, only with his very being, was an outcome of this project I could have never presumed. I am lucky to have discovered yet another treasure in a man who is full of them.

INTRODUCTION

⊷⊶⊷⊶◦⊷⊶⊷⊶

I HAVE ALWAYS LOVED CHEESE. I even used to dream about it. Visions of melted cheese would keep me warm at night, lending comfort in a way that no ordinary blanket could. When my grandmother made her eggplant Parmesan, I would dig my way through the tomato sauce, push it aside, and grab a forkful of melted mozzarella along with some of the fried and breaded exterior of the eggplant. It was my own version of fried cheese, and it fulfilled every cheese fantasy I might ever have had.

Later I went off to college and probably became the only student in dormitory history to request recipes from the cooking staff. The Sunday morning cheese strudel was the one thing that could lure me out of my bunk bed onto the cold, hard floor and outside into the foggy morning. Stumbling to the dining hall, I had visions of oozing cheese mixed with fresh lemon juice, encased in pillows of sweet dough. That recipe made it to my mother's kitchen, where she joyfully reduced the size from five hundred servings to four.

I have discovered that I am not alone in my passion for cheese. The American Dairy Association conducted a survey that asked Americans about their number-one food craving. The answer: cheese (chocolate was second). Combine this with the fact that Americans have increased their annual cheese consumption from about twenty-six pounds in 1996 to over thirty pounds in 1998, and a pattern begins to emerge. A growing percentage of that cheese consumption consists of specialty and handcrafted cheeses, often made at small farms throughout the United States. Americans are now recognizing the exceptional craftsmanship and flavor of these cheeses.

When I first told people I was writing a book about American cheese, I met with considerable skepticism. From the less cynical, the reaction was a heartfelt "Why?" I welcomed such responses because they gave me a chance to expound on the extraordinary advancements that have been made in cheesemaking in the United States in just the past few years.

Cheese made in this country now has as much flavor, depth, complexity, and pure artistry as any cheese made in parts of the world where the traditions are hundreds of years old. Our cheesemakers are relatively new to the craft, but they have been hard at work building a specialty that is on the verge of becoming the next great food revolution in America. Additionally, Americans' increased interest in artisanal and specialty cheeses parallels our growing desire to learn more about both the sources and the quality of our food. Increasingly people want back-to-basics, unprocessed food, and nothing fits that bill better than handcrafted cheese.

A relative of mine from Germany recently told me that when she came to this country in the mid-1960s, she could find few foods that matched the flavors of what she was used to back home; the coffee, the

OPPOSITE: An assortment of cheeses from Cypress Grove Chèvre in McKinleyville, California. The lines in the cheese are made of a thin layer of edible vegetable ash.

bread, and the cuisine were all inferior in this country. Now, she says, all of those and more, including the cheese, are far better here than in Europe.

That is because today cheese and many other foods in the United States are being made with serious focus, care, and equally important, passion. Hearty, crusty fresh-baked breads now fill the markets as skilled bakers return to this ancient art. Coffee beans are roasted with the same precision and science that winemakers apply to their wine; farmers' markets are popular fixtures in the midst of urban centers because they feature fruits and vegetables grown by farmers who have gone to great lengths to grow good-tasting food, and to grow it responsibly. Now handcrafted cheese is being sought after because it represents these same qualities of flavor and care in the making of the product. It, too, is unquestionably a reflection of its human maker, not a machine.

Since the early 1990s, the number of specialty cheesemakers in the United States has grown from a nominal number to at least two hundred—that we know of. And there is no sign of this growth slowing down. All across the nation, cows, sheep, and goats dot the landscape, lending their milk for cheeses that used to be made primarily in other countries. While specialty cheeses were certainly made within the borders of the United States in earlier times, they were hard to find and were usually known only by those who frequented farmers' markets or were lucky enough to have a cheesemonger that stocked these "boutique" cheeses.

Although American-made specialty cheeses are beginning to appear more regularly, it has been a long road for the cheesemakers toward gaining the respect, recognition, and patronage they have deserved. Fortunately, this nation has many cheesemakers whose families have been in the business for generations, and they have helped pave the way for today's artisans. People like Ig Vella, and his father before him, of the Vella Cheese Company in California; the Viviani family of the Sonoma Cheese Factory in California; Sid Cook of Carr Valley Cheese in Wisconsin; the Mossholder family, makers of Mossholder cheese in Wisconsin; the Peluso family, makers of Teleme cheese in California; and while not family-owned, America's oldest cheese plant, Crowley Cheese Company in Vermont, have all contributed to the high standard of cheesemaking that now exists in this country.

In addition, many individuals have struggled to make cheese when no one else was doing it, when there was no equipment to be found, and when they had no one to teach them. Laura Chenel is chief among these pioneers. She, more than anyone, introduced goat cheese to the national palate. Ricki Carroll, owner of New England Cheesemaking Supply, is no less important to cheesemaking today, because it was she who brought the equipment to the United States, outfitting cheesemakers with the necessary tools and teaching them how to make cheese. Both she and Chenel continue their crafts in an exemplary manner today.

Like a lot of grassroots efforts, specialty cheesemaking has never been especially well funded, even though it is a particularly expensive undertaking. It is also immensely hard work. As a result, cheesemakers have had to rely on word of mouth, self-taught business and marketing skills, some good luck, and membership in organizations to help bring them the necessary attention. Often they are just too busy to garner it on their own. Yet getting their message out is key to educating the American public about specialty cheese.

Until recently, it has been an uphill battle. First, the majority of cheese made in the United States is still manufactured entirely by machine. This is the cheese that ends up at the supermarket, and this is what

people buy. Specialty cheeses, however, are made and marketed in small quantities, and are often made by hand. They are sold primarily in cheese shops, gourmet food stores, and upscale grocery stores, although that is slowly changing. More and more formerly hard-to-find cheeses are making their way onto the shelves of mainstream markets. Still, exposure to these cheeses remains limited.

Also, because most shoppers are unaware of the quality of domestic cheesemaking, they still often seek out imported cheeses when they want a specialty cheese. This is simply a matter of education. Now that domestic cheesemakers are so highly skilled, the more important considerations are how and where the cheese is made, the quality of the milk used to make it, and, ultimately, how it tastes. Since the cheeses are now made close to home, finding these answers is much simpler. Besides, American cheeses are beginning to be recognized as every bit as good as their European counterparts. Like the California wines that were introduced in France in the 1970s, American cheeses are winning prestigious awards in world championships when placed side by side by with their foreign competitors.

Indeed, in the United States, cheesemakers have painstakingly worked to improve their craft, many traveling to Europe to work with cheesemakers there. My German relative was astonished to learn that the rustic-looking sheep's milk cheeses and perfectly ripened goats' milk cheeses that I was serving one evening were actually all from Vermont. She was certain they must have been imported.

In this country, cheese operations are defined in different ways, depending on the process by which the cheese is made. Besides bulk manufactured cheese, we have *artisanal* or *handcrafted* cheeses. These are, as the name implies, handmade. This almost always means that the cheesemaker makes the cheese from start to finish with little or no mechanization. This can pertain to both small and large cheesemakers, because many of the larger outfits still make all of their cheese by hand. They may or may not, however, be using their own animals' milk. If they are, then the term "farmstead" is used. "Farmstead" refers to cheeses that are made exclusively from the milk of the cheesemaker's own animals.

Another category of cheesemaking is *specialty* cheese. All artisanal cheese is specialty cheese, but not all specialty cheeses are handcrafted; an increasing number are now being manufactured. The milk selected for specialty cheese is of very high quality, the type of cheese is made in small quantities and is often designed for a niche market, but little or none of it is done by hand. The cheese that results can be as good as its handmade counterpart or it can fall well short. It simply depends upon who is making it.

For many people, the often higher price of handcrafted foods is daunting. To put it simply, many American-made artisanal cheeses are not cheap. But as any cheesemaker will tell you, they are not getting rich. The amount of labor involved in making and aging cheese results in a more expensive product. But it is one that is in an entirely different category than its machine-made counterpart. Compared to bulk cheese, a few ounces of handcrafted cheese give far more bang for their buck in flavor and in satisfaction.

This book features recipes using specialty and handcrafted cheeses. Understanding how to use these cheeses in different ways should create an emboldened specialty-cheese-buying public. As you will see, the recipes have one thing in common: they showcase each cheese rather than obscure it. It is not worth buying an expensive cheese if you aren't able to taste it—that's a waste of cheese *and* money.

Very few of the recipes combine meat with cheese. This is mostly a personal preference; I find that meat can easily dominate the flavors in cheese. It is like putting a young, mild cheese with a big wine: the cheese gets lost. On the other hand, those recipes that do feature meat and cheese showcase the main

ingredients equally, as counterpoints for one another in flavor, texture, or both.

In the following pages, you will meet some of the cheesemakers who are making names for themselves in this country and around the world. They are people to celebrate and to admire, for they have raised the bar for all of us who enjoy cheese and good food in general. Many of these cheesemakers are new to their craft—some have been in business for less than a year. All of their stories bring to life the crucial connection between the farm and the table.

By no means is the number of great American cheesemakers confined to those described in this book. Indeed, having to limit the profiles was a challenge. So many cheesemakers in this country are well worth noting, and their numbers increase every day. For this reason, an expanded list of specialty cheesemakers follows at the end of the book. This will provide a starting point for anyone who is interested in contacting their local cheesemakers.

Also in these pages you will find a comprehensive list of cheese tasting terms. These are provided to help you build a vocabulary for describing some of the flavors that are found in cheese. This is just a guideline; invent your own terms or whatever might help you to remember and enjoy different cheeses. You will also find the colorful story of the history of cheesemaking in America; you'll learn how cheese is made, how cheese fits into the diets of those who might be lactose intolerant, how to create your own cheese course, and how to pair cheese with wine and other beverages. You will also find an extensive glossary to help make sense of the ever-growing language of cheese.

Cheese is a complex, labor-intensive, exquisite food to which American cheesemakers are giving new meaning. In the following pages, a picture will emerge of the delicacy of cheesemaking and of the backbreaking work true cheesemaking entails. You will see why its handcrafted nature results in each cheese being slightly different from the other. In a land where food uniformity is prized, enjoying handmade products implies a certain attitude shift. Just as organic farmers have been working hard to educate us to the notion that smaller fruit is often better and a blemish or two is part and parcel of this type of farming, so can we come to accept a slight imperfection in a handmade cheese and minor variations from batch to batch. These types of distinctions actually create the romance in cheeses since, by their very nature, they cannot be boring. They are exciting, always new, and intensely satisfying.

In writing this book, I was continually amazed by the exceptional quality of the cheese being made across the land. Each time one would arrive in the mail, no matter what time of day or night, I would carefully unwrap it (unveil it, really), delicately cut a piece, and eagerly sample it. The only disappointment I ever experienced was when I didn't have friends or family around to join me in these epiphanous moments. And they were epiphanous, each and every one of them.

I hope you will begin to have similar experiences as you read the stories of the cheesemakers and as you begin your exploration of American handcrafted cheese. A trip to your local cheesemonger is all it takes to start the journey. Once you say "American" and "cheese" in the same sentence, a dialogue will ensue, and you will be introduced to some of the finest cheeses made anywhere in the world. Welcome to The *New* American Cheese.

ALL ABOUT
CHEESE

HOW TO TASTE, BUY, AND STORE

ALWAYS FARM FRESH

THE CHEESE COURSE

SINCE 1620

CHEESE AND WINE

MADE IN THE U.S.A.

THE EVOLUTION OF
CHEESEMAKING IN AMERICA

MUCH HAS BEEN WRITTEN about cheese and its early beginnings in North America. Unfortunately, much of the information is conflicting. But short of time traveling, we have to rely on the existing documents that tell of our forebears' eating habits. As almost every school-age child can attest, a history lesson about the first settlers in the New World often begins with the Pilgrims. It is the same with cheese.

The year was 1620. A group of people aboard the ship known as the *Mayflower* had reached the shores of Cape Cod, having traveled across the Atlantic from England. Briefly the travelers anchored at Provincetown, but after a bit of exploration they decided to set sail across the bay and land permanently at Plymouth. This intrepid group became known to future generations as the Pilgrims.

The Pilgrims have landed in this book, however, because they carried some relevant cargo: goats.

Historians at the Plimoth Plantation in Plymouth, Massachusetts, say that the first Thanksgiving, or Harvest Festival as it was called then, featured fresh goat cheese. The English were fond of their curds and whey, which they obtained from their easily transported goats.

It is well documented that the Pilgrims also had hard waxed cheeses called "Holland" cheeses with them when they sailed, but some say that these cheeses never made it to North America; chances are the cheese was consumed before the ship reached the shore. They also brought a cheese called "Slotten," which was a very hard skim milk cheese. In 1624, however, "three heifers and a bull" came sailing into the new colony. After that, cows' milk cheeses began to be made.

The first inventory lists we have are from 1633 and list items including cheese presses and trays, indicating that cheesemaking was being done in the Bay Colony on a broader scale than just for home consumption.

While brief compared to other countries, America has an illustrious cheese history. A few decades after the Pilgrims arrived, Spanish missionaries were moving up from Mexico into California and introducing cheese to the western half of the continent. Soon after, cheesemaking began to develop in pockets throughout the country, setting the stage for the cheesemaking that is going on today.

Dry Jack cheese aging at Vella Cheese Company in Sonoma, California.
The dark coating is a mixture of cocoa, black pepper, and oil.

CHEESEMAKING IN NEW YORK

Much of American cheesemaking began in New York. Shortly after the Pilgrims were settled in Massachusetts, the Dutch began arriving in the Hudson River Valley. With them came cattle, farming know-how, and a dairy tradition. Among their talents was cheesemaking. Dutch women made a fresh cheese similar to cottage cheese, called Schmierkäse, which they also aged to be sliced for other uses. Documentation of other types of cheeses includes hard cheeses as well as one that had spices added to it. By the mid-17th century, Dutch dairymen had earned the title "milk and cheese men."

While the Dutch were going about their business in the Hudson Valley, the English (New Englanders) joined them, deciding that it would be a good place to develop dairy lands of their own. They did the same on Long Island, where the Dutch had also settled first. Lush grassland in both places provided perfect grazing for cattle, and not surprisingly, women went to work making the cheeses of their homeland.

The late 1700s and early 1800s was a boom time for dairy farms in the state of New York, and much of what was produced was, of course, cheese. By the mid-1800s, cheesemaking was growing so much that cheesemakers were beginning to move their operations out of the barns and into special facilities. The New York State Agricultural Society even held a contest for the best design of a cheesemaking facility to encourage greater efficiency.

Many of the cheesemaking facilities at this time were large, and notably most of them employed at least one woman to be the cheesemaker. She was paid $1 to $2 a week and was given room and board. In some cases she was also responsible for the housework. In other situations, the "girls," as they were called, had afternoons off, having started their day milking the cows early in the morning. The allure of the female cheesemaker was that she was considered neat—and possibly most important, could be hired for little money.

As cheesemaking began to be big business, the transition from farm to factory was inevitable. One man in particular, Jesse Williams of Rome, in Oneida County, is credited with having transformed farm-house cheesemaking into large-scale cheese production. Although others had figured out ways to increase production, Williams' system of associated dairying is what distinguished his method.

In this system, local farmers would milk their cows and supply Williams with that milk for the cheese. All would share in the profits from the cheese. Up until then, a cooperative system of that type hadn't existed on any scale. In addition, Williams created machinery that improved cheese manufacturing, and he was apparently quite happy to share his innovations with anybody who asked. This in turn helped cheesemakers from New York and beyond to improve their own cheesemaking methods.

Williams and his wife, Amanda, made cheese commonly known as New York State cheddar, Yankee cheese, or American cheese. Their experimentation led them to travel to dairy farms throughout New York to try to learn how to make the best cheese they could. It apparently paid off. Their son, George Williams, who was also a dairyman, joined his herd with his father's. This led to a partnership that included Williams' other son, Dewitt, and together they erected two buildings for cheesemaking and storage. The machines were turned on for the first time in 1851, and cheese production began.

Williams' innovations remain a blueprint for many of today's cheesemaking procedures. The milk was carried to the facility by wagon and sent through a tube to a vat inside. A coagulant, rennet, was added, the mixture was heated, the curds were formed and then cut, and the cut curds were removed to a rack to drain off the whey. They were salted and placed in wooden hoops, pressed, and drained some more. The 150-pound cylinders of cheese were then "bandaged," or wrapped, and pressed once again. They were brought to the curing room, where they were turned every day except Sunday. Four such cheeses were made every day. By the time Williams died in 1864, five hundred cheese factories were in operation in New York alone.

A few other cheese factories existed in the East and Midwest, but many of these were set up for curd production only. In this case, the curds were shipped to factories elsewhere, and there they were made into cheese. The most famous example of this type of production occurred in 1801 when the people of Cheshire, Massachusetts, wanted to impress President Jefferson. They decided to make him a cheese wheel—though not just *any* cheese wheel. They collected curds from individual farms and from those curds created a whopping 1,235-pound cheese. They were apparently anxious to show the president their appreciation for the victory of the Democrats over the Federalists.

Legend has it that it is from this event that the expression "the big cheese" originated as a phrase used to describe an important person. At least two other presidents., Martin Van Buren and Andrew Jackson, received such a dairy gift. Jackson, in particular, was purported to be a huge fan of cheese.

Cheeses from Carr Valley Cheese in La Valle, Wisconsin.

While New York was known mostly for its cheddar cheese, one Swiss immigrant, Emil Frey, was busily trying to emulate a German cheese called Bismarck Schlosskäse. Three years of frustrating attempts did not yield that cheese, but in 1891 Frey's efforts resulted in an even better cheese. He christened it "Liederkranz," which means "wreath of song"—the cheese was named after a distinguished choral group that was reputed to adore its flavor.

Demand for the cheese soared. To meet that demand, a factory was built in Ohio, but the manufacturers could not duplicate the flavor of the Liederkranz made in New York. Finally it was determined that the problem was related to the bacteria that was unique to the cheesemaking room in Monroe, New York, where the cheese had been made previously. Without that bacteria, the same flavor could not be achieved. As the story goes, they therefore dismantled the cheesemaking room in New York, transported it to Ohio piece by piece, smeared the remains of the last New York-made Liederkranz on the walls to reintroduce the bacteria, and achieved the desired result! In 1929 the factory and the recipe for Liederkranz were sold to Borden, which later sold it to another company. If Liederkranz is still being made, it is being done on a small scale only, although rumors persist that Liederkranz production may resume. Perhaps history will repeat itself in the 21st century.

While New York was fast becoming a cheese state, Wisconsin, California, Vermont, and other states were busily establishing their own cheese histories, including the invention of cheeses that are uniquely American.

CHEESEMAKING IN WISCONSIN

The production of cheese in Wisconsin began later than it did in New York since settlers didn't begin arriving until the 1830s. Along with the new settlers came a few cows and sheep. At the same time, people from many parts of Europe, including Germany, Switzerland, Holland, Belgium, Scandinavia, Italy, and the British Isles, began arriving in Wisconsin, able to reach the area via the newly opened Erie Canal. They set about clearing the trees and prairie grasses and planting wheat. In doing so, they transformed Wisconsin into the second-largest wheat-producing state by 1860. At this time, there were no dairy products to speak of.

Wheat remained the dominant crop in Wisconsin well into the 19th century, but production began to fall off due to the lack of crop rotation and poor weather, among other factors. At the same time, attempts at dairying were made, but with little success. One reason was that dairying was more closely associated with "women's work." Few farmers wanted to make their living off something that was traditionally female. Despite economic necessity, farmers stubbornly held off until just after the Civil War before they finally made the plunge into dairying for a living.

Once the decision was made, dairy farmers approached their new business with vigor. The Wisconsin Dairymen's Association was formed, and members began to devise a marketing plan for their cheese. An example had been set in 1866, when New Yorkers formed the American Dairy Association to help market their cheese. The Wisconsin farmers were clever enough to recognize that the demand for different types of cheese was partly determined geographically. For example, New Yorkers wanted a slightly dyed, harder cheese and Chicagoans were concerned more about the size of their cheese.

At this time, cheese was being produced primarily in the home. Factories were few and far between. Mostly, whatever cheese was made came from the milk of the farmer's own cows. One exception was a man named James Picket, from Lake Mills, Wisconsin. A decade before New Yorker Jesse Williams became known for his associated dairying method, Picket was already using it. Milk from a few cows belonging to nearby farmers supplemented the milk he got from his own cows, and it all came together to form his cheese. His operation grew, and cattle owners and cheesemaker alike enjoyed the profits.

Although cheesemaking in Wisconsin got off to a slow start, it is estimated that by 1880 there were 700 cheese factories, and by 1890 over 1,100. At this time, more cheeses were beginning to be produced, including Swiss and Limburger. These choices made sense since the Swiss, in particular, had generations of cheesemaking in their blood. They knew what good cheese tasted like and how to make it. They also knew what the cows needed to eat to create the best-tasting milk (and subsequent cheese), and with that, the Swiss planted clover and grass.

Factories finally came to Wisconsin with the help of a transplanted New Yorker. Nicholas Gerber built a Limburger cheese factory in 1868 and a Swiss cheese factory in 1869. Eventually he owned fourteen factories, laying the groundwork for Wisconsin to produce over one-quarter of America's cheese by the turn of the century, nearly one-half by 1909, and nearly two-thirds by 1919. Today Wisconsin is the nation's largest cheese producer, with California close behind.

Although most of the cheese made in Wisconsin, and in the rest of the United States, is based on cheese from other countries, three cheeses were invented in the state: Colby, brick, and a loose combination of the two created by a man named Otto Mossholder. The name of that cheese comes as no surprise: it is called Mossholder.

Colby is a washed-curd cheese that was supposedly born out of a mistake. In 1885 a man named Joseph Steinwand was making cheddar cheese, but for some reason it wasn't working. To correct what he thought was the problem, Steinwand washed the curd with cold water and then drained it. Steinwand's makeshift method resulted in a cheese that was moister and milder than cheddar. He named the cheese after a nearby town.

Invented in 1875, brick cheese has jokingly been called the "married man's Limburger" because it is a toned-down version of the very pungent German cheese. It is called "brick" because of the shape of the presses used to extract moisture from the cheese—or perhaps because of its final shape. Whatever the origin of its name, it definitely measures high on the "daring" scale as it ages. When young, brick is a mild high-moisture cheese. But after being dipped daily in whey for a couple of weeks and then wrapped in foil, it enters into "stinky" territory.

Otto Mossholder created his cheese in the 1920s by following recipes for several Colby and brick cheeses and cooking them together on his kitchen stove. Mossholder cheese is still made in the traditional loaves in the town of Appleton, Wisconsin, by the Mossholder family (see page 74 for more about Mossholder).

In the early 1900s, as cheesemaking became a serious business, Wisconsin cheesemakers were required to have a license. At the same time, innovations in cheesemaking were being developed. Among those was the Babcock Milk Test, which measured the amount of fat in the milk—a key indicator of the quality of the milk. Another innovation, important in the cold-winter states, was the silo. Since there was no grass in the wintertime, silos were built to store corn that would then ferment and turn into cattle feed. This meant that the cattle could produce decent milk for cheese all year long, although not everyone agreed that the milk was of adequate quality. Eventually, however, silos came into common use and were fairly well accepted by the dairy community.

After World War II, mechanization came into being. The result was not always favorable. The farmers would hook their animals up to the mechanized milking machines, but they weren't always conscientious about the cleanliness of the machines. This led to many cheesemaking disasters due to contaminated milk, but it also led to a crackdown on cleanliness in both the milking and the cheesemaking process.

Despite innovations and its firm foundation as a cheese state, Wisconsin has seen its number of cheese factories diminish to fewer than 150. Part of that change was unavoidable. It used to be that most of the cheese produced in the state was sold within the state, often to people in the immediate area. But once cheese became a big industry and demand for milk increased, the small farmer could no longer meet that demand. Also, the larger dairy farmers were buying Holstein cows, which produce the most milk, replacing the Brown Swiss, Jerseys, and Guernseys whose milk was considered more desirable but was less plentiful. That helped the wealthier farmers to increase production still further. This type of mass production, along with the strong emphasis on dairying and cheesemaking in the late 1800s, has led to the inextricable association between the state of Wisconsin and cheese.

While dairy development was going on in Wisconsin, dairying and cheesemaking were well under way in California. The early settlers in California were Spanish missionaries who had come up from Mexico. Starting in 1769, they traveled from Mexico to California, bringing with them cows, goats, and sheep. With those animals they brought milk production, and eventually cheese, to California.

CHEESEMAKING IN CALIFORNIA

The first known California cheese was something called "Queso del Pais," or "country cheese," which was a soft, creamy cheese. It is said to be the forerunner of Monterey Jack. While the missionaries were making their way north in California, a Russian colony north of San Francisco was tending its own herd of cattle. From the milk they produced butter and cheese, which they sent to their hungry troops stationed in Alaska. Although technically not an export, that shipment of cheese is seen as the beginning of cheese exporting from California.

Once again, women figured prominently in cheesemaking. Women tended the cows, churned the butter, and in some cases, made fresh cheese such as cottage cheese. Later, after the Gold Rush began in 1848, demand for just about everything, including milk, exceeded supply. A woman named Clarissa Steele, who had come from Delaware County, New York, commissioned someone to round up the wild cattle near her property in the hopes of milking them. She did, and she began to make cheese from a recipe she found in a cookbook that had belonged to her English grandmother. The recipe was for cheddar cheese. In 1864 the Steele family produced what is believed to be the largest wheel of cheese ever made in California: 21,800 pounds, 20 feet around and 18 inches thick. Chances are, few have tried to duplicate such a feat. The cheese was sold in pieces at a fair to raise money for charity.

Other cheesemaking operations were beginning at about the same time. One, created in 1865, is known today as the Marin French Cheese Company. It is located in Marin County, north of San Francisco. By 1900 the company was producing soft-ripened cheeses like Camembert as well as other soft and washed-rind cheeses. They continue to make these cheeses today.

Farther south, in Monterey County, a businessman and landowner named David Jacks wanted to make cheese. His Portuguese and Swiss dairymen were certainly familiar with cheesemaking, and drawing from old mission recipes, they produced a soft white cheese. It was shipped by rail to San Francisco and became known as Monterey Jacks' (the "s" and the apostrophe were eventually dropped). This American-invented cheese, like Colby, remains a big player in the country's cheese-buying habits.

Around the time of World War I, a "new" cheese was created from Monterey Jack cheese. It was called Dry Jack and, like Colby, was an unexpected variation on an established cheese. A cheese wholesaler had a large order of Monterey Jack in storage for a long time. It was wartime and he had no one to sell it to. To try to preserve it, he had his workers turn and salt it every few days. When he went to check on the cheese, he discovered that it had hardened, but instead of turning to mass pieces of mold or drying out like a rock, it had developed a sweet, nutty flavor. This discovery coincided with the local Italian community's unrequited desire for the hard cheeses of their homeland. Dry Jack quickly was embraced as an alternative to the grating cheeses from home. It is still one of the finest cheeses made in California.

OTHER CHEESE STATES

Many other regions in the United States have their own cheese histories as well. Vermont is home to the oldest continually operating cheese plant in the United States. Located in Healdville, the Crowley Cheese Company made its first cheese in 1882. Crowley cheese is also unique, falling somewhere between a Colby and a cheddar, although it is said to have been invented before the Wisconsin Colby. (See pages 162-163 for more about Crowley.) Other cheese companies were not far behind Crowley, including Grafton Village Cheese Company, which began in 1890 and is famous for its cheddars, and Cabot Creamery, which is now Vermont's largest cheese producer. (See page 251 for more about Grafton.)

In addition to cows' milk cheeses, many sheep's and goats' milk cheeses are being made now in Vermont, and the relatively new Vermont Cheese Council is working hard to promote Vermont as a cheese destination for travelers.

Ohio, too, got its start as a cheese producer well over a century ago when Swiss immigrants settled there. Attracted to the rolling hills reminiscent of home, the Swiss began making Emmentaler as early as 1833. At that time, groups of farmers would get together and build small cooperative cheese factories that

produced one or two wheels of cheese a day. They did not operate during the winter.

Cheesemaking went on in this way for nearly a hundred years, until modern manufacturing became the rule. By 1986 Ohio had become the largest producer of Swiss cheese, and it still holds that distinction today. Small cheesemaking operations, many of them family-owned, continue to make Swiss and other cheeses as well.

On the West Coast, settlers traversed the Oregon Trail in the 1850s and staked their claim in Bandon, Oregon, near Coos Bay. Local dairy cows and river boats transporting goods on the nearby Coquille River provided a constant supply of milk in Bandon, which led to the first cheesemaking in southwest Oregon in the 1890s. The Bandon Creamery still operates, producing cheddar, Jack, and flavored cheeses.

Oregon's most famous cheese settlement is in Tillamook County. A Canadian by the name of Peter McIntosh arrived there in 1894 and taught local dairymen how to make cheese. The dairy farmers then pooled their resources and built the first of several cheese plants in the area. There would be as many as twenty-six such plants by the early 20th century. In 1909 the new company chief, Carl Haberlach, made the unprecedented move of registering the first cheese brand in the country. It was called Tillamook. In 1990 a state-of-the-art fully automated plant was built, and today the Tillamook County Creamery Association produces an impressive 60 million pounds of cheese annually. Tillamook is, in fact, the trade center of the Oregon dairying region.

PROCESSED CHEESE

A chapter on the history of cheesemaking in America would not be complete without the mention of processed (also called process) cheese. Processed cheese has played a huge role in introducing Americans to cheese, even though some would argue that processed cheese is really not cheese at all. By definition, processed cheese is not made the same way as artisanal cheeses, although it apparently takes skill to create the combination of ingredients that will result in a good-tasting processed cheese.

In 1916 a man named John Kraft figured out that by grinding and blending cheddar cheeses, heating them, adding a little salt, and packing the result in foil containers, he would have a cheese that always tasted the same and needed no refrigeration. It became an instant hit and single-handedly transformed America's cheese-eating habits.

Since then a number of other processed cheeses have been created, including pasteurized processed blends, spreads, and imitation spreads. The latter are usually lower in fat, and all have less nutritive value than unprocessed cheese.

The abundance of processed cheese as well as so-called commodity cheeses—mass-produced cheeses—plays a big role in America's appetite for cheese. But the downside of these cheeses is that they also diminish the appetite for more flavorful and often less predictable cheeses or those that fall into the category of specialty and artisanal cheeses. Fortunately, though, that is slowly changing, and a new chapter of American cheesemaking is just beginning. That chapter began in the late 1970s and now, in the 21st century, is hitting its stride thanks to a few pioneering cheesemakers.

THE NEW GOAT CHEESE

Among those pioneers is a woman named Laura Chenel. In the early 1970s Chenel, along with Alice Waters, owner of the famed Berkeley, California, restaurant Chez Panisse, introduced American goat cheese to the restaurant-going public. Waters had founded her restaurant on the notion that cooking seasonally and supporting local food producers were essential to perpetuating small farms and local food production. She was equally intent on introducing people to the concept of "farm-fresh" and its relation to flavor. Chenel's locally made cheese fit right in.

Chenel's battle was not an easy one (see pages 116-117), and like all innovators, she struggled to find ways to make a superior product. She finally accomplished that and in so doing set an example for other prospective goat cheese makers. It is not an overstatement to say that she launched a small industry. As one goat cheese maker puts it, "Laura Chenel is the mother of us all."

It is also no surprise that this chapter of American cheesemaking was also begun by a woman. Although some men were making goat cheese, notably Bob Kilmoyer, who with his wife, Letty, founded Westfield Farm in Massachusetts (see pages 193-194), it was primarily women such as Chenel (and well before her, the Pilgrims), and a little later Judy Schad of Indiana and Mary Keehn of California, who created the extraordinary goat cheeses that we now enjoy. Another woman, Ricki Carroll, founder of New England Cheesemaking Supply, was equally important in this evolution because she taught people how to make goat and other cheeses and brought the equipment with which to make it into the United States.

The acceptance of Chenel's product was symbolic of something much greater that was going on in this country. It was at that time that "organic produce," "sustainable agriculture," and other "back-to-nature" concepts were being embraced. Again, Alice Waters was at the forefront of this movement, and she introduced the idea that by supporting local growers and small farmers, we would not only be keeping people in business, we would also be supporting a way of life that is integral to all of us. That way of life would result in our enjoying fresh farm products, supporting environment-friendly farming practices, and ultimately having a long-lasting, healthy food source.

Cheese was an integral part of this philosophy and remains so today. The amount of attention paid to cleanliness in cheesemaking, the flavor of the cheese, the fact that some cheesemakers have gone organic, and the careful raising and tending of the animals—all these elements are indicative of these times and of a real concern about our food sources. Cheese buyers care more than ever about these factors, and that is leading to a whole new direction in American cheesemaking.

SHEEP'S MILK CHEESEMAKING: A BRIEF HISTORY

Another relatively new direction in American cheesemaking is sheep's milk cheese. This goes only as far back as the early 1980s. Some of those who started the industry are still involved in it—such as Sally Jackson of Washington (see page 141) and Jane North of Northland Sheep Dairy near Marathon, New York (see page 226)—but other industry pioneers, like Joan Snyder, who ultimately sold her Hollow Road Farm, and Lucie and Roger Steinkamp of Minnesota, are no longer making cheese. At least for now. Although more sheep are milked than any other type of animal around the world, sheep's milk cheeses haven't been made in this country in any quantity primarily because we haven't had the number of dairy sheep that other countries do. Some sheep dairy owners, as well as sheep research facilities, are working to change this, however.

Additionally, sheep give less milk than cows or goats. Although the butterfat content of sheep's milk is high, which translates to more cheese per pound of milk, the overall amount of milk a sheep gives is relatively low. This contributes to the high cost of making sheep's milk cheese. Difficulties notwithstanding, several people, particularly in Vermont and to a lesser extent in Wisconsin, are starting to do more sheep dairying and cheesemaking. In turn, as people taste domestically made sheep's milk cheeses, they are beginning to demand more of it.

THE FUTURE OF AMERICAN CHEESEMAKING

American cheesemakers are breaking new ground every day, and as we look back at the evolution of cheesemaking in this country, this doesn't seem unusual. Our history is full of innovators. Fortunately the cheesemakers of today are concerned not only with making cheese but also with the quality of the milk they use, with the way the animals—the milk sources—are treated and what they are fed, and with the delicate alchemy that turns the milk into cheese.

As for the next chapter in American cheesemaking, it could easily be called "The Rebirth of Cheesemaking in America." In a way, cheesemaking has gone *back* a century or two by recapturing the handmade and artistic aspects of the craft. Yet it now has the added advantage of today's sophisticated palates as well as a much better understanding of the science of cheesemaking and of animal husbandry. That combination is one that will make the next phase in American cheese a tremendously exciting one. And, we will all have the chance to become part of that history as we make the switch to American-made cheeses.

HOW CHEESE IS MADE

WHEN WE BUY CHEESE, we are buying the result of breathtakingly hard work. Even more, we are experiencing first-hand one of nature's most precious examples of the interplay between science and art. Without science, cheese would not be; and without art, it would not be as we know it. From the milk to its final form, cheese is a natural wonder that is coaxed along by the artistry of the cheesemaker combined with his or her knowledge of how cheese is made. While the basics of cheesemaking are fairly easy to understand, cheeses—like pie crusts—vary tremendously, depending on their maker.

The basic steps for making cheese are fairly standard:
1. A starter is added to the pasteurized or raw milk to sour it.
2. Rennet is then added to curdle the milk, which begins the process of separating the solids (curd) from the liquids (whey).
3. The curds are usually cut to help further expel the whey.
4. The whey is drained off.
5. The curds are handled in any number of ways, depending on the specific cheese being made.
6. The cheese is either ready for market or is aged for a specific period of time, which can range from days to years, before it is sold.

Of course, if it were this simple, we'd probably all be cheesemakers. But here is where art and science intersect. The types of starters and rennets used, the length of time the curds and whey sit before being cut, the amount of time the curds are left to drain, and how the curds are handled from that point on, all determine the final product. The individual cheesemakers make the decisions about all of these steps, and one misstep can create a vat of disaster. But at the same time, the right sequence of steps and ingredients can create one of the most heavenly foods in the world: great cheese.

Think about cheesemaking as the transition from liquid to solid, mild to flavorful. Add to that the chemical transformations that make this happen, and eventually you've got cheese. The first transformation occurs when the lactase enzyme, found in all milk, converts to lactic acid as a result of the addition of bacteria. This bacterial addition is called the starter. The lactic acid is essential to the coagulation of the milk protein, or casein. While some lactose remains in the cheese, most of it is eventually drawn out in the whey. (See "To Your Health" for more on lactose.) The milk is now beginning to "ripen."

Next, the rennet is added, causing the curds to coagulate further. Rennet, a coagulating enzyme used to curdle milk, is key to the making of a cheese. Until fairly recently, rennet was almost always derived from the stomach lining of a calf, goat, or lamb, depending on which type of cheese was being made. While these remain a source of rennet, and for some cheesemakers still the preferred source, vegetable rennets (derived from plants) and genetically engineered microbial rennets have become increasingly popular alternatives for cheesemakers and cheese consumers as well.

For vegetarians, these non-animal types of rennet are a necessity. For cheesemakers, the rennet yielding the best-tasting cheese is almost always the guiding force. However, the increase in the number of vegetarians as well as a general awareness about food sources has caused many cheesemakers, especially American cheesemakers, to switch to non-animal rennets. Since that involves an entire recipe change for the cheese, the transition is not always easy nor necessarily successful. The rennet is integral to the final flavor of the cheese, as is the starter, and changing either one of these "ingredients" can result in an entirely different, and in some cases inferior, cheese.

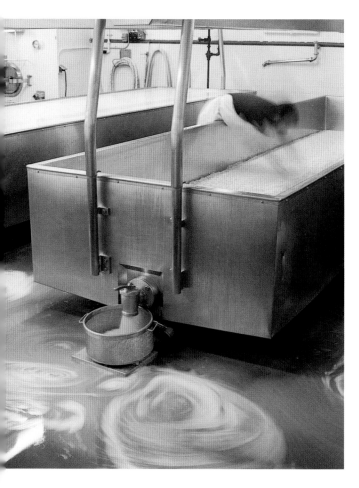

Once the curds (solids) and whey (liquid) have begun to separate from each other, the whey is drained off. The curds are then turned into cheese.

Usually within an hour of the rennet being added, the curds are cut. Whether by hand or by machine, a device with either vertical or horizontal wires (or both) cuts through the coagulating milk, helping to expel the whey as well as to create uniform pieces of curd. Some cheeses, however, require no cutting and are simply scooped into perforated molds. Gravity then works to press the whey through the holes, leaving behind concentrated curds.

The size of the cut curd is based on the cheese that is being produced. If a harder cheese is the goal, then the cheesemaker will get rid of as much whey as possible by cutting the curds into tiny pieces. Likewise, the curds will be kept larger to retain more moisture for softer cheeses.

At this point, the curds undergo a heating process that can range from very little heat to fairly extreme temperatures. Generally speaking, the curds for the longer-aged, harder cheeses are heated to high temperatures, or "cooked" as it is sometimes called, to create smaller curds and to release more whey. Swiss and Gruyère cheeses, among others, fall into this category. In the case of most soft cheeses, the temperature is kept fairly low to keep the curds a little more jelly-like. Following the heating process, the whey is then usually pumped out or, in smaller quantities, dumped out, leaving the coagulated curds behind.

What happens next depends upon the cheese

that is being made. Mozzarella, Queso Oaxaca, and Provolone, among others, are collectively known as *pasta filata,* or stretched-curd, cheeses. In this category of cheeses, the curds are cooked and then allowed to mat together. They are then broken into pieces and immersed in a hot-water "bath" that softens the curds. While soft, the curds are literally stretched or molded into shape and then placed in plain or salt water to cool. This is what creates the stringy quality in these cheeses, including string cheese.

Curds for cheddar cheese, on the other hand, are not cooked, though they are heated. They then go through a process, not surprisingly called cheddaring, which is essentially further acidification of curds (begun when the starter was added), and the expulsion of whey. The curds are first left to drain, during which time they bind together to form sheets of curds. These sheets are stacked to facilitate further drainage, since the weight of the stacked curds naturally presses out the moisture. The sheets are then cut into pieces only to be drawn together again, and relayered to drain still more. The curds are then cut up into tiny pieces, or milled, before they are salted and molded.

Salting is another step in the process that creates distinctions among cheeses. It also performs some important functions. First, salt retards the ripening of a cheese, allowing the aging phase to be more carefully controlled. It also helps leech out any remaining whey, facilitating the aging process, and naturally it provides flavor. To derive these benefits, cheese and salt are introduced to one another in a variety of ways.

Some cheeses are salted when they are still in curd form and before they are molded, such as with cheddar. Others, like Vella's Dry Jack cheese, Winchester Gouda, and most feta cheeses, are molded and then placed in a saltwater or brine bath for anywhere from a few hours to several days or months. Still other cheeses are salted only on their surfaces to preserve them and to facilitate the formation of a natural rind. Finally, so-called washed-rind cheeses are rubbed by hand with a saltwater or other solution, such as wine, beer, or apple cider. The resulting rind can be soft and pungent or hard and crusty. Certain blue cheeses and some soft-ripened cheeses fall into this category, as do many aged cheeses.

Because cheese is salted at varying stages based on the type of cheese, the molding step may occur before or after the salting process. The molding and pressing stage accounts for the shape of the cheese as well

The cut-up, or milled, curds for Dry Jack cheese are poured into muslin cloth which allows for further drainage of the whey and forms the shape of the cheese.

as for further moisture loss. The curds are placed in the molds and are mechanically pressed or pressed by weights. They may be left that way for twenty-four hours or longer before they go on to the aging stage. What happens in the aging room will determine the speed at which moisture loss occurs as well as the amount of moisture that is lost.

Aging rooms have carefully controlled temperature and humidity levels. Temperatures usually hover around 50°F, while the humidity level varies according to the type of cheese that is being ripened. In the case of soft-ripened cheeses, the humidity level can reach nearly 100 percent to promote the growth of the bacteria on the surface of the cheese. It also keeps the cheese from drying out. Harder cheeses tend to be placed in a room with a humidity level of about 85 percent down to almost zero humidity, depending on the desired result. In both cases, the idea is to bring about the slow breakdown of the

The curd-filled muslin cloth is formed into a round, placed on boards, and stacked. The weight of the stacked boards helps press out most of the remaining whey and further forms the shape of the cheese.

cheese's main constituents: protein, sugar, and fat. This, in turn, creates the unique flavor of the cheese.

It is during the aging process that the artistry of the cheesemaker is tapped once again. While there are general rules about aging, the way the cheesemaker, or occasionally the *affineur* (the cheese finisher), handles the cheese at this stage is often what gives the cheese its final mark of distinction.

In the case of soft-ripened cheeses, such as a Camembert-style cheese, the cheese ripens from the outside in. This means it begins softening, or ripening, on the outside first. This ripening is aided by a bacterium that is sometimes sprayed onto the cheese to form what is called a bloomy rind. (Other bacteria are added earlier in the cheesemaking process as well.) The bacteria promotes mold growth, which in turn promotes aging. Although the idea of "mold" may be unappetizing, in this case the mold is harmless and in fact is partly responsible for the cheese's flavor.

The same is true for blue cheeses. In these, a different mold, *Penicillium roqueforti*, is introduced to the cheese. The cheese is then poked with holes to allow oxygen to penetrate and, in turn, allow the mold to grow. This is what accounts for the blue veins in blue cheese.

The harder cheeses generally ripen as the result of their starter bacteria, not surface bacteria. This accounts for the ripening occurring from the inside out. However, for a cheese to ripen evenly, it usually

Crottins, or small disks of goat cheese, are aged up to three weeks at Redwood Hill Farm in Sebastopol, California.

must be turned every so often to distribute the remaining moisture in the cheese. Sometimes hard cheeses are surface-dried, waxed, or cloth-wrapped. These cheeses need little more than to be turned.

Some semi-hard and hard cheeses are treated with a special coating. Vella Dry Jack cheese, for example, has a coating consisting of cocoa powder, coffee, and vegetable oil that is brushed on at the beginning of the aging cycle. Other cheeses have a wiped and/or brushed rind. One such cheese is Gruyère, in which the rind is literally scrubbed and washed of any bacteria and enzymes that might influence the flavor of the cheese. And finally, the washed-rind .cheeses require "washing," or wiping with a brine solution at intermittent stages of the ripening process to help facilitate the growth of a natural rind.

How long a cheese is aged is the next consideration for the cheesemaker. Since the softness or hardness is based on the amount of moisture still left in the cheese, cheesemakers base decisions about the ripening phase on the type of cheese being made. Of course, so-called fresh cheeses are not ripened at all.

Soft-ripened cheeses, such as Old Chatham's Camembert or Cypress Grove's Humboldt Fog, will be aged from about ten days and up to three months, while a semi-hard cheese, such as a Prima Käse Gouda or Grafton cheddar, might be aged anywhere from one month to three years. A cheese that is aged past about eight months begins to approach the hard cheese stage, since most of its moisture will have been lost. Many good grating and eating cheeses fall into this category, including Vella Dry Jack, Antigo's Stravecchio, and Bellwether's Pepato and Toscano, among others.

The cheesemaking process can be done entirely by machine, as it is with most bulk manufactured cheese; it can be done using a combination of machine and manual labor, as it is with the many specialty cheeses and artisanal cheeses; or it can be done entirely by hand, as it is by most farmstead operations.

The many decisions that a cheesemaker makes go far beyond the universe of science and well into the realm of art. Though in this case, without science there would be no art. As cheese-lovers, we can appreciate both disciplines and be grateful that there are people in this country who are capable and willing to straddle the line between the two, and as a result bring us magnificent cheese.

TO YOUR HEALTH

WHEN PEOPLE HEAR THE WORD "CHEESE" they often run for the nearest low-calorie door. "Cheese?" they say. "Oh, I love the stuff, but I stay away from it." It is an understandable response—no one ever said that cheese is low in calories. But if calories were the only thing that counted, then we likely wouldn't eat nuts, other whole-milk products, salmon, or many other foods with a higher fat content. But calorie count doesn't tell the whole story. There are tremendous health benefits in all of these foods, but moderation is the key. Cheese is no exception, but compared to many other higher-fat foods, small portions of it pack a lot more nutritional punch.

Cheese is one of the best available sources of both calcium and protein, as well as phosphorus. Talk about "bang for your buck." One ounce of cheese provides 20 to 30 percent of the recommended daily allowance of calcium, depending on one's age, and although it varies according to the type of cheese, the protein found in most cheeses provides an average of around 10 percent of a person's daily needs. It is well known that calcium helps stave off osteoporosis, or the breakdown of the bone structure, but recent studies indicate that calcium may also be an important factor in protecting against colon cancer as well as premenstrual syndrome and high blood pressure. Cheese also has a fair amount of phosphorus, which is a bone builder right alongside calcium.

You may think that none of this matters, or that you'd rather get your calcium and protein from other sources, opting not to deal with the calories and cholesterol found in cheese. But again, eaten in small amounts, the benefits of cheese far outweigh its detractions. Even the cholesterol in cheese, while not cheese's finest attribute, is not necessarily a deal breaker, with the possible exception of those who are on a very low-cholesterol diet. But even then, some cheeses, such as cottage cheese, are naturally low in cholesterol, too.

A one-ounce portion of cows' milk cheese, on average, contains somewhere between 15 and 30 milligrams of cholesterol. Since it's okay to consume as much as 300 milligrams of cholesterol per day, you can see that it would take a lot of cheese to put the average person into the danger zone. In addition, the short- and medium-chain fatty acids in goats' and sheep's milk cheeses, which are different than those in cows' milk, might actually *aid* cholesterol metabolism. Besides, it's the saturated fat more than the cholesterol in cheese that is of greatest risk to those concerned about their health.

Saturated fat contributes to the levels of so-called bad cholesterol, or low-density lipoprotein cholesterol (LDL), in your body. As the word "bad" implies, LDL's, if too abundant in the bloodstream, will increase the risk of heart disease since they clog the arteries. However, for most people, some amount of saturated fat in the diet is permissible, as long as it makes up no more than 10 percent of the total daily fat intake. The other fats, which should add up to about 20 percent of the total fat intake, ideally should come from monounsaturated and polyunsaturated fats.

Another consideration when eating cheese is sodium. Sodium levels are rather high in many cheeses,

and while not a cause for concern for the healthy person, this is something that anyone trying to maintain a low-salt diet should be aware of. The cheeses highest in sodium are processed cheeses, while skim-milk ricotta cheese has very little. It is best to check the labels, but as a rule of thumb a cheese that sits in a salted brine, such as feta, is obviously going to have more salt than, say, a fresh mozzarella, which is made with little or no salt.

Before it becomes cheese, sheep's milk contains the highest amount of butterfat and solids. This does not, however, translate to a more fattening cheese because a higher content of solids simply means it takes less of it to make the same amount of cheese. For example, it takes 10 pounds of cows' milk to make 1 pound of cheese. It takes only about 4½ pounds of sheep's milk to make 1 pound of cheese. Ultimately, the ratio of solids to liquid depends on the type of cheese being made, as well as the length of the aging process, since it is the aging that determines the amount of moisture remaining in the cheese.

The *solids,* or the nonwater components, that remain in the cheese are measured to determine the fat in the cheese. This will vary according to how the cheese is made because it might be made with whole milk, skim milk, or some portion of each. In the United States the dry, nonwater components, or cheese solids, are referred to as "dry matter." This means that the butterfat is determined by the portion of the cheese that is the nonwater part. This may be less than 30 percent of the total cheese, or it can be much higher, depending on the cheese. For example, a creamy type of cheese, such as a Camembert, may have less butterfat as a percentage than a hard cheese, since the latter has far less moisture than a Camembert. Mostly what remains in a hard cheese are the solids and therefore a higher percentage of butterfat. (An exception is when some soft-ripened cheeses have cream added to them to become a double- or triple-crème cheese. This type of cheese is naturally higher in fat.)

The childhood advice about good things coming in small packages may also hold true when eating cheese: smaller amounts are infinitely more satisfying than big quantities. If the consumption of cheese at one sitting is excessive, then the special qualities of the cheese become less noticeable and its healthful qualities are diminished as well.

LACTOSE: WHEYING IT OUT

Many people complain of being lactose intolerant. This is a condition where the body doesn't produce a sufficient amount of the enzyme lactase to break down the natural sugar, lactose, found in milk and other dairy products. News of this condition, however, may have been greatly exaggerated. Most food scientists now agree that milk and other dairy products, when consumed in small quantities, are digestible for many people who have lactose intolerance.

There are, of course, exceptions. For example, certain ethnic groups, most predominantly Asians, Native Americans, and African-Americans, have proven to be genetically ill-equipped to handle lactose in significant quantities as adults. Most people, regardless of genetic background, lose (or perhaps never had) the ability to digest lactose as they get older. Nonetheless, many people who believe they are lactose intolerant can still enjoy cheese and other milk products. The reason lies in the whey.

In the cheesemaking process, the milk is curdled, which causes the separation of the curds from the whey. When this happens, most of the whey is removed and the curds are ultimately made into cheese. Since lactose resides only in the whey, much of the lactose is gone long before the curds become cheese.

One exception is ricotta cheese, which is usually made mostly from whey and is best avoided by lactose-intolerant people. Hard cheeses have the least amount of whey since they have the least amount of moisture, and therefore they have a negligible (if any) amount of lactose.

Typical symptoms of lactose intolerance include gas pains, bloating, and/or diarrhea. These symptoms, however, can often be controlled once the condition is diagnosed. One way is by taking over-the-counter lactose pills, which are essentially synthetic lactase, the enzyme that breaks down lactose. These pills facilitate digestion of milk, fresh cheese, and ice cream, often allowing symptom-free enjoyment of these products. Likewise, many milk products are now made specifically for lactose-intolerant people. In these, the lactose has already been broken down into its digestible components.

A milk allergy is an entirely different problem since it usually comes about as a reaction to the proteins found in milk. Symptoms can range from a runny nose, itching, and watery eyes to more severe symptoms, including skin rash, the inability to breathe, and vomiting. But because the proteins in cows', sheep's, and goats' milk differ, an allergy to one type of milk does not necessarily mean an allergy to all types. A person who is allergic to a cows' milk cheese may not be allergic to goats' or sheep's milk cheeses. Determining the cause of the allergy might give a clean bill of health for certain cheeses and other dairy products. However, some people are simply dairy intolerant, meaning they can consume no milk products whatsoever. It is wise to consult a doctor to determine whether an allergy exists and if so, to which type of milk and/or cheese.

In fact, it is best to check with your health care provider when trying to determine the cause of any dairy-related problems. But it is also important to understand that milk allergies and lactose intolerance are two very different health issues and must be treated as such. In general, milk allergies are important to diagnose because allergic reactions to any foods can be very serious. Lactose intolerance is certainly uncomfortable, and for some very serious, but it is usually remedied easily. And it often requires no remedy at all—just moderation.

REDUCED-FAT CHEESES

For those who are on a weight-loss or fat-reduction program, reduced-fat cheeses offer a way to have your cheese and eat it too. Some cheeses, like Sonoma Cheese Factory's reduced-fat flavored Jack cheeses, taste almost like their full-fat counterparts and are perfectly acceptable substitutes. Others, especially nonfat cheeses, tend to be tough and far less flavorful. That toughness results from the reduction of fat globules. The relative lack of globules accentuates the more rubbery qualities of the protein structure of the cheese.

Fortunately, there are many cheeses that are naturally low in fat. These are usually fresh cheeses, such as ricotta, fromage blanc, cottage cheese, and part-skim mozzarella cheese. Some cheeses that are made with skim milk, however, are not always low in fat. Parmesan cheese is one such example. Its main ingredient is skim milk, but it is by no means a low-fat cheese. On the other hand, because Parmesan is so concentrated, a small amount offers a lot of flavor. This is particularly good for anyone who is trying to watch their fat or cholesterol.

In the United States, fat-free (nonfat), low-fat, reduced-fat, and "lite" versions of foods have strict definitions. *Fat-free* means just that: virtually no fat in the product and no added fats or oils. *Low-fat* means that the product must have 3 grams or less of fat in each serving size of 2 tablespoons or more, or if the

serving size is less than 2 tablespoons, then it must have no more than 3 grams of fat per 50 grams (about 2 ounces) of product. *Lite* or *light* means that the amount of fat in the product must have been reduced by a minimum of one-third if less than 50 percent of the calories in the product come from fat. It must be reduced by half if more than 50 percent of the product's calories come from fat. *Reduced-fat* means the product's fat must be cut by a minimum of 25 percent from its regular amount.

When it comes to cooking, generally speaking it is best to use low-fat and nonfat cheeses in their simplest, uncooked form, with the exception of *fresh* cheeses. These are very versatile due to their creaminess and melting qualities. Firmer low-fat and nonfat cheeses fare less well in the kitchen. For example, placing a reduced-fat cheddar or reduced-fat Swiss cheese directly under a broiler or in a toaster oven will turn it to rubber rather than creating the more desirable soft, melted consistency. On the other hand, adding low- or nonfat cheese to a sauce can be a little more successful, although it might take a little longer to melt. No matter what you are making, it is important to grate reduced-fat cheeses because that will help them melt more easily.

If given the choice, it is usually best to eat a smaller amount of a full-fat cheese than a larger amount of a low-fat or nonfat cheese because the latter will add up quickly in calories while offering less flavor. Still, reduced-fat cheese is made across the country and provides a perfectly acceptable alternative to anyone who is counting calories or fat.

A NOTE ABOUT PASTEURIZED VERSUS RAW MILK

Much has been made about the use of raw, or unpasteurized, milk, in cheesemaking. In the United States, any cheese made with raw milk must be aged a minimum of sixty days. This includes domestic and imported cheeses. It has been determined that after that time, any possibly unhealthful bacteria that might have existed in the raw milk will likely have dissipated. (Pasteurized milk is heated, which kills off any potentially harmful substances in the milk.)

For centuries, cheese has been made in Europe using raw milk since it is believed that it often produces a cheese with better flavor. Even today, a visit to a cheesemaker in the countryside of France or Italy might well mean a taste of a cheese made just yesterday with raw, unpasteurized milk. Traditional Camembert and Brie are made with raw milk, and if bought in France, will have been on the shelves for less than sixty days. Most cheesemakers around the world—large and small—are fastidious about the purity of the milk they use for their cheese. In turn, this means safe cheese consumption most of the time.

Nonetheless, there is a move afoot in the United States to ban raw-milk cheese in order to eliminate any possibility of contaminated dairy products from entering the food supply. Yet many American cheesemakers rely on raw milk to create their unique cheeses, placing them at odds with the government. What is more, some scientists firmly believe that pasteurizing milk actually allows for certain harmful bacteria to survive because those bacteria's natural enemies have been eliminated through the pasteurization process. It is a subject of great debate. But the goal on both sides of the issue is the same: to create good-tasting healthful cheese. It remains to be seen how this will be worked out, but it is an issue that is particularly important to the future of cheesemaking in the United States as well as the rest of the world.

The American Cheese Society is working to educate the public as well as the government on the raw-milk issue since, as a body, they believe that it is something that should remain an option for cheesemakers and consumers. If you would like to learn more about this issue, or to take a side in it, contact the American Cheese Society (see the Resources section).

OPPOSITE: Classic milk bottles on display at
Bass Lake Cheese in Somerset, Wisconsin.

HOW TO TASTE CHEESE

⊱┄┄⊰○⊱┄┄⊰

WHEN YOU DESCRIBE THE TASTE of something to another person, chances are you use a general term like sweet, sour, salty, or bitter. Or you might compare the taste of what you're eating with another similar food. "This codfish tastes kind of like red snapper." But in reality, when we're tasting our food what we're doing is absorbing its *flavor*. Taste has to do with the way a food hits our tongue; flavor is a combination of a large number of sensory inputs that come from food. These include the smell, taste, texture, and even the appearance and sound. What does all this have to do with cheese? Everything. To fully enjoy the many flavors within cheese and to increase your knowledge of cheese, it is essential to understand how to go about "tasting" it.

First, the idea of "flavor" rather than "taste" does not mean ignoring the taste buds. It is just that the taste buds are slightly overrated when it comes to their overall importance in evaluating the flavor of food. Nonetheless, taste receptors for salty, sweet, bitter, and sour reside on and around the tongue, and they are there for a reason. They unquestionably contribute to our response to a particular food.

A fifth taste or sense—*umami*—is slowly being added to our taste vocabulary. *Umami* is loosely equated with "savory," since that is the closest English translation of the Japanese term. The actual definition, however, corresponds to the naturally occurring form of monosodium glutamate (MSG), of which salt is a major component. ("Naturally occuring" is key, since *umami* does not apply to foods to which the artificial form of MSG is added.) It is a sense that the Japanese have long acknowledged and one that Americans and other cultures are just now beginning to appreciate. It also helps explain the flavor sensations we get from those foods that do not fall neatly within the four other taste categories. Some hard cheeses, like cheddar, are considered to have *umami*. So, too, are tomatoes, mushrooms, ham, some shellfish, and many, many other foods.

Unquestionably, our taste buds are helpful when tasting cheese, but the sense of smell is equally important to our appreciation (or condemnation) of certain cheeses. After all, the smell of a cheese can mesmerize or terrorize. It can also help define the flavors of the cheese we're tasting, since a swallow of cheese isn't complete without taking note of how the "taste" fills the nasal passages.

The olfactory sense, or sense of smell, is inextricably linked with our sense of taste. Think about when you get a cold. You probably say that you can't taste anything. In fact, you can't *smell* anything. Without our sense of smell, our sense of taste is severely diminished. But that sense of smell comes from two places: outside our nose and inside our mouth.

The outside, or orthonasal, pathway carries a cheese's aroma through the air and into our nasal passages. This alone may entice or repel us. Once we put the piece of cheese in our mouth, however, we may get an entirely different smell. That is because the aroma qualities in the cheese are coming through the "back door," or from our mouth and throat area, to the nasal receptors. This is called retronasal. The aroma in the cheese may now seem very different than it did before chewing it.

The easiest way to test this for yourself is to smell a cheese. Next, taste it, but before swallowing it, hold it in your mouth and breathe in. Pay attention to the flavors you're getting. Swallow that piece and take another. This time, pinch your nose while you swallow. With the nasal passages blocked, the taste will be diminished. Take one more bite and don't hold your nose. Note the different flavors you pick up.

Dry Jack from Vella Cheese Company in Sonoma, California.

The sense of smell is also integral to how a cheese is usually described. If you ask a cheesemonger to tell you about a certain cheese, he or she will probably begin by telling you one or two things about its flavor characteristics but then will invariably use a few adjectives to describe that cheese's aroma. It might be pungent, strong, sweet, or any other number of possibilities, but all cheese has some aroma, and again, it is an essential element of the cheese.

Other components of flavor—texture, visual appeal, and sometimes even an aural quality (think crunchy, as in potato chips)—are important to our overall perception of how a food tastes. When it comes to cheese, the texture and the appearance are both extremely important. Usually the texture is equated with something called "mouthfeel," while the look of a cheese includes many factors.

The definition of mouthfeel is what it sounds like: how the cheese feels in the mouth. Is it granular? Smooth? Creamy? Rubbery? Although judges in cheese competitions are acutely aware of this component, since it provides a window into the method used to make the cheese, it also helps the average cheese consumer develop a better understanding of cheese. For example, if a semi-soft cheese feels granular in the mouth, that could be an indication that something is wrong. Conversely, if a cheese billed as a hard cheese has a soft mouthfeel, you may not be buying what you thought, and that supposedly hard cheese probably hasn't been aged as long as it should have been.

The appearance of a cheese is no less important than its taste, but it takes a little experience to know what differentiates the good from the bad. Begin by asking your cheesemonger. If that isn't possible, then try to determine for yourself how healthy you think the cheese really looks. The rind, for example, may be showing signs of severe cracking or even rotting. That might not be a good choice. On the other hand, many rinds are natural and deliberately haven't been smoothed in the aging process. To a novice, one of these might look downright scary. But if the cheese is cut and the inside looks uniform and healthy, then chances are the cheese is in good shape. (See "How Cheese Is Made" for more about rinds.)

Monterey Jack cheese pairs beautifully with fresh or dried fruit.

When it comes to tasting cheese, certain characteristics are common to certain cheeses. Knowing what these are helps broaden your basic understanding. For example, fresh goat cheese naturally has a lot of acid, resulting in a tangy flavor, while an aged sheep's milk cheese usually has a more pronounced, earthy flavor. Aged cheeses in general, devoid of most of their moisture, are often saltier and stronger, while a young cows' milk cheese might be a little tangy. A cheddar is often nutty, as is a Gruyère and some Goudas. As for blue cheese, the salt factor often distinguishes the style and age of the cheese. The point is that as you begin to see patterns among cheeses, your understanding will rise exponentially and your overall enjoyment of cheese will soar along with that. Just remember that much of that understanding comes from using *all* of your senses to "taste" cheese.

Most important, have fun. Unlike wine, cheese has never been a source of intimidation for Americans, nor should it become so now. Develop a cheese vocabulary or not, but most of all, derive the full enjoyment that cheese has to offer. That is all that really matters.

THE ART OF CHEESE TASTING

So how do you taste cheese? First, there's no substitute for putting it in your mouth. A simple glance at a cheese won't help. Nor will taking a whiff. You must taste it. Don't be afraid to ask retailers for a sample. They're usually ecstatic when a customer wants to learn more. But if you're stymied about what to do with the cheese once it's in your hands, here are a few hints:

• First, tell the retailer what style of cheese you like. Then ask for one or two recommendations.

• Try several cheeses in the same category. Don't try a blue cheese and then a fresh goat cheese. Instead go from mild to strong, soft to hard, within the same category of cheeses.

• A cheese should always be at room temperature before sampling. A cold cheese has muted flavors and aromas and cannot be appreciated at its full value.

• If the cheese is not at room temperature, take a small piece and rub it between your thumb and index finger. Then smell it. By rubbing it, you're warming it up and you're also helping to release some of its aromas, which will in turn further your evaluation of the cheese. The aroma is just as important as the taste, and this is the simplest way to coax out this essential component in the cheese. Also, by rubbing it between your fingers you will begin to get a visceral understanding of the differences between semi-soft, semi-hard, and hard cheeses. There's nothing like touching a cheese to understand its moisture or dryness.

• Take your time. It is important to really pay attention to what you're tasting.

• If you can, taste with people who know more than you. They can help educate you and your palate.

• Look at the cheese. Its visual appeal is not only an aesthetic consideration but also one of the best indicators of the condition of the cheese. If, for example, a hard cheese is cracking and has some blue mold in the middle of it, it might be over the hill. On the other hand, if a soft-ripened cheese is beginning to sag a little, it's simply in the process of ripening and could very well be at its peak. Ask your cheesemonger to guide you.

• Treat cheese tasting a little like wine tasting: What is the color of the cheese? What is its texture? Swish it around in your mouth and see how your different taste receptors respond to the nuances in the cheese.

• Try not to sample the cut side of a cheese if it has been exposed to plastic wrap. Sometimes plastic can impart a flavor that will alter the taste of the cheese. (See "How to Buy and Store Cheese.")

• Sample cheese from its center to its rind. Even if you're eating a cheese that doesn't have an edible rind, it will taste different at its core, or its paste (or *pâte* as it is called), than it does closer to the area that is more exposed to air. This is a good way to gain an appreciation for the particular subtleties existent within the same cheese.

• "Listen" to what you're tasting. Don't chew rapidly and swallow. Instead, chew slowly and work the cheese through your mouth, from the front of the mouth to the back. What is the first sensation you get? Is it salty? Bitter? Strong? Sweet? Press it against the roof of your mouth. What is its texture? Keep a small amount of the cheese in your mouth and take a breath through the mouth, exhaling through the nose. This will bring the flavor and scent of the cheese through your nasal passages, which will help you to understand and appreciate both the taste and the smell of the cheese.

• Try not to talk along the way. Just listen to what your senses are telling you. This will help you get in touch with the intricacies of cheese. Most cheeses are more complex than we give them credit for.

• Eat another piece of cheese and, again, pay attention to what happens to the lingering flavors in your mouth. Your taste buds extend throughout the mouth and throat area and may give you some surprising messages about the cheese as it makes its way down. Also, the flavors will linger on the tongue and often those flavors will give you the truest results of your tasting. Ultimately they will help you judge whether the cheese gets added to your shopping basket or left for someone else's cart.

• If you're tasting cheeses at home, don't taste them with other foods. Palate cleansers, such as bread or unflavored crackers, are okay, but crackers with spices, lots of salt, or cheese flavor will impede your ability to really taste the cheese. One palate cleanser that works rather nicely is sweet melon. However, bear in mind that melon is very filling.

• Drink water only. Other beverages, such as wine, are fine if you're doing a wine and cheese pairing, or if you're just in the mood to eat cheese rather than really *taste* it, but if you're tasting cheeses with an eye toward educating yourself about them, keep other flavors to a minimum.

CHEESE-TASTING VOCABULARY

Like wine tasting, cheese tasting has a vocabulary that can be useful in helping to define the characteristics within the cheese, desirable or not. Many of the flavor characteristics of cheese are similar to those in wine and are thus described similarly. But most of us have not been exposed to that vocabulary when it comes to cheese, nor do we know how to use it.

The following list is not scientific, but it does draw from a variety of scientific papers, culinary artists, cheese distributors and vendors, and dairy sources as well as from abundant personal experience. It is mainly to help you get started in the world of cheese tasting by expanding not only your vocabulary but also your understanding of the world of cheeses that come with the "Made in the U.S.A." label.

The list is categorized by aroma, flavor, mouthfeel/texture, and visual appeal. Each of these categories begins with a list of favorable descriptive terms followed by less favorable terms. Sometimes a characteristic of a cheese can be favorable in certain cases and unfavorable in others. For example, a blue cheese will have mold, but hopefully a Swiss cheese will not. In this case, mold is favorable in one case and unfavorable in another. As a result, several of the terms are followed by the phrase "depending on the cheese."

As you'll see, many of the descriptive adjectives appear in more than one category. This happens because of the close relationship between our senses. The senses of smell and taste are not easily differentiated and, as noted earlier, work hand in hand. But more important, this crossover in terms probably helps to explain why so many people love cheese: it is complex and it satisfies several of our senses at once. Now *that's* a food worth eating.

DESCRIBING CHEESE

AROMA

FAVORABLE

Barnyardy (depending on
the cheese)
Earthy
Floral
Fresh
Fresh milk
Fruity
Gamy (depending on the cheese)
Garlicky
Moldlike (depending on
the cheese)

Musty (depending on
the cheese)
Nutty
Oniony
Perfumy
Smoky
Subtle
Sweet
Truffly
Vegetal

LESS FAVORABLE

Acrid
Ammoniated
Barnyardy (depending on
the cheese)
Gamy (depending on the cheese)
Pungent
Sour
Sour milk

FLAVOR

FAVORABLE

Acidic (depending on
the cheese)
Applelike
Balanced (milk/acid)
Barnyardy (depending on
the cheese)
Butterscotch
Buttery
Citrusy
Clean
Coffee
Complex
Creamy
Delicate
Earthy
Explosive
Farmlike
Feed (flavors of the animal feed
come through milk)
Fresh milk
Fruity

Grassy
Hay
Hazelnut
Herbaceous
Herb-flavored
Lemony
Moldy (depending on
the cheese)
Mushroomy
Musty (depending on
the cheese)
Muttonlike
Nutty
Peppery
Piquant
Rich
Ripe
Robust
Rustic
Savory (*umami*)
Sharp
Smoked

Smoky
Spicy
Springlike
Strong (depending on
the cheese)
Sweet
Tangy
Tart
Toffee
Truffly
Vegetal
Wine-cured
Yeasty
Zesty

LESS FAVORABLE

Acidic (depending on
the cheese)
Acrid
Ammoniated
Artificial
Barnyardy (depending on
the cheese)

LESS FAVORABLE (continued)

Bitter

Fermented

Flat

Garlicky

Metallic

Moldy (depending on
the cheese)

Oily

One-dimensional

Overpowering

Overripe

Plastic-wrap

Pungent

Rancid

Soapy

Sour

Strong (depending on
the cheese)

Sulfurous

Watery

Waxy

Weedy

TEXTURE

FAVORABLE

Body

Buttery

Crumbly

Crystallized

Dense

Firm

Fondant-like

Hard

Open

Runny

Silky

Smooth

Soft

Supple

Velvety

LESS FAVORABLE

Acidic

Burning

Chalky

Curdy

Gummy

Pasty

Rubbery

Slimy

Tough

VISUAL APPEAL

FAVORABLE OR NEUTRAL

Bloomy rind

Cloth-wrapped

Cream-colored

Crumbly (depending on
the cheese)

Delicate

Fresh-looking

Furry (depending on the cheese)

Ivory

Leaf-wrapped

Natural rind

Open

Orange

Runny (depending on
the cheese)

Smooth (depending on
the cheese)

Solid

Uniform

Veiny

Waxy (depending on the cheese)

Well shaped

LESS FAVORABLE

Bumpy

Cracked

Cryovac'd

Dried out

Dull

Faded

Furry (depending on the cheese)

Holey (depending on the cheese)

Ill-shaped

Lopsided

Moldy (depending on the
cheese)

Mottled

Off-colored

Oily

Pale

Plastic-wrapped (depending on
the cheese)

Red-hued rind

Rind rot

Saggy

Slimy

Unappetizing

Uneven

Unnatural color

Waxy (depending on the cheese)

HOW TO BUY AND STORE CHEESE

IT USED TO BE THAT A TRIP to the local cheese store meant a romp through a few varieties of cheddar, Jack, or mozzarella. While those choices still overflow on the store shelves, they're being increasingly crowded by cheeses with names like Camellia, Trade Lake Cedar, and Orb Weaver. Without an American cheese directory, these names have little meaning. That's where your sense of adventure, along with a good retailer, comes in.

As with wine, developing your cheese palate as well as your cheese-buying skills takes experience. One thing is certain: there is no substitute for tasting. Without trying cheeses, you cannot know what they taste like, and more important, whether you like them. (See the preceding chapter for more on how to taste cheese.) Most retailers are ecstatic when a customer wants to learn more about cheese. Because of that, they're usually trimming off a piece for you to taste long before you have had the chance to ask. But if that isn't the case, don't be afraid to ask. A good cheese shop wants to educate you and knows that the best way to do that is to let you try their products.

If you don't have any idea of what you want, simply state that. The retailer will probably begin by asking you how you plan to use the cheese. Or a cheesemonger might take a quick glance at the cheeses that fill the counter and then cut off a small chunk from one of those cheeses for you to sample. Your reaction becomes the starting point for the conversation and ultimately the cheese-buying transaction.

Good retailers will continue by asking you a few more questions in an effort to zero in on your tastes and needs. For example, what time of day will the cheese be served? Is it to be served before dinner? After dinner? On a picnic? For breakfast? Is the cheese an ingredient in a recipe? If so, what is the recipe? Will the cheese be served along with other foods or by itself? Is the cheese part of a cheese course? (See "The Cheese Course" for more information.)

These types of questions help you, the customer, to become more focused on what you might be looking for and to become comfortable with the cheese-buying process. If you are shopping for cheese at a local market where there is no cheesemonger available, then these are excellent questions to ask yourself. You can then buy your cheese with a lot more confidence.

Appearance is also important, since the physical character of the cheese may very well determine its quality. But buying with your eye takes experience. For example, if the cheese you're buying is a Swiss and it has the creamy color you're looking for, you might think it's perfectly fine. But look again: the color may appeal to you, but is the cheese itself cracking? Are there dull or grayish spots on the cut surface? Is there mold on the cut surface? Are the signature Swiss cheese holes missing? If so, this cheese may not have been made well and/or cared for properly.

Sometimes, however, a questionable appearance might be deceptive if you don't know what you're looking for. For example, a soft, runny cheese, such as California's Peluso Teleme, is at its best when it is oozing rather than when it is in its square, molded form. Some people might think there's something wrong with a cheese if it's running all over the place. The only way to be sure is to ask your cheese vendor.

In fact, "ask and taste" is probably the best credo to live by when learning about cheese. As a practical matter, however, it may not be possible to stand at a cheese counter for an extended period and try a dozen or more cheeses at one time. Because of this, consider buying very small amounts of three or four cheeses, taking them home, tasting them, and taking notes on what you've tried. Pretty soon you will have developed your own personal cheese diary, which will quickly help you understand the different cheeses and, most of all, determine what you like. Again, as with wine, your cheese tastes will change, evolve, and become more finely tuned as you add more and more cheeses to your repertoire.

STORING CHEESE

I don't know about your refrigerator, but mine is home to more half-eaten pieces of cheese than I care to admit. Invariably, I buy two or three cheeses at a time, having made great plans for them, and then somehow I don't use them up. Of course it is nice to have leftover cheese, but it's just that the cheese part of my refrigerator becomes slightly unruly after those two or three become nine or ten. As a result, I've learned a few things about storing cheese and using small pieces of cheese that help prevent the garbage disposal from being the ultimate cheese consumer in my home.

One easy, if not creative, way to take care of all of your cheese scraps is to make something the French call *fromage fort*, or literally, strong cheese. Fromage fort is a blend of cheese scraps (rind, hard spots, and mold cut out), optional herbs and spices, a little butter, and a little white wine (see page 75 for a recipe). The particular cheeses don't matter, as long as they are trimmed. However, if you do not want to create a cheese du jour, then learning about storing cheeses is essential.

Knowing how to store cheese means understanding what happens to cheese once it is cut from its protective coating or rind. A cheese is usually made in the form of a wheel or a block. That wheel or block has some sort of rind, coating, or wax that keeps the cheese fresh as well as somewhat moist, depending on the age and type of the cheese. Once a piece of cheese is cut from that wheel or block, it no longer has that protective rind—only a portion of it. This means it must be wrapped in the way that will best preserve it.

In addition, cheese, whether whole or cut, is in a constant state of moisture loss, or aging. This simply means that cheese gets harder as it gets older because it continuously loses moisture. The same aging process continues in your refrigerator, and knowing how to wrap and store cheese will help retard moisture loss and extend the life of the cheese.

Ideally, "pretend you are creating a cellar environment" when storing cheese, says one cheesemonger. This means that you want a cool place, away from drafts, yet with some air circulation. Unless you're lucky enough to actually have a cellar or a cheese aging room, attempting to simulate that environment is the next best thing. This means allowing your cheese to breathe yet retain its moisture. How do you do both?

There are a few ways. First, wrap cheese in waxed paper or parchment. Both of these materials let in a small amount of air, allowing the cheese to breathe. At the same time, you are allowing the cheese to maintain some of its moisture because the moisture loss will take place slowly.

One exception to this is when you are storing a hard grating cheese, such as an Asiago or a dry Jack. Because these cheeses are already dry to begin with, you want to minimize the amount of air they get. In

OPPOSITE: A wedge of aged cheddar from Shelburne Farms in Shelburne, Vermont. Shelburne Farms also makes a rare, English-style cloth-wrapped cheddar.

this case, plastic wrap is the best choice. Be aware, however, that plastic can impart a subtle flavor of its own. Also, it should be changed often since it not only keeps *out* the air but also keeps *in* the bacteria.

In fact, it is important to take into account the type of cheese before deciding on the appropriate wrapping material. Semi-soft cheeses are best stored in waxed paper or parchment paper. They'll continue to age (that is, lose moisture), but that is natural. Likewise, soft-ripened cheeses, such as a Camembert-style cheese, should be in some type of breathable environment. Soft-ripened cheeses ripen from the rind, or outside, inward, and if they are wrapped in plastic wrap, the moisture will get trapped and the rind will die. The rest of the cheese will die, too. You can also try placing a soft-ripened cheese in a plastic container with a few pinholes poked into it. This allows the cheese to breathe, but it creates a slightly warmer environment at the same time. Be sure to check the cheese often to make sure it has enough air. Otherwise, it will quickly become ammoniated.

Iowa's famous Maytag Blue.

It may sound confusing, but it really comes down to common sense plus a little experience. If a cheese is hard to begin with, then try to limit its exposure to the air. If a cheese is moist to begin with, then let it breathe a little or its moisture, if trapped, will end up suffocating the cheese. It is probably better to err on the side of wrapping a cheese too loosely, or with too breathable a material, than wrapping it too tightly, or with a material that doesn't breathe, such as plastic wrap. If, however, you notice that one of your cheeses seems to be drying out more than you would like, wrap it in plastic. That will slow down its moisture loss.

Any time you buy a cheese that has been vacuum-packed, be sure to place it in waxed or parchment paper, or unwrapped in a plastic container, after you have taken it out of its packaging. The vacuum-packed process is good for preserving the cheese during shipping, but it will not keep a cheese in good condition for very long once you have brought it home.

Temperature is another consideration when storing cheese. In general, cheese should be placed in the warmer parts of the refrigerator, toward the top or in the drawer, away from any fans. It is best not to use the designated "cheese" compartment if it is on the door of the refrigerator because the door is opened and closed frequently, subjecting the cheese to unwelcome temperature changes. In an ideal world, most cheese would be stored for a short time at around 53°F, but most home refrigerators run seven to ten degrees cooler than that. That's why the drawer compartments, usually designated for produce, are good for cheese—since they are slightly warmer.

If you're a little adventurous, you can try keeping your cheese out on the kitchen counter instead of refrigerating it. Of course, this is not the best way to store cheese if it is the middle of the summer and you are sweltering. Your cheese will swelter, too. But in moderate climates, a cheese can be kept on the countertop, covered, for two to three days, allowing for a perfect eating temperature at all times. The type of environment used to protect the cheese can be anything from a bread box to a cake plate with a glass or plastic cover to a terra-cotta pot that has been moistened. The cheese should be set on a plate so that air can circulate *underneath* as well—place a piece of chicken wire, a small cooling rack, or some other type of metal grid on top of the plate. Place the cheese on top of the rack and cover it. Regardless of its environment, cheese does not respond well to wide variations in temperature, so if your kitchen is not fairly temperate, it is probably best not to try storing your cheese outside of the refrigerator.

Also, if you choose to try the countertop method, try to buy no more cheese than you think you will be able to use in the two or three days that it will be on the counter. Otherwise, the cheese might be wasted. Of course you can always put the cheese in the refrigerator at any time, and indeed you should if the kitchen temperature is changing or if the cheese is ripening too fast.

It is a good rule of thumb to buy no more cheese than you think you can use in one or two sittings. Sometimes that is hard to judge, and the amount you buy is entirely dependent on its intended use. If it is for a cheese and wine tasting, where only a small amount of other food, if any, is being served, then you will probably want to allow as much as 6 ounces of cheese per person. This is a large amount, and not everyone will eat this much, but it is amazing how quickly people will work their way through cheese, especially when it is the "main course." If you are buying two or three cheeses to sample and learn about at home, then allow about 2 ounces of cheese per person. If the cheese is to be used in a recipe, the recipe will specify the exact amount you will need.

In general, you should check your cheese every few days and change the wrapping material at the same time. If the cheese has begun to get moldy, simply cut off the mold (wiping the knife or cheese cutter after each slice to avoid spreading the mold on the rest of the cheese), and be sure to change the wrap. If you cut off the mold without changing the wrap, the mold spores on the wrapping material will reinfect the cheese.

Sometimes a cheese cannot be salvaged. If it looks, smells, and tastes questionable, throw it away. On the other hand, some cheese can be saved, even when it might not seem like it. For example, if a cheese has become slightly ammoniated (literally, it smells like ammonia), try opening it up and letting it sit, uncovered, in the refrigerator or on the countertop for a couple of hours. If the ammonia smell is still there after two hours, then the cheese is probably no longer good. But you might find that all the cheese needed was some air.

Likewise, you may buy a cheese that started out as a semi-hard cheese and, as it has lasted in your refrigerator, become harder. This "new" cheese can be truly wonderful, although you might have to shave away a little bit of mold before uncovering the healthy cheese. In the course of its moisture loss, it may have become a flavorful grating cheese.

Remember, cheese is an organic, evolving product. Part of that evolution might mean a little mold, but it's usually harmless. The character of a cheese changes from day to day, and so do its texture and taste. That's part of the intrigue of cheese as well as its complexity. It is also part of the fun. In fact, you might discover that the cheese you accidentally left in the back of your refrigerator can easily be the gourmet centerpiece on your dinner table tonight.

STORING CHEESE AT-A-GLANCE

SOFT OR FRESH CHEESES = HIGHEST MOISTURE = PLASTIC CONTAINER

Young blue cheese	Fresh goat cheese	Quark
Cottage cheese	Fromage blanc	Queso fresco
Crème fraîche	Mascarpone	Ricotta
Feta	*Pasta filata* cheeses, such as mozzarella or Oaxaca	

SOFT-RIPENED AND SEMI-SOFT CHEESES = HIGH MOISTURE = WAXED OR PARCHMENT PAPER, OR PLASTIC CONTAINER WITH HOLES

Beer Käse	Crescenza	Limburger
Brick	Crottin	Mossholder
Brie	Gorgonzola	Muenster
Butter Käse	Havarti	Provolone (some)
Camembert	Jack (some)	Teleme

SEMI-HARD TO HARD CHEESES = MEDIUM TO LOW MOISTURE = BREATHABLE WRAPPING MATERIAL (WAXED OR PARCHMENT PAPER) OR, TO RETAIN MOISTURE, PLASTIC WRAP

Asiago	Crowley	Gruyère
Baby Swiss	Edam	Jack
Blue cheese	Emmentaler	Swiss
Cheddar	Fontina	Tilsit
Colby	Gouda	

HARD CHEESES = LOWEST MOISTURE = LESS BREATHABLE MATERIAL (PLASTIC WRAP)

Asiago (some)	Enchilado	Romano
Cotija	Parmesan	
Dry Jack	Ricotta salata	

PAIRING CHEESE AND WINE

⊱—⊷—✦—⊶—⊰

THE OLD SCHOOL OF THOUGHT about cheese and wine pairing used to be simple: eat cheese with red wine. Period. Now, however, that has changed. While some red wines are indeed good cheese wines, they are far more difficult to match with many cheeses. White wines, on the other hand, tend to be more cheese friendly because of the relative lack of tannins (the astringent quality in many red wines), and because they are often cleaner, simpler, and sweeter. But whether it's white or red, the matching of wine with cheese is not as intuitive as it might seem. This is because both wine and cheese have highly distinguishable characteristics that taste excellent on their own but together might be disastrous. Also, as agricultural products, cheese and wine often vary from season to season. The same cheese from the same cheesemaker might taste different at various times of the year due to changes in the diet of the animals whose milk is being used for the cheese. Also, the handcrafted nature of specialty cheese naturally leads to slight variations from batch to batch.

Likewise, the same bottle of wine from the same producer and vintage might taste slightly different from one bottle to the next, not because the wine itself varies, but because the experience around the wine varies. The first time the wine is served it might accompany a roasted leg of lamb. The next time a bottle from the same vintage, same grape, and same winemaker is opened, it might be paired with lasagna. Although the wine itself is probably no different, its characteristics will seem different because of the food being served alongside it.

What's more, the memories of the same wine can be vastly different depending on the events that surrounded the drinking of the wine. The wine served during a wonderful evening may be remembered as fantastic. A not-so-good evening, where the same wine is offered, might inadvertently taint the memory of the wine.

It is difficult to overstate how subjective cheese and wine pairing really is. What one person may think is a great or "classic" combination may taste downright awful to another. That said, there are some general rules that are worth following to help create successful cheese and wine pairings, and more—to create evocative, sensual memories of the perfect food experience.

Cheeses and wines should be paired either because they share similar characterics or because they have contrasting but complementary characteristics. How can you know which is which? Wine can best be understood by looking at its components. Basically, wine is made up of acid, alcohol, sugar, and tannins. The variation of these components, as well as production factors and aging, is primarily what gives each wine its unique flavor. Cheese shares some of the components found in wine, including acid, but it is also made up of protein and fat. The concentration of these components contributes to the final flavor of cheese, and leads to the successful or unsuccessful marriage with certain wines. One classic pairing is sauvignon blanc with fresh goat cheese. In many sauvignon blancs (occasionally called fumé blanc), the acids in the wine are kept high to bring out the crisp, clean qualities in the sauvignon blanc grape. Fresh goat cheese also has a high acid level, which is partly what gives it its tangy flavor. Put the two together and you have a seamless blend of flavors—an example of cheese and wine sharing similar characteristics.

Other examples of complementary cheese and wine pairings would be a California chardonnay, which has a lower acid level, alongside a somewhat older cheese that also has a lower acid level. These could range from a medium-aged Gouda or cheddar to several of the mountain cheeses, including Gruyère, Emmentaler, and Swiss cheese. The slightly higher salt content in each of these cheeses, along with their earthy, nutty flavors, helps them to pair with the buttery, oaky qualities typical of a California chardonnay.

A classic contrasting pairing would be a salty blue cheese with a sweet dessert wine. The reason is simple: salt and sugar are the predominant characteristics, and in this case, result in complementary flavors. On the other hand, you do not want to try pairing a strong cheese with a light wine. That is an example of a contrast that will end up quashing the wine and exaggerating the already strong characteristics of the cheese.

In fact, it is important to remember that cheese influences the taste of wine much more than wine influences the flavor of cheese. As a result, pairing a strong cheese with an older, mellow wine will likely result in a flavorless wine. Likewise, pairing a highly acidic cheese with a low-acid, light-bodied wine will probably make the wine taste bland.

Keep in mind that creamy cheeses, or those with a high fat and protein content, will almost invariably soften the tannins in a wine. This means that if you are drinking a big, bold cabernet sauvignon, a Camembert-like cheese, a creamier-style blue cheese, or an aged hard cheese like dry Jack or Antigo's Stravecchio will coat the palate and make way for the tannic wine to find a smooth passage through the mouth.

The owners of Brie & Bordeaux, an exemplary cheese and wine shop in Seattle, spend much of their day helping people create the right cheese and wine combinations. Co-owner Alison Leber says that for red wines, she generally has the greatest luck matching cabernet sauvignon, syrah, and merlot with cheese because these wines are fairly predictable in style (based on where they are from and how long they have been in the bottle). Pinot noir, on the other hand, has no fewer than 1,000 clones, according to Leber, and that makes matching it with cheese—or any other food for that matter—far more challenging. The right pinot noir-cheese combination, however, is unbeatable.

Another good cheese wine is Gewürztraminer. *Gewürz* means spice, and with its crisp characteristics, Gewürztraminer pairs well with a variety of cheeses, including young goat cheese and an aged earthy cheese such as Vermont Shepherd. Brie & Bordeaux's Leber underscores the notion that the special characteristics in Gewürztraminer tend to bring out the fruit flavors in a cheese like Vermont Shepherd, bringing them into balance with that cheese's more forward earthiness. And as a general rule, according to John Ash, culinary director at Fetzer Vineyards in California, sweeter white wines will work with cheese more often than dry white wines do. An example of this might be chenin blanc, which is a light, somewhat fruity cheese-friendly grape. It matches particularly well with light cheeses, but it will also stand up to some stronger cheeses because of its relative fruitiness.

Trying to match cheese and wine by region, as is often done in Europe, is a virtual impossibility in the United States. In France, many goat cheeses are made in the Loire Valley, where Sancerre is also made. Sancerre is made from the sauvignon blanc grape, which is the classic match with fresh goat cheese. By contrast, the majority of wine made in the United States comes from California, while the majority of cheddar cheeses are made in Wisconsin. The areas where we make cheese do not necessarily go hand in hand

OPPOSITE: Long Island's Sagpond Emmentaler has a natural accompaniment: a glass of Sagpond Vineyards wine.

with our wine production areas, and matching the two consequently is more challenging.

Below are a few guidelines for wine and cheese pairing. Keep in mind that these are very general, since both wine and cheese are ever-changing. What might work today could change entirely with next year's vintage or that season's cheese.

- Light cheeses with light wines (young cows', goats', or sheep's milk cheese with chenin blanc)
- High-acid, younger cheeses with high-acid white wines (fresh goat cheese with sauvignon blanc)
- Low-acid, more aged cheeses with low-acid white wines (aged cows' milk cheeses with oaky chardonnay)
- Stronger cheeses with stronger wines (aged cheddar with syrah)
- Strong, salty cheeses with dessert wines or fortified wines (blue cheese with late-harvest Riesling)

It is a little harder to pair wine with several cheeses at one time, as in a cheese course. For this reason, the selection of cheeses should be kept to no more than three, unless you plan to offer more than one type of wine. For example, you could pair two or three high-acid cheeses, such as fresh goat cheeses, with a sauvignon blanc or a non-oaky chardonnay. If, however, the pairing isn't terribly important, then feel free to serve as many cheeses—and wines—as you like.

Many people like to drink champagne. With its bubbles, its sugar, and its yeastiness, it would seem that it might not be a cheese-friendly beverage. *Au contraire*. Champagne works beautifully with many soft-ripened cheeses, including Camembert and Brie-style cheese, as well as with some hard cheeses. In addition, many cheese aficionados are passionate about blue cheese with sparkling wine. They love the salty and earthy qualities of the cheese in combination with the bubbly, earthy qualities of the wine. If you think about the classic combination of champagne and (salty) caviar, it begins to make sense.

CHEESE AND OTHER BEVERAGES

In addition to wine, there is a wide range of beverages that go with cheese. Beer fans salivate at the prospect of putting together a sharp cheddar with an amber ale or a stout. After all, this is a tradition that is still in full swing in the British Isles as well as in Belgium (home of at least 300 beers and ales) and Germany, among other countries. Drinking beer with cheese can be a filling proposition but a rewarding one nonetheless.

Like wine, beer has numerous characteristics that can turn it into a cheese companion or a cheese enemy. For example, some beers have very strong foodlike flavors, such as butterscotch or caramel. These qualities could make such beers a nice match for an aged Gouda. On the other hand, it could just as easily be a disastrous match since those flavors in the beer might very well compete with the butterscotch components of the cheese rather than complement them. The foolproof way of determining what works is to try different combinations.

The "rules" for beer and cheese pairing mostly parallel those for matching wine with cheese. Light-bodied beers should be paired with lighter-style cheeses, while stronger aged cheeses will find a friend in the darker beers, ales, and stouts. Yet for every rule there is an exception. The Wisconsin Milk Marketing Board, for example, suggests pairing a dark lager with a fresh mozzarella. This is an example of a contrasting, rather than complementary, pairing, and it is also an example of a rule-breaker that works. The Wisconsin Milk Marketing Board has actually developed a handy guide to beer and cheese pairing that will

help anyone who is interested in these combinations (see the Resources section).

Finally, there are myriad nonalcoholic beverages that fold right into the flavors of cheese. Like sauvignon blanc and goat cheese, apple cider (nonalcoholic or alcoholic) and soft-ripened cheese is an age-old tradition from the Normandy area of France that certainly works just as well in this country. Likewise, carbonated water is a great palate cleanser and works perfectly well with cheese of any kind. Soft drinks are too sugary to pair with most cheeses, and acidic juices, such as orange or grapefruit juice, will generally kill or alter the flavors of cheese in unfavorable ways. However, nonalcoholic grape juices, such as those that are being made increasingly by wineries, offer some of the same characteristics of regular wine, although they will naturally be sweeter and in some cases less cheese-friendly.

For every guideline or rule about cheese and beverage pairing, there is usually another guideline, rule, or suggestion to counter it. Nonetheless, two rules are ironclad: Experiment with different combinations, and do not be intimidated about asking cheese, wine, or other beverage retailers for their suggestions.

It is exciting to discover the perfect cheese and beverage combination, and the way to do that is to have fun with the process. Experimenting will lead you to some great discoveries, and the knowledge you acquire along the way will increase your confidence when it comes to serving cheese with any type of beverage at home.

THE CHEESE COURSE

PUTTING TOGETHER A CHEESE COURSE, or cheese board as it is often called, is limited only by your imagination. The grouping can be thematic, it can be systematic, or it can be eclectic. Some combinations will work better than others, but the best way to find out is to try them.

Here are a few suggestions for putting together a cheese board that will make for a fun, flavorful, and festive course. The one important guideline to remember is that it is best to sample cheeses in sequence from soft to hard and from mild to strong. Starting out with a strong cheese will disable your palate for anything left to come.

SELECTING THE CHEESES

• Choose cheeses with a variety of textures. This might mean a soft, fresh goat cheese, a semi-hard mountain-style cheese, such as a Gruyère, and a hard and flavorful cheese like an aged Jack or Parmesan-style cheese. You might choose two cheeses within each category to give a nice variety as well as an interesting lesson in how similar cheeses can be very different.

• Choose several versions of the same cheese made by different producers. This works with any kind of cheese, and it makes for a wonderful learning situation. For example, blue cheeses vary widely, depending on

the maker and the method of production. There is no better way to learn about their differences than by sampling them in one sitting. You'll be surprised to discover how some blue cheeses taste stronger, while others might be saltier, while still others might be more creamy.

Clockwise from top: Old Chatham Sheepherding Company Camembert, Maytag Blue Cheese, Vermont Shepherd, Vella Dry Jack, and Capriole Wabash Cannonball (center).

• Assemble a cheese board by choosing cheeses made from the three main types of milk: goat, sheep, and cow. You might include a fresh cheese like fromage blanc, a soft-ripened cheese made from sheep's milk, and an aged cheese made from goats' milk. Again, you might opt to include several cheeses within each category.

• Choose a cheese board based on the wine you are serving. If you are serving a young, highly acidic wine, then choose young, highly acidic cheeses. If you are serving more than one wine, try to serve cheeses that might go with the various wines. This is a little trickier, but it makes for a fun learning experience. If you are serving a big, bold red wine, serve creamy and/or salty cheeses since both will complement the wine.

• Select a theme. Maybe you live in Maine and would like to try California cheeses. Obtaining a few California-made cheeses through the many wonderful cheese shops and mail-order sources could make for a fun and educational cheese course. Another theme might be farmstead cheeses—cheeses that are made only with milk from the cheesemaker's animals. It might be interesting to compare the various farmstead sheep's milk cheeses made in Vermont.

• Don't mix several strong cheeses. A smoked cheese, for example, will overtake almost every other flavor. For this reason, it should probably not be served as part of a cheese board. If you are intent on serving a smoked cheese, serve it on its own. A strong washed-rind cheese, such as an aged brick cheese, will compete for attention with another strong cheese, and both cheeses will lose. Choose one or the other but not both.

BASICS FOR PLANNING AND SERVING

• Allow two to six ounces per person, depending on when the cheese course is being served. If it is a course following dinner but preceding dessert, allow about two ounces per person. If it is the only food being served, allow four to six ounces per person.

• Serve no more than six cheeses, preferably less. Fewer is better because it is easier to concentrate on the flavors of a few cheeses.

• Bring all cheeses to room temperature before serving.

• If you are serving individual portions, it is easier to cut the soft cheeses while they are still cold. Bring them to room temperature after they are cut. If you are presenting the cheeses on one cheese platter, do not cut them in advance. Simply cut them as needed, but again, be sure they're at room temperature.

• Have several serving utensils available if you are serving large pieces of different types of cheese. A spoon might be necessary for a soft, runny cheese while a sharp, sturdy cheese knife might be necessary for a hard cheese. There should be as many utensils as there are cheeses. Don't plan to use one knife for three cheeses; the cheeses will become intermingled in the cutting process.

• It seems there is a cheese knife for just about every type of cheese. For hard cheeses, a cheese "shaver" or plane works best. This is a straight-handled rounded V-shaped wide blade with a horizontal opening in the middle that is for shaving the cheese. The sides of the blade can be used for cutting. (A vegetable peeler also works nicely for shaving hard cheeses.) For soft cheeses, the aptly-named cheese knife, also called a skeleton knife due to the holes in the middle of the blade, works best. Those holes prevent the cheese from sticking to the knife. Both a skeleton cheese knife and a regular cheese knife (one that doesn't have the blade holes) have two prongs at the tip for spearing the cut piece of cheese to put on a plate or napkin. Wire slicers work well for semi-soft to semi-hard cheeses, especially to make uniform-sized slices, and short stubby knives are best for digging out chunks of extra-hard cheese from a wheel.

• Serve simple fruits, vegetables, and breads with the cheese. You can even try matching a fruit or vegetable with a particular cheese. For example, dried dates and aged, salty cheeses form an addictive combination. A thin piece of walnut toast is a great host for a fresh goat cheese. And the licorice flavor in a piece of fennel provides a gentle contrast with a fresh cows' milk cheese or even a young Emmentaler.

• Refrigerate any leftover cheeses as soon as possible. Certain cheeses, such as the soft-ripened ones, may be difficult to wrap if they have spread out from being at room temperature. In this case, use a spatula to transfer the cheese to a plate, cover it tightly with plastic wrap, and refrigerate it just until it is chilled, about half an hour. Then remove the plastic wrap and place the cheese in a plastic container or wrap it with waxed or parchment paper for longer-term storage.

• Have fun.

COOKING WITH CHEESE

⊱──⊰

"**M**ANY'S THE LONG NIGHT I've dreamed of cheese—toasted mostly," said Robert Louis Stevenson. But who hasn't dreamed of creamy melted cheese on bread, or on top of a pizza crust, or oozing from lasagna after that first poke of a knife? All of these images are what makes cheese the sought-after comfort—and cooking—food that it is. At the same time, cooking with cheese can be a slightly greater challenge than it might seem. Just as easily as cheese melts, it also can become a stringy or curdled mess.

Cheese is essentially a mass of protein that is quite content to stay that way. When heated, it rebels and tries desperately to cling to its fellow proteins. In so doing, it separates just enough to create strings, or something we try to avoid: curdling. This usually happens as the result of any one of four factors: the temperature is too high for the particular cheese being used; the cheese has been exposed to high temperatures for too long; there isn't a sufficient amount of acid (lemon juice or wine, for example) to prevent the cheese from curdling; or the dish does not have the proper amount of starch to prevent coagulation.

Fortunately, there are ways to avoid this.

• Before cooking with them, grate all cheeses that fall within the semi-hard to hard range. This allows the cheese to melt faster, reducing the need for a long cooking time. When cooking with soft and semi-soft cheeses, cut them into very small pieces.

• Grate the cheese that will be added to a dish after it comes off the stove or out of the oven. Because grating results in quicker melting, it ensures that the dish will be hot. Pasta is a perfect example, where cheese is often added after the dish is removed from its heat source.

• Cold cheese is much easier to grate than room-temperature cheese. Keep the cheese in the refrigerator until you are ready to grate it. Once the cheese is grated, bring it to room temperature for cooking, since room-temperature cheese cooks more evenly.

• Grate cheese over waxed paper. You can then simply lift the waxed paper and, holding the short ends together, make a chute through which the cheese will slide directly into a bowl or measuring cup.

• Add a little starch to cheese dishes that will be cooked for a long time. For example, the flour in the sauce for macaroni and cheese virtually eliminates the chance of the cheese becoming stringy when it is added.

• In general, harder cheeses work better at high temperatures than softer cheeses do. The broken-down protein structure in hard cheeses allows for this. Such cheeses include everything from Parmesan-like cheeses to Gruyère and Emmentaler.

• Use wine or another acidic ingredient, such as lemon juice, when making fondues and other cheese dishes that will be subject to an extended period of heat. This lowers the boiling point and helps prevent the stringiness that would otherwise result from the constant heat.

• Most cheese should not be subjected to very high heat except for a brief period of time. The

Mushroom and Camembert Crostini (pages 110–111) get a short heat treatment under the broiler. Likewise, the pizzas (pages 128, 131, 133, and 136) are baked in a 500°F oven, but only for about 15 minutes.

• Use blue cheese sparingly in cooked dishes—a little goes a long way.

• Use creamy cheeses, such as fresh goat cheese, fromage blanc, or blue cheese, instead of cream or milk to create a thick, creamy consistency in such dishes as cooked spinach or even mashed potatoes. Make sure the cheese is at room temperature before using.

• If you are using cheese in a sauce, add the cheese after the sauce comes off the heat. Both hard and soft cheeses can be used in a sauce. Higher-moisture cheeses, or those with more water and fat than hard cheeses, are slightly more tricky, but added little by little to a sauce off the heat will result in a creamy, velvety sauce.

COOKING MEASUREMENTS

• 4 ounces cheese, grated and loosely packed, is the equivalent of about 1½ cups

• 2 ounces soft, fresh cheese, loosely packed, is the equivalent of about ⅓ cup

GRATING CHEESE

When it comes to grating cheese, the type of grater you use really doesn't matter as long as it will make the proper-size pieces. Just use the grater with which you are most comfortable. I find myself using the drum type of grater quite often, but a standing four- or five-sided box grater, a flat grater, and the grater blade on a food processor all work perfectly well. There is a fairly new type of grater called a rasp that is narrow, about one foot long, and is designed for grating cheese very fine. It's wonderful. But it is probably best to have a grater that offers at least two hole-size options since recipes calling for hard cheeses generally demand a finer grate than semi-hard or semi-soft cheeses, which usually call for a coarse or larger grate.

A NOTE ON FREEZING CHEESES

As a rule, it is not a good idea to freeze cheese. However, certain cheeses can be frozen with some success. Among those are goats' and sheep's milk cheeses, which, because of their protein structure, tend to hold up fairly well in the freezer. Conversely, cows' milk cheeses have a larger protein structure, which breaks down when frozen; when the cheese is defrosted, it is dry and crumbly. One way around this is to grate the cheese before freezing it, although the cheese will lose a substantial amount of flavor in the process.

Fresh cheeses, particularly fresh cows' milk cheeses such as mascarpone and fresh mozzarella, are best left unfrozen. Likewise, soft-ripened cheeses, such as a Brie or Camembert, should never be frozen because they become watery and flavorless. A hard grating cheese, such as Parmesan, can be frozen successfully either grated or whole, but like other cheese, its flavor will be diminished.

Defrost all cheese slowly in the refrigerator rather than bringing it to room temperature right away, and do not freeze any cheese for longer than one or two months. If frozen for long periods, cheese loses its wonderful creaminess and milk flavor. One exception: dishes that have been made with cheese, such as lasagna or cheese enchiladas, can be frozen with little consequence to the overall taste.

A NOTE ABOUT CHEDDAR CHEESE

As most people know, cheddar is often orange-colored. But as most people also know, that is not the color of the milk that is used to make the cheese. Instead, some cheesemakers create the coloring using annatto seeds. In cooking, the age of the cheese matters more than the color because the age most often determines the flavor as well as its cooking properties. For the cheddar recipes in this book, both white and orange will work unless otherwise specified. As a general rule, use the cheese you like the most, since you will like the final dish more as well. White cheddar or orange cheddar is simply a matter of personal (and regional) preference. In Wisconsin most of the cheddars are orange; in Vermont they are white.

HISPANIC-STYLE CHEESES

Cheeses throughout the world reflect the cultures that make them. In this country, we have cheeses from all over the world because our citizens are from all corners of the globe as well. One particular group of cheeses, however, is making its way to the forefront of cheesemaking in America: Hispanic-style cheeses. The reason is that the Hispanic population in America is growing at breakneck speed. Their indigenous cheeses are naturally following suit.

In the United States, Cacique USA in California is one of the largest producers of Hispanic-style cheeses, but others, such as Marquez Brothers in California and Tropical in New Jersey, are producing millions of pounds of Latin- and Caribbean-style cheeses as well. These cheeses are often unfamiliar to non-Hispanic people, but they are increasingly being incorporated into the diets of all Americans, not just those of Latin or Caribbean descent.

Among the best known Hispanic-style cheeses are *queso fresco* and *queso blanco fresco*. These are both mild cows' milk cheeses that have myriad cooking applications. *Queso fresco* is a soft, moist cheese that does not melt when heated. It is best used as a crumbling cheese and is a great addition to ripe tomatoes, enchiladas, or beans. It is a particularly nice crown on an avocado filled with a mixture of bay shrimp, chopped white onion, cilantro, lime juice, and tomato.

Queso blanco fresco is a firm yet moist cheese that is also a crumbling cheese, often used in salads or soups. It is more firm than *queso fresco* and holds its shape when heated. Because of this, it can also be used for frying. In this case, it is called *queso para freir* or "Frying Cheese." This type of cooking method has its roots in Central America.

Queso blanco is a more aged version of *queso blanco fresco* (fresco means fresh), and can be categorized as a semi-soft to semi-hard cheese. Like other semi-soft and semi-hard cheeses, it melts well and becomes a perfect ingredient in a simple quesadilla or an old-fashioned grilled cheese sandwich. It is mild in flavor.

Another increasingly popular cheese is called *panela*. This is a pressed, low moisture cheese that, like *queso blanco fresco*, holds its shape when cooked because it does not melt. Like most other Hispanic-style cheeses, *panela* has a mild flavor and works equally well with savory and sweet dishes. (See recipe on page 214). When whole, it is also an interesting looking cheese because it is pressed in a loosely woven basket and takes on the basket's contours as the moisture drains.

Cotija is an aged cows' milk cheese that is a salty, hard cheese. It is similar to feta cheese and can be used interchangeably with it. The main difference, apart from the fact that most feta is made with either sheep's or goats' milk, is that *cotija* is not immersed in brine. *Cotija* is also known as *queso añejo*.

Oaxaca, or *queso Oaxaca,* is a fresh cheese that is almost identical to mozzarella. It is a *pasta filata,* or stretched curd cheese, and is distinguished by its shape: a braid. Its cooking applications are also identical to mozzarella because of its melting properties and its mild flavor.

Enchilado is another Hispanic-style cheese that is very similar to *cotija* except that it is coated in paprika or chile powder. Like *cotija*, it can be crumbled and used to top a tostada, vegetables, soups, or salads.

There are several other Latin American and Caribbean cheeses and other dairy products that are making their way into mainstream supermarkets as people from these parts of the world continue to move northward. They are bringing with them exciting flavors and are weaving a beautiful new thread into the tapestry of American cheese.

OLEMA ROUNDS
COWGIRL CREAMERY

FROMAGE BLANC WITH FRESH
HERBS MADE BY SUE CONLEY $4.50
ORGANIC

QUICK REFERENCE GUIDE

⊱ ⟞⟝ ○ ⟞⟝ ⊰

FOLLOWING IS A LIST of generic cheeses that are made in the United States. It is organized by the age of the cheese, from fresh to long-aged. This should be especially useful when determining cheese substitutions for recipes or when putting together a cheese course. Some of the cheeses fall into more than one category because they are sold at different stages in their ripening process. A Provolone, for example, might be sold at two months and it might also be aged and sold after one year. The recipes in this book specify the age of the cheese (for example, "hard grating cheese").

Many specialty cheesemakers have their own names for their cheeses, which is why, at the end of each category, it says "Many specialty sheep, cow, and goat cheeses." For example, the primary cheese made at Orb Weaver Farm in Vermont is called "Vermont Farmhouse Cheese." It happens to be similar to a Colby, but it is important for the cheesemakers at Orb Weaver Farm, as it is for most American cheesemakers, to have a uniquely named cheese that represents their farm, their region, or something else that is particular to themselves or their cheese.

Many cheesemakers use established names for their cheeses when they follow the methods that have been used for centuries to make those types of cheeses. For example, a Gruyère cheese made using the traditional method will most likely be called a Gruyère.

The best way to become familiar with the cheeses being made by American cheesemakers is to seek them out. Ask your cheesemonger if he or she has any cheeses from your local area or a neighboring state. Or ask if there are any cheeses from the opposite end of the country. You'll be surprised at the number of states that are represented at your cheese counter.

FRESH CHEESES (NOT AGED OR RIPENED)
Good cooking cheeses

Bakers' Cheese	Mascarpone	Queso blanco fresco (also
Chèvre (fresh goat cheese)	Mozzarella	called queso para freir)
Cottage cheese	Oaxaca	Requeson (similar to ricotta)
Crème fraîche	Panela	Ricotta
Farmer cheese	Pot cheese	Scamorza
Feta (some)	Quark	
Fromage blanc	Queso fresco	

OPPOSITE: An array of American cheeses, including Cowgirl Creamery's Olema Rounds, are sold at Tomales Bay Foods in Point Reyes, California.

SOFT-RIPENED AND SEMI-SOFT CHEESES (AGED 1 WEEK TO 3 MONTHS)
Good eating cheeses. Semi-soft are also good cooking cheeses

Asadero
Beer Käse (also spelled
   Beerkaese and Bergkaese)
Brick
Brie
Butter Käse (also spelled
   Butterkaese)
Camembert

Colby (some)
Crescenza
Crottin (goat cheese)
Gorgonzola
Havarti
Jack (some)
Limburger
Mossholder

Muenster
Plymouth (some)
Provolone (some)
Teleme
Many specialty sheep, cow,
   and goat cheeses

SEMI-HARD CHEESES (AGED 1 TO 12 MONTHS)
Good cooking and melting cheeses

Asiago (some)
Baby Swiss
Blue cheese (some)
Cheddar (some)
Chontaleño
Colby (some)

Crowley
Edam
Emmentaler
Fontina
Gouda
Jack (some)

Kasseri
Menonita
Plymouth (some)
Queso blanco
Tilsit
Many specialty sheep, cow,
   and goat cheeses

SEMI-HARD TO HARD CHEESES (AGED 3 MONTHS TO 2 YEARS)
Good cooking and melting cheeses

Blue cheese (some)
Cheddar (some)
Emmentaler

Graviera
Gruyère
Swiss

Many specialty sheep, cow,
   and goat cheeses

VERY HARD (USUALLY GRATING OR CRUMBLING CHEESES) (AGED 6 MONTHS AND UP)
Good for baked dishes and pasta toppings

Asiago (some)
Cotija
Enchilado

Dry Jack
Parmesan
Ricotta salata

Romano
Many specialty sheep, cow,
   and goat cheeses

RECIPES
AND
PROFILES

APPETIZERS AND SALADS

PASTAS AND POLENTAS

ALWAYS FARM FRESH

MADE IN THE U.S.A.

CLASSICS AND DESSERTS

PIZZAS AND VEGETABLES

SINCE 1620

STARTERS and APPETIZERS

Bruschetta with Fig Puree and Blue Cheese

This recipe comes from Brian Streeter, the highly talented chef at Cakebread Winery in the Napa Valley. Brian has an enviable ability to put some of the earth's simplest foods together in memorable ways, while at the same time using very few ingredients to create that effect. Naturally, he uses wine in much of his cooking. Dolores Cakebread, matriarch of the family, has a tremendous passion for gardening and has created an extensive vegetable and herb garden on the Cakebread property, just a stone's throw from Brian's kitchen. That means that all year long, he has an impressive bounty from which to choose his ingredients. This recipe is a good example of how "simple" can ultimately be the most satisfying.

Although the recipe calls for placing the cheese on top of the fig puree and then slightly heating the cheese, I have found that a nice variation is to place the cheese on the bread first and then top it with a thin layer of puree, not bothering to heat the bruschetta. It's interesting how the same ingredients, when used in a different order, can yield an entirely different flavor. Either way, this is a lovely and elegant bruschetta.

STARTERS AND APPETIZERS

1 pound dried Black Mission figs, stems trimmed
3 cups merlot or other smooth red wine
¼ teaspoon anise seeds
1 cinnamon stick (about 2 inches long)
2 bay leaves
1 loaf country-style bread (1½ pounds), cut into ½-inch-thick slices, or two 3-inch-wide baguettes, cut into ½-inch slices
Olive oil for brushing
4 ounces blue cheese (Maytag works particularly well), thinly sliced
¼ cup chopped flat-leaf parsley

Preheat the broiler.

In a medium saucepan, combine the figs, wine, anise seed, cinnamon stick, and bay leaves.

Bring to a boil and simmer for 5 minutes. Remove from the heat and allow to steep for 20 minutes. Remove the cinnamon stick and bay leaves, and puree the fig mixture in a blender or food processor. Set aside.

Arrange the bread on a broiler pan, and toast both sides under the broiler. Brush one side of each slice with olive oil, and then spread a thin layer of the fig puree on each slice. If you are using country-style bread, quarter each slice. Top each with a thin slice of blue cheese. Place under the broiler just long enough for the cheese to begin to melt, about 45 seconds. Remove, and garnish with the chopped parsley. Serve hot or at room temperature.

Makes about 4 dozen

Note: The puree can be kept in an airtight container in the refrigerator for up to 3 months.

OPPOSITE: Teleme, Squash, and Onion Galette (see page 82).

VELLA CHEESE COMPANY

MENTION "DRY JACK" AND YOU'RE REMINDED not only of a remarkable cheese but of an entire family history. The Vella Cheese Company in Sonoma, California, fifty miles north of San Francisco, has been operating for nearly seventy years—having transformed itself from a brewery into a cheesemaking facility during Prohibition.

Today Ignacio ("Ig") Vella runs the operation, as he has for much of its existence (he traded in cheese for local politics for a few years). Ig's father, Tom, started the business in 1931.

Like many wonderful foods, Dry Jack cheese is the result of both luck and design. A Sonoma cheese dealer was having a hard time selling his supply of Monterey Jack during World War I. He began stacking his cheeses in his basement, between wooden boards, since he had no place else to put them. He tended to the cheeses, adding a little salt to them and turning them every week. What resulted was a dry, aged cheese that particularly appealed to the new Italian immigrants who were searching for a hard grating cheese. (Italian cheeses were not being imported at the time.)

Ig Vella is tireless in his promotion of high-quality cheese. He still dons a rubber apron and like the rest of his workers, gathers the curds, ties them in muslin, and places the muslin sack of curds and remaining whey between his belly and the side of the cheese vat, squeezing out as much moisture as his strength will allow. It's then bundled and tied to drain further on wooden slats.

The term "dry" comes from the fact that unlike regular Jack cheese, this one is aged to allow much of the moisture to evaporate. While the majority of Dry Jack cheese is aged for about a year, a few wheels can be found that are as much as four or five years old. At that point they have transformed into a beautiful golden color with a rich, sweet, nutty flavor that is unlike any other cheese. It is truly exquisite.

A unique feature of Vella Dry Jack is its rind, which is coated with a mixture of cocoa, pepper, and oil. This dark brown rind not only adds a bit of spice, it also protects one of America's most soulful cheeses.

WHAT THEY MAKE

Asiago

Monterey Jack: block form, grated dry, high-moisture, dry, Golden Bear (dry Jack aged 3½ to 4 years), seasoned, Special Select Dry (aged 1 to 2½ years)

Cheddar: flavored, mild, mild raw milk, sharp, sharp raw milk

Fontinella (Italian Table Cheese)

HOW TO REACH THEM

Sonoma, California
800-848-0505
707-938-3232
707-938-4307 (fax)

While this cheese has equal parts flavor and history, many of the other Vella cheeses are noteworthy as well. Ig Vella is quick to credit his cheesemaker, Charlie Malkassian, who has been with him for eighteen years, for the quality of these cheeses. Malkassian's skill with the variety of Vella Cheese Company cheeses is truly impressive. Of particular note are the raw milk cheddar and the Fontinella.

The cheddar is the only raw milk cheese that Vella makes. It is a robust white cheddar that is a bit sweeter than many cheddars but is rounded out with a balanced milk/acid flavor. Its consistency is firm but pliable, and because it is not super-sharp, it becomes a mildly addictive cheese.

The Fontinella, sold on the wholesale market as Italian Table Cheese, is modeled after Italian Fontina. It does not have the earthiness of an aged Fontina d'Aosta, but it does have a lovely mix of nuttiness, clean and fruit flavors, and a savory component as well. It is, as its name suggests, a table cheese, but it is also a perfect melting cheese. A pizza is all the better for it.

As if the Vella Cheese Company were not enough, Ig Vella also spends much of his time at the Rogue River Valley Creamery in Oregon. Founded by his father, it is mostly dedicated to making Oregon Blue Cheese. This used to be a highly regarded blue cheese, but over the past two years the cheese has faltered due to lack of attention. Vella is now deciding where this cheese plant's future lies.

In the meantime, the Vella cheeses are alive and well. Vella's Golden Bear cheese, the elder statesman of Dry Jack, ranges from three and a half to four years old. Its nuttiness and buttery qualities are unsurpassed; its golden flavor surely mirrors its name; and its very hard texture means that it is more easily chipped off the wheel than cut. The effort is more than worth it, though its rarity makes it available to on-site visitors only.

Chili-Pecan Biscotti with Dry Jack Cheese

Although biscotti are traditionally sweet, meant to be dipped in coffee or dessert wine, I see no reason why they can't be enjoyed in a savory style as well. "Biscotti" means twice-baked, and that's why they usually have to be dipped: otherwise, they are teeth-breakers. But these biscotti, while still twice-baked, remain crumbly and easy to eat. They're also easy to make, though you have to be a little patient when you cut the dough after it has been baked the first time. It tends to crumble a little. Not to worry, though. Their rustic look suits their assertive flavor. Although you don't need a liquid to dip these in, an icy margarita alongside would be a welcome accompaniment.

You can serve these alone, or alongside the Black Beans with Cotija Cheese (page 182).

FOR THE PECANS

2 teaspoons canola oil

¼ teaspoon coarse (kosher) salt

¼ teaspoon ground cumin

⅛ teaspoon ground coriander

Freshly ground pepper

¾ cup pecan halves

FOR THE BISCOTTI

½ cup boiling water

¼ cup sun-dried tomatoes (not oil-packed)

2 cups all-purpose flour

2 teaspoons very hot chili powder

1½ teaspoons baking powder

1¼ teaspoons kosher salt

½ cup (1 stick) unsalted butter, softened

2 tablespoons sugar

2 eggs

2½ cups coarsely grated Vella Dry Jack cheese (or use aged Asiago or domestic Parmesan)

To prepare the pecans: Preheat the oven to 325°F.

In a small bowl, whisk together all the ingredients *except* the pecans. When blended, add the pecans to the bowl and coat well. (It won't look like much coating, but don't worry. It is enough.) Spread the pecans out in a small baking pan and bake until they start to release a nutty aroma and are beginning to turn a light brown color, about 8 minutes. Remove from the oven and let cool completely. Then chop the pecans and set them aside. (The pecans can be made 3 days in advance and kept in an airtight container at room temperature, or 1 month in advance and frozen.)

To make the biscotti: Increase the oven temperature to 350°F.

In a heatproof bowl, pour the boiling water over the tomatoes. Let stand for 10 minutes. Drain

STARTERS AND APPETIZERS

well, and chop into pieces about the size of a raisin.

In a small bowl, mix together the flour, chili powder, baking powder, and salt. Set aside.

In the bowl of an electric stand mixer, cream the butter at high speed until very smooth. (Alternatively, use a large bowl and a sturdy wooden spoon for the steps in this process.) Add the sugar and mix until well blended and creamy. Add the eggs and mix at high speed for 5 minutes. (They may not thoroughly integrate with the butter and sugar, but don't worry about it.) Set the mixer on low speed and add the flour mixture. When the flour mixture is almost fully incorporated, add 2 cups of the cheese and the chopped tomatoes. Mix for 30 seconds. By now, the dough will have formed a solid ball. (If it's still crumbly, add 1 to 2 tablespoons cold water.) Keeping the mixer at a low speed, add the chopped pecans and mix just until all of the ingredients hold together. (If the pecans end up at the bottom of the mixing bowl, simply remove the dough from the bowl and place it on a work surface. Put the errant pecans on the work surface as well and work them into the dough by hand.)

Remove the dough from the mixer, and on a lightly floured board, shape it into two logs about 3 inches wide and 6 to 7 inches long. Round the tops slightly. Place them about 2 inches apart on an ungreased baking sheet. Sprinkle the tops with the remaining ½ cup

cheese. Bake for 20 minutes, or until the logs are brown around the edges and the cheese has melted (the cheese will not brown). Remove from the oven and let cool for 10 to 12 minutes.

Reduce the oven temperature to 325°F.

Place one log on a cutting board. Using a long, sharp knife, cut the log into ¼-inch-thick slices, slightly on the diagonal. (The slices may crumble a bit, but if you cut the dough with a rapid motion rather than "sawing" it, your slices should remain intact.) Repeat with the other log. Place the slices, cut side down, back onto the baking sheet. They may be placed close together (though not touching), since they will not spread; use two baking sheets if necessary. Bake for 15 minutes. Turn the slices over and bake until the edges are browned, 10 or 15 minutes. Place the biscotti on a cooling rack and cool to room temperature.

Makes 30 to 36

Note: These can be kept in an airtight container at room temperature for 2 days, or in the freezer for up to 3 months. Freshen the frozen biscotti in a preheated 325°F oven for 5 to 7 minutes.

Do not double this recipe; even a stand mixer will not be able to handle that much dough. Instead, make the dough in two batches. Form all the logs and bake them on two baking sheets, rotating the baking sheets for even baking.

Helen's Tiropitas

Melted cheese encased in thin, buttery sheets of dough is the stuff of dreams. These appetizers bring that dream to life by mixing together four cheeses, folding them between layers of butter-brushed filo dough, and baking them to a golden brown.

This recipe is adapted from one given to me by one of the best cooks I know: my mother-in-law. In her eighties, she has a sophisticated palate and when she gives a dinner party, she cuts no corners. These tiropitas are elaborate and beautiful, and are surprisingly easy to make. They do take a little time since each one has to be folded individually, but they can be assembled ahead and frozen.

If you've never worked with filo dough, you'll be surprised at how easy it is. Just remember that it is essential to keep a slightly damp towel over the dough or it will dry out quickly.

---

4 ounces mozzarella cheese, coarsely grated
4 ounces Monterey Jack cheese, coarsely
 grated
1 cup (about 8 ounces) ricotta cheese
¼ cup finely grated aged cheese, such as
 Asiago, Stravecchio, or Parmesan
2 eggs, lightly beaten
1 teaspoon salt
½ teaspoon freshly ground pepper
12 sheets frozen filo dough, defrosted
 according to package directions
1 cup (2 sticks) unsalted butter, melted

Preheat the oven to 375°F.

In a medium bowl, mix together the cheeses. Add the eggs, salt, and pepper. Mix well and set aside.

Unroll the pastry sheets and cover with a damp towel. (They will dry out quickly if left uncovered.) Lay one sheet of filo on a work surface.

Brush it liberally with melted butter. Cut the sheet into thirds lengthwise. Cover two of the strips with a damp towel, and on the third strip place 1 heaping tablespoon of the cheese filling about ½ inch from one end. Fold the strip up as if you were folding a flag, beginning by folding the filled end at 45° to make a triangle. Continue folding flag-style until you reach the end of the filo strip. Seal the edge with some melted butter. Brush the tiropita with more melted butter and place it on a baking sheet. Continue until all of the filo strips and cheese mixture are used up.

Bake for 15 minutes, or until the butter is bubbling and the triangles are golden brown. Serve hot.

Makes about 36

Note: You can freeze the tiropitas after assembling them, for use at a later time. When you're ready to bake them, just take the frozen tiropitas and place them on a baking sheet. Do not defrost. Bake them at 375° for about 30 minutes.

STARTERS AND APPETIZERS

Peppered Goat Cheese Crackers

When I first made these crackers, I actually did so with the intent of making croutons. But when I decided to make some a little thicker than croutons, I realized that they made delicious crackers that could be served on their own or even with other cheeses, chutneys, or anything else that crackers are used for. They are very rich since they're mostly butter and cheese, but their texture is flaky, similar to shortbread. In fact, I like to think of these as a savory type of shortbread with a pepper kick. They can be stored in an airtight container for about a week or in the freezer for up to six months.

10 ounces fresh goat cheese, at room temperature
6 tablespoons (¾ stick) butter, softened
1⅓ cups all-purpose flour
1¼ teaspoons kosher salt
2 teaspoons very coarsely ground fresh pepper

In a food processor or with an electric mixer, beat the goat cheese and butter together until smooth. Add the flour and salt and beat until well blended. Divide the dough in half, and place each half on a piece of plastic wrap about 18 inches long. Gently roll the dough back and forth, using the countertop as a base, to create two 12-inch logs. Carefully unwrap the dough and sprinkle the pepper over the logs. Wrap each log in plastic and refrigerate for at least 3 hours and up to 3 days.

When ready to cook, preheat the oven to 325°F. Take one log out of the refrigerator, and using a serrated knife, cut it into ½-inch-thick slices. On an ungreased baking sheet place the slices cut side down, 1 inch apart. Repeat with the second log and another baking sheet. (Or if using only one baking sheet, keep the second log in the refrigerator until you're ready to bake it.)

Bake for 30 minutes. Turn and continue baking until the crackers are a rich golden color, 15 to 20 minutes more. Transfer them to a cooling rack and let cool completely.

Makes 4 dozen

Note: While you may eat these warm, I have found that the flavors really develop if you let them cool for at least an hour.

To make croutons, slice the logs ⅛-inch thick and bake for 25 to 30 minutes, turning halfway through.

MOSSHOLDER CHEESE

ALTHOUGH COLBY, BRICK, AND MONTEREY JACK are the cheeses most often cited as American originals, Mossholder cheese could certainly be counted among them. Otto Mossholder was an Ohio transplant who made his living buying run-down creameries and refurbishing them. In the 1920s, he settled in Appleton, Wisconsin, and set up his own "creamery" at home. He and three others experimented with recipes for two popular Wisconsin cheeses—brick and Colby—and came up with a cheese he confidently called Mossholder.

Mossholder is a brick-style semi-soft cheese that is made from unpasteurized milk. It has characteristics of Swiss, brick, and Colby all in one, but unlike brick, it does not have a "gooey" rind. Instead, the cheese is rolled in salt once it is pressed into brick form. It then sits before it is wrapped in plastic wrap. The ends are waxed to keep the air out, and the brick is wrapped with another layer of plastic. Lois Mossholder explains that this extra layer of plastic keeps the wax from cracking. No doubt it preserves some of the moisture in the cheese as well.

This unique cheese is produced in the same basement where Otto Mossholder first made it. Larry and Lois Mossholder have carried on the tradition, living in the same house and making the cheese in almost the same way. Now, though, they have modern-day conveniences such as a vat with a hot-water jacket. The nearly 100,000 pounds they make annually is all aged downstairs as well. Unlike most Wisconsin cows' milk cheese producers, Mossholder is a farmstead operation. They own forty Holsteins and produce all of their cheese with the milk from their cows.

Because it is made with raw milk, the cheese is aged for at least sixty days. The cheese is sold at various ages, up to two and a half years. Unlike brick, it does not get nose-holding strong as it ages, but it does become a little more pronounced in flavor and develops a bit of a kick. It can be eaten alongside a rustic bread with fresh apple slices, or the younger version goes nicely between a couple of slices of pumpernickel. It is a great melting cheese or it makes the perfect addition to the recipe for Fromage Fort that follows. The Mossholders also make flavored versions of their cheese.

Because they are a small operation, they sell their cheese on site at their store and at a couple of other stores in Wisconsin and Illinois. They'll happily do mail order, though, and if "unique" sounds appealing, then getting a taste of Mossholder is a must.

WHAT THEY MAKE
Mossholder: mild, medium-aged, extra-aged
Flavored Mossholder: caraway, crushed red pepper,
    dill weed, jalapeño, chopped onion, vegetable blend

HOW TO REACH THEM
Appleton, Wisconsin
920-734-7575
920-734-7696 (fax)

Fromage Fort

A catch-all for cheese leftovers, fromage fort, or "strong cheese," is a great way to use up small pieces of cheese. You can clean out the cheese compartment of your refrigerator, and at the same time create something wonderful to eat. In France, the home of fromage fort, it is a little more elaborate than simply leftover cheese. Traditionally leftover cheeses were mixed together and then allowed to ferment in a liquid such as milk or vegetable broth. Wine or oil was then added to stabilize the mixture, and herbs, salt, and more wine were added to season it. It was often put in a stoneware pot to age, and when it was time to eat it, apparently the word fort took on a whole new meaning. Fromage fort is still made in France, but usually with just one cheese—which is determined by the region where it is being made. Because of its runny consistency, it is sold by the ladleful.

For this version, try to balance the types of cheeses you use. For example, do not use more than one especially salty cheese, as it will make the mixture too salty. Do not use blue cheese unless you want that to be the dominant flavor; it will overtake all other flavors. Because of fromage fort's relatively neutral character (depending on the types of cheese you use), it can be livened up with almost any type of herb or flavoring you like—or none at all, since the combination of cheeses, no matter what they are, take on a flavor of their own. Serve it with bread, crackers, or slices of oil-brushed toasted baguette.

---

1 pound assorted leftover cheeses, at room temperature
¼ cup white wine
3 tablespoons unsalted butter, softened
2 tablespoons fresh herbs (such as thyme, sage, flat-leaf parsley, tarragon, marjoram, or basil; optional)
1 clove garlic (optional)

Remove the rind, hard spots, and any mold from the cheese. Cut the cheese into ½-inch cubes, and grate any hard cheeses.

Combine the cheeses, wine, butter, and optional herbs and garlic in a food processor and blend until very smooth and creamy, 3 to 5 minutes. Serve immediately, or refrigerate for at least 1 hour if you would like a firmer consistency. The mixture can be kept for up to 5 days in the refrigerator.

Makes about 2½ cups
Serves 10 to 12

Chili-Rubbed Pork and Oaxaca Cheese Quesadillas
with Chipotle Crème Fraîche

Southwest cuisine lends itself to cheese like nothing else. There's a good reason: Dairy, whether it be milk or cheese, soothes the heat that the chiles create in this fiery cuisine. In this dish, both the cheese and the crème fraîche do their part to tame the spiciness.

Oaxaca is a pasta filata, *or stretched-curd cheese, nearly identical to mozzarella in both texture and taste. When melted between the layers of tortillas, it provides the mild and chewy host for the spicy pork and chipotle crème fraîche. For the chipotle chiles, use the canned ones called "chipotle chiles en adobo." Adobo is a smoky sauce that will also be used in this recipe. If you can't find the canned chipotles, use minced jalapeños. Both types of chiles are high on the "hot" scale, although chipotles have a very smoky flavor while jalapeños have a sharper, crisper flavor. Both are excellent in this dish.*

Serve these quesadillas alone or accompanied by Black Beans with Cotija Cheese (see page 182).

(see page 182)

FOR THE CHIPOTLE CRÈME FRAÎCHE
⅓ cup plus 2 tablespoons crème fraîche
1 canned chipotle chile, minced, or
   1 medium-size fresh jalapeño, roasted,
   skinned, seeded, and minced
1 teaspoon adobo sauce
1 teaspoon fresh lime juice
Salt to taste

FOR THE PORK
1 pork tenderloin (about 1¼ pounds)
4 cloves garlic, minced
1 tablespoon finely chopped fresh oregano
   leaves
1 tablespoon sesame seeds, toasted (if you
   have black sesame seeds, use half black
   and half white)

2 teaspoons medium-hot chili powder
1½ teaspoons kosher salt
1 teaspoon ground cumin
1 teaspoon ground coriander

FOR THE QUESADILLAS
6 flour tortillas (about 7-inch diameter)
6 ounces Oaxaca cheese, coarsely grated
   (about 1½ cups; or use mozzarella)
2 tablespoons canola or vegetable oil
¼ cup chopped fresh cilantro, for garnish

To make the chipotle crème fraîche: Two hours before serving, mix all the ingredients together in a small bowl. Refrigerate the mixture, but bring to room temperature before serving. This will keep, refrigerated, for about a week.

To prepare the pork: Place the pork in a glass baking dish. If it is too long to fit, cut it in half crosswise. Combine the remaining ingredients and mash until they form a paste. A mortar and pestle is the most effective way to get the proper consistency, but you can also place the ingredients in a bowl and use the back of a fork to mash them. Using your fingers, spread the spice rub on all sides of the pork. It will not cover the pork entirely. (If you have trouble making the rub stick, lightly oil the pork and then pat the rub on.) Let it sit for about 30 minutes.

Prepare a grill or preheat the broiler.

If broiling, transfer the pork to a broiler pan. Broil or grill the pork, turning it occasionally, until medium rare, about 15 minutes. Remove it from the heat and cover loosely with foil. Let sit for about 15 minutes.

Cut the pork crosswise into ¼-inch slices.

To assemble: Place one tortilla in front of you. Sprinkle ¼ cup grated cheese over half the tortilla. Top the cheese with 3 slices of pork. Fold the other half of the tortilla over the cheese-pork mixture. Repeat with the remaining tortillas, cheese, and pork.

Line a baking sheet with paper towels.

In each of two large sauté pans, heat 1 tablespoon oil over high heat. (Or just use one pan, if that is all you have.) Place two quesadillas in each pan, but do not let them overlap. Cook until the bottoms of the quesadillas are golden brown, 2 to 3 minutes. Flip the quesadillas over and cook on the other side until golden brown. Transfer to the paper-towel-lined pan to soak up a little bit of the oil.

Place the quesadillas on serving plates and drizzle with the crème fraîche. Garnish with the cilantro. If you are serving them as a first course, serve one per person. Otherwise, cut each quesadilla crosswise into five equal-sized strips to serve as an appetizer.

Serves 6 as a first course, or 8 to 10 as an appetizer

Note: To keep the quesadillas warm, set the oven at 325°F. Place the quesadillas in a single layer on a baking sheet and put it in the oven until you have finished making the remaining quesadillas. Try not to keep them in the oven for longer than 15 minutes or the tortillas will dry out.

Ricotta-Stuffed Grape Leaves with Caponata

This colorful appetizer brings home the best of the flavors of the Mediterranean: tomatoes, fresh herbs, cheese, capers, nuts, and grape leaves. The caponata, an eggplant mixture, is best made a day in advance to allow the flavors to meld together. Grape leaves, which come in a jar filled with brine, can be found in many grocery stores as well as in specialty and Middle Eastern stores. For this dish, the leaves must be parboiled to rid them of their toughness. Once the leaves are stuffed, you may refrigerate them overnight before cooking them. Note that they take a while to cook. Serve them with good crusty bread to mop up any extra caponata.

If you do not wish to use grape leaves, the caponata and the cheese filling are also wonderful encased in filo dough and baked. Follow the instructions for Helen's Tiropitas on page 72, placing 1 teaspoon of caponata and 1 teaspoon of the cheese mixture side by side on the filo strip. Fold and bake as directed.

FOR THE CAPONATA

2 eggplants (1 pound each), peeled, cut into
½-inch slices, then cut into ½-inch cubes
Kosher salt
½ cup olive oil, plus more as needed
2 yellow onions (about 8 ounces each), finely
chopped
⅔ cup canned tomato puree
5 tablespoons red wine vinegar
4 teaspoons sugar
¼ cup capers, rinsed and drained
3 tablespoons dried currants, covered with
hot water, plumped for 20 minutes, and
drained
Salt and freshly ground pepper

FOR THE GRAPE LEAVES

1 jar (8-ounce) grape leaves in brine
2 cups ricotta cheese, drained well
2 tablespoons milk
½ cup slivered almonds, toasted
¼ cup chopped fresh basil leaves, plus
extra for garnish
Cracked pepper
Olive oil

To make the caponata: Place the eggplant cubes in a colander, sprinkle with salt, and let stand for about 1 hour. Rinse and pat dry.

In a large sauté pan, heat the olive oil over medium-high heat. Add the eggplant cubes and sauté until very tender and completely cooked through, about 20 minutes. Remove with a slotted spoon and drain on paper towels. Set aside.

In the same pan, add 1 to 2 more tablespoons olive oil if needed, and add the chopped onions. Cook over medium heat until the onions begin to soften, about 10 minutes. Add the tomato puree and cook over medium-low heat for 5 minutes. Return the eggplant to the onion-tomato mixture, and add the vinegar and sugar. Cook for 5 more minutes. Add the capers and currants, stir well, and cook until the vinegar has cooked off slightly and the ingredients are well blended, about 15 minutes. Add salt and pepper to taste. Set aside, or let cool and then refrigerate overnight. Bring to room temperature before continuing.

To prepare the grape leaves: Rinse the grape leaves and pat dry. (This is important because the brine is very salty.)

Bring a large pot of water to a boil. Add the grape leaves and boil for 2 minutes. Remove them from the water and place on paper towels to drain. (The grape leaves will probably twist and fold in the boiling process. Don't worry—they unfold easily.)

In a medium bowl, combine the ricotta, milk, almonds, ¼ cup of the chopped basil, and cracked pepper to taste. Mix well.

To assemble: Preheat the oven to 225°F. Oil a large ovenproof pan or glass baking dish.

Place one grape leaf on a work surface with the smooth side down and with the stem side closest to you. The tip of the leaf will be farthest from you. Take 1 tablespoon of the cheese mixture and place it ¼ inch from the bottom of the grape leaf. Fold the bottom over the cheese mixture. Next, fold in both sides of the grape leaf and roll from the bottom toward the tip. The cheese should be completely encased. Continue with the remaining grape leaves and cheese mixture.

Brush the tops of the grape leaves with oil and cover the pan with foil. Set the pan in a larger pan and put them in the oven. Fill the larger pan with hot water to reach halfway up the sides of the baking dish. Bake for 1¼ hours. Remove from the oven and let sit, still covered, for 15 minutes.

To serve, place three or four stuffed grape leaves on each plate. Drizzle 2 to 3 tablespoons caponata over the grape leaves, and garnish with a little chopped basil. Serve immediately or at room temperature.

Serves 8 to 10

PELUSO CHEESE COMPANY

WHEN 1 PERCENT OF YOUR BUSINESS makes up 90 percent of your reputation, the likelihood is that the 1 percent is stellar. In the case of the Peluso Cheese Company, Peluso Teleme cheese practically defies description. It is creamy, almost molten, and tastes like a thick, liquid version of a slightly fruity Jack cheese. Although other cheeses go by the name Teleme, Peluso Teleme is almost certainly unique in this country.

The origins of Teleme are slightly confusing. It is technically a Greek cheese, but the Pelusos' style of Teleme is more like cheeses from other parts of the Mediterranean that go by different names. According to Peluso Cheese Company owner Franklin Peluso, a true Greek teleme is closer to a feta cheese.

Teleme got its start in this country in the 1920s. A Greek cheesemaker founded an outfit called the Standard Cheese Company in Pleasanton, east of San Francisco, where he produced a cheese that was similar to one he was familiar with back home.

Not long after, a man named Frank Peluso started his own cheese factory in northern California. Although he had never made Teleme before, he was able to study this superb cheese made by Standard Cheese and to replicate it, giving Standard Cheese its first competition. Upon graduating from high school in the early 1930s, Frank's son went to work as the manager of the plant and there learned how to make the prized Teleme. The recipe and the cheesemaking responsibilities were passed down, and in the 1960s, the present owner, Franklin Peluso, stepped up to the plate. At that time, though, he was making other cheeses. Teleme production didn't resume until 1980.

This heralded cheese is made in a place called Los Banos. This is in the heart of California's Central Valley, where a normal summer day will register three digits on the thermometer and the winters are defined by the thick white Tule fog. It is also where farming and agriculture still dominate the local economy. It is the sole production site of the square-shaped semi-soft cheese that comes in a cardboard box.

After a month or two of ripening, the Peluso Teleme must be eaten with a spoon. This runny quality naturally lends itself to cooked dishes since it is nearly melted before it's ever exposed to heat. The *galette* in the following recipe is an ideal showcase for this cheese because of the buttery crust and the matching buttery quality of the

---

WHAT THEY MAKE

Chihuahua
Chontaleño
Cotija
Panela

Queso crema
Queso fresco
Requeson
Ricotta
Teleme

HOW TO REACH THEM

Los Banos, California
209-826-3744
209-826-6782 (fax)

cheese, but Peluso Teleme also adds a silken quality to an omelet, as a topping on grilled summer squash, or in almost any hot dish that calls for cheese. Naturally, a cows' milk cheese as creamy and sweet as this is also excellent with simple accompaniments. The dripping cheese can be scooped up with slices of pear or spooned over ripe figs.

Another distinctive feature of Peluso Teleme is its light dusting of rice flour. This tradition began with the European workers who, Peluso theorizes, may have been trying to duplicate the white mold that they were accustomed to seeing on their cheese in Europe.

In addition to Teleme, Peluso Cheese Company makes Mexican and Central American cheeses to meet the huge demand in the border states. Those cheeses comprise the bulk of the business. Although they are made on a much wider scale than the Teleme, many of them are still specialty cheeses since they are made in relatively small quantities and are for a niche market.

A three-generation California family is not necessarily commonplace in the Golden State. In the case of the Pelusos, the distinct advantage is that a rarity like the Teleme recipe was not left behind with the family's past. Cheese aficionados can be grateful, since this cheese is a prime example of American cheese-making at its best.

Teleme, Squash, and Onion Galette

If the words "buttery" and "crunchy" conjure up positive food images for you, then this recipe is a can't-miss. A pastry dough rather than a pizza dough, a galette is a thin, free-form pastry that has plenty of butter and does not need to rise. This dough definitely makes for a rich dish, but it also creates a delicate, flaky crust for the cheese and vegetables. The Teleme really makes this dish, and I would highly recommend you go the extra mile to find it. If you can't, then use Monterey Jack, mozzarella, or a young Provolone. This entire recipe can be doubled easily. Or you can double just the dough recipe and keep half of it frozen for later use.

FOR THE DOUGH
1 cup all-purpose flour
⅛ teaspoon salt
⅛ teaspoon sugar
6 tablespoons (¾ stick) unsalted butter, very cold, cut into ¼-inch cubes
¼ cup ice water

FOR THE TOPPING
1 tablespoon olive oil
½ yellow onion, thinly sliced
¼ pound yellow squash, sliced into ¼-inch rounds
1 tablespoon fresh thyme leaves, or 1½ teaspoons dried thyme
Salt and freshly ground pepper, to taste
¼ pound *young* Teleme cheese, coarsely grated (see Note)
1 tablespoon milk or cream

To make the dough: In a large bowl, mix together the flour, salt, and sugar. Using a pastry cutter or two knives, cut the chilled butter into the flour mixture just until the butter is the size of small gumballs.

Make a well in the middle of the dough. Pour a small amount of ice water into the center, and using a fork, bring some of the flour-butter mixture into the water. Continue until all of the water has been well incorporated. The mixture will be slightly crumbly, but it should hold together. If it doesn't, add more cold water, 1 tablespoon at a time.

Press the dough into a ball and then flatten it into a disk about 5 inches in diameter. Wrap in plastic wrap and refrigerate for 2 hours or up to 24 hours. The dough can also be frozen.

To make the topping: Preheat the oven to 425°F. Place a rack in the lower third of the oven. Do not place in the lowest slot or the bottom of the galette will burn before the topping is done.

In a medium skillet, heat the olive oil over medium-high heat. Add the onions and squash and sauté for about 2 minutes, stirring constantly. Add the thyme, salt, and pepper and continue to cook until the onions and squash are translucent but not brown, about 5 minutes. They should be slightly underdone. Remove from the heat and set aside.

To assemble: Remove the dough from the refrigerator, and on a well-floured surface or on a floured piece of parchment, roll it into a circle 8 to 9 inches in diameter and ⅛ inch thick. Place the dough in a shallow baking or pizza pan. (Do not use a rimless baking sheet, or you'll likely end up with melted butter on your oven floor.) Spoon the onion-squash mixture onto the center of the dough, leaving a 1½-inch border. Top with the cheese. Next, fold the 1½ inch border of the galette toward the center to encase part of the filling, crimping the edges a little as you go. You should end up with a "window" of filling about 5 inches in diameter, with the crust overlapping the edges of the filling.

Brush the folded-over edges with the milk or cream. Bake until the border is golden and the cheese is bubbly and golden brown, 25 to 30 minutes. Serve immediately.

Serves 4 as a first course, or 6 to 8 as an appetizer

Note: If the cheese is ripe and runny, then use spoonfuls of the cheese or instead use grated Monterey Jack, mozzarella, or a young Provolone.

STRAUS FAMILY CREAMERY

AS THE FIRST CERTIFIED ORGANIC DAIRY WEST OF THE MISSISSIPPI, the Straus Family Creamery is setting an example. The family-owned dairy has been organic for five years, but it took at least that long to become certified. While the Straus Family Dairy makes some cheese, they appear here because of their commitment to producing the highest quality milk. Not a lot of cow dairies are doing this, even though high milk quality leads to the best cheese.

The creamery, dairy, and surrounding pastures are in the heart of a traditional dairy area on the western coast of northern California where Marin and Sonoma counties meet. It is about an hour north of San Francisco, but it is a world apart. The hills roll endlessly and are lined with carpets of grass, rising and falling against the horizon. Paradoxically, black-and-white cows add color to the otherwise green landscape, and the only predictable feature in this wild, windswept coastal land is the thick morning fog that rises like a curtain to reveal the turbulent waters of the Pacific Ocean below.

The drama of the land could be said to reflect the difficulties of the transition to an organic dairy. Although the Strauses weren't using pesticides, they still had to take several steps to become certified organic. The first was to raise money. They had to feed their cows organic feed for one year. They also had to treat them with homeopathic remedies rather than antibiotics when the need arose, leading to a retraining of the local veterinarian. These changes were costly. In addition, milk was fetching lower prices than ever, making dairying a money-losing prospect.

Their perseverence paid off. At about the time the Straus Family Creamery became certified organic, the controversial bovine growth hormone was introduced. This was a fortuitous event for the Straus family

because concerned consumers scrambled for milk that didn't contain BGH. Their distinguishable milk-in-a-bottle won over consumers, despite the higher price. Many of those consumers became permanent converts.

The Straus Family Dairy was started fifty years ago by Bill Straus, an immigrant from Germany who wanted nothing more than to own his own farm. His Dutch wife, Ellen, had the same dream, and together they built their dairy. Their son, Albert, had his own dream of bottling the dairy's milk (his parents sold the milk before it was bottled), and it was his idea to create an organic dairy.

WHAT THEY MAKE
Cheddar and Monterey Jack cheese
Butter
Milk: whole, low-fat, nonfat, chocolate
Plain yogurt

HOW TO REACH THEM
Marshall, California
415-663-5464
415-663-5465 (fax)
website: www.strausmilk.com

The Strauses' milk is pasteurized, but it tastes like no other milk. It is richer, with very slight earthy overtones, and the consistency is generally thicker than regular milk. Even the nonfat milk has a thickness that is closer to commercial whole milk than to other nonfat milks. Additionally, the absence of antibiotics in the animals, along with the organic feed given to them, provides extra assurance to those who are seeking a pure product.

Straus now supplies all of the milk for the Cowgirl Creamery in nearby Point Reyes, which makes 100-percent organic cheeses from it, including fromage blanc (see pages 215–216). The Strauses are now making a delicious organic chocolate milk with their lowfat milk, and they make one of the richest yogurts available. They also commission a small amount of cheese to be made with their milk and under their own label, but they do not have a cheesemaking facility themselves.

Additionally, Ellen Straus makes cheesecakes for Cowgirl Creamery using Ellen's Nonfat Quark, their German-style cheese named in her honor. The cheesecakes are sold at the Cowgirl Creamery facility known as Tomales Bay Foods.

As a 660-acre property, the Strauses' ranch is considered medium-size in California. Their ambition, however, is much larger. They have always been dedicated to the ideal of a dairy where the resources are reusable and the milk is kept as close to its natural form as possible (non-homogenized, for example), but they have broken new ground in the Golden State and have provided consumers with choices they never had before.

Spicy Cheese Spread with Rye Toasts

This easy-to-make spread combines two wonderful cheeses to pack a surprising amount of flavor. It might be thought of as the modern-day equivalent of the cheese ball, but the use of caraway and spicy Hungarian paprika takes it into the realm of the exotic. In addition to rye toasts, the spread goes well with relatively neutral accompaniments, such as fresh vegetables. That way, the full flavors of the spread are highlighted. You can substitute almost any herbs and spices you like, including ground fennel seed and black pepper, or cumin and chili powder for a Mexican flavor.

Because of the saltiness of the feta, it is important to use unsalted butter in this recipe. Also, be sure to give the spread plenty of time for the flavors to meld, preferably overnight, since the salt in the feta needs time to mellow. Bring to room temperature before serving.

¼ **pound feta cheese**
6 **tablespoons (¾ stick) unsalted butter,**
    softened
2 **ounces (¼ cup) fromage blanc, at room**
    temperature (or use ricotta)
1¼ **teaspoons ground caraway seeds**
½ **teaspoon dry mustard**
1½ **teaspoons Hungarian paprika**
1 **scallion, white and light green parts,**
    minced (optional)
10 **slices rye bread, cut ¼ inch thick**

In a bowl, mix the feta, 4 tablespoons of the butter, and the fromage blanc with an electric mixer until smooth and creamy. Add the caraway seed, mustard, and paprika, and continue mixing until well blended. Mix in the scallion, if using. Place the spread in a mold of any shape (a 1½-cup ramekin works nicely) or simply place it in a bowl. Cover and refrigerate for at least 6 hours and preferably overnight.

About one hour before serving, carefully unmold the cheese onto a serving platter. (If you didn't use a mold, simply leave the spread in the bowl.)

Preheat the oven to 400°F.

Place the bread slices in a single layer on a baking pan and bake until one side is nicely browned, 8 to 10 minutes. Turn the slices over, and spread the remaining 2 tablespoons butter over them. Put back in the oven and bake until the butter has melted and the slices are nicely browned, 5 to 8 minutes. Let cool slightly, and then cut the bread slices crosswise into thirds. Put in a basket or other serving bowl or plate. Serve the cheese spread with the rye toasts.

Makes about 1½ cups of spread
Serves 8 to 10

Note: You can serve the spread as a dip with blanched fresh vegetables such as asparagus, broccoli, or artichokes, or with raw vegetables such as carrots, celery, and jicama.

STARTERS AND APPETIZERS

NEW ENGLAND CHEESEMAKING SUPPLY

A BOOK ON AMERICAN CHEESEMAKERS could not exclude Ricki Carroll. While she does not make her living making her own cheese, she has helped more American cheesemakers to make their cheese than any other individual in this country.

As the co-founder and owner of New England Cheesemaking Supply in Ashfield, Massachusetts, Ricki has been supplying cheesemaking equipment to cheesemakers for the past twenty-five years. She started her business when very few people were making artisanal goat cheese in this country, and those who were, were struggling to find the proper equipment. In addition she too was making cheese and learning the capricious nature of the art first-hand. This education bolstered her expertise, putting her in a good position to help other cheesemakers. She has been doing so ever since.

It is not, however, only established cheesemakers whom Ricki assists. She also helps aspiring cheesemakers, home cooks, and hobbyists who are simply interested in making their own cheese. She does this in part by selling low-priced cheesemaking kits. The basic kit contains the necessary materials for making mozzarella and ricotta along with simple instructions. All the cheesemaker has to do is buy the milk.

For those who have never made cheese, these kits couldn't be more rewarding. There is nothing like buying a gallon of milk at the grocery store, taking it home, and over the course of an hour or two, turning it into ricotta cheese. While a cheesemaking kit isn't a prerequisite to making ricotta, it makes it a lot easier. The same is true for the mozzarella, which is a more complicated cheese to make at home. In this case, though, it is as simple as following a recipe. Once home cheesemakers have mastered the basic technique, they can get cheesemaking supplies and do more cheesemaking on their own.

Ricki says she and her then-husband, Robert, started their business after discovering that the equipment they needed to make cheese could be found only in Europe. They began importing that equipment for themselves as well as to help others get started in cheesemaking. They actually learned cheesemaking in England, but they never intended to make cheese to sell. Later they began to conduct cheesemaking workshops as their expertise coincided with the growing curiosity about cheesemaking—among goat owners in particular.

Now Ricki Carroll is the "answer-woman" whom cheesemakers call for advice when a batch of cheese is a failure, for tips on how to improve their cheese, and for supplies. Hobbyists call for supplies like starters, rennet tablets, citric acid, or other components necessary to make cheese. Ricki has carved out a small niche and in the process has created an invaluable resource for professional and nonprofessional American cheesemakers.

NEW ENGLAND cheesemaking SUPPLY COMPANY
85 MAIN ST., ASHFIELD, MA 01330
www.cheesemaking.com

HOW TO REACH THEM
Ashfield, Massachusetts
413-628-3808
413-628-4061 (fax)
website: www.cheesemaking.com

BREAD and CHEESE

PRIMA KÄSE

THE GOLDEN AGED GOUDA made by Randy Krahenbuhl of Prima Käse in Monticello, Wisconsin, is an award-winning cheese that has rightfully brought recognition to Krahenbuhl and to the cheesemaking talents within America's midst. This extraordinary cheese won a world championship in 1998, beating out the Dutch, who invented the cheese.

Krahenbuhl, along with his wife, Shelley, has been making cows' milk cheese most of his adult life in his century-old factory and home. Not much has changed in this factory, nor in the living quarters upstairs, which started as a home for Limburger cheese in 1863. It was later remodeled when two other cheese factories came on board in 1898. Since then it has been the site of numerous cheesemaking endeavors, including a stint as a larger Swiss cheese factory in the early 1990s. In 1993 Krahenbuhl bought back the factory and once again began making the variety of cheeses for which Prima Käse is known.

Today Prima Käse specialty cheeses are made in old-fashioned copper kettles and in stainless-steel vats, depending on the cheese. These are fired up sometime after midnight, about the same time Randy lumbers out of bed to begin making cheese. The cheesemaking continues into the afternoon and early evening, leaving little time for sleep.

The Prima Käse aged Gouda is one of those cheeses that manages to fill all of the senses. The aroma is

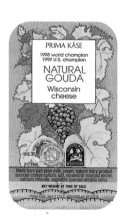

sweet, the taste is buttery with hints of caramel, and its golden hue is beautiful and enticing. It is made in a traditional Gouda style, in which the curds are formed, pressed, cut into pieces, and then put into their round forms. They are brined overnight, after which a coating is applied, "similar to Elmer's Glue," says Krahenbuhl (it is the same coating as is used in Holland). Finally, it is waxed. The Goudas are aged anywhere from three to eight months.

Since Prima Käse is a small operation, some of their specialized cheeses are not widely distributed. However, others, such as the trademarked Sweet Swiss, is sold as private label cheese to stores throughout the country. This cheese, created by Krahenbuhl, (who holds the recipe under lock and key), is sweeter than regular Swiss cheese due to its lower acid level. It is similar in flavor to the Norwegian Jarlsburg cheese. Blue cheese is next on the agenda for Krahenbuhl. In addition to the twenty-some cheeses Prima Käse already makes, this, too, will be a cheese to watch.

WHAT THEY MAKE

Asiago
Butter Käse
Cheddar
Cheddar curds
Edam
Fontina
Gorgonzola: extra creamy
Gouda: young and aged; raw
  and pasteurized, smoked

Grigotto
Havarti: plain and dill
Ricotta
Saga blue
Swiss: baby Swiss, block,
  Sweet Swiss (plain and
  smoked)
Swiss Emmentaler

HOW TO REACH THEM

Monticello, Wisconsin
608-938-4227
608-938-1227 (fax)

OPPOSITE: Red Pepper Gougère (see page 90).

Red Pepper Gougère

The original "cheese puff," a gougère *is a* choux *pastry (a pastry dough that's made with boiling water, butter, and eggs) with cheese and a few optional seasonings. It's easy to make, and the result is a golden brown, puffy pastry that looks like a cross between a soufflé and a circular loaf of bread. (Unfortunately, just like a soufflé, it will fall slightly.) A gougère works equally well in individual puffs or in one large ring. See note below.*

BREAD AND CHEESE

1 cup water
½ cup (1 stick) butter
1 cup all-purpose flour
4 eggs
1 teaspoon Dijon mustard
½ teaspoon dry mustard
¾ teaspoon crushed red pepper flakes
1½ teaspoons kosher salt
1½ cups coarsely grated Emmentaler or Swiss cheese, such as Prima Käse (about 5 ounces)
2 tablespoons finely grated Dry Jack cheese (or use any other hard grating cheese)

Preheat the oven to 425°F. Grease a baking sheet and set it aside.

In a saucepan, slowly bring the water and butter to a boil. Once it is boiling, remove it from the heat and add all of the flour, mixing vigorously with a wooden spoon until the mixture comes together and forms a ball. Beat in the eggs one at a time. When well incorporated, add the mustards, crushed red pepper, salt, and cheeses. Mix thoroughly.

Put one third of the gougère mixture into a pastry bag fitted with the widest tip (or a self-sealing plastic bag with a ½-inch hole cut out). Pipe the gougère mixture onto an ungreased baking sheet in a ring about 8 inches in diameter. Overlap that ring with the next one third of the dough; repeat with the remaining dough. You will end up with a three-layer ring that will meld into one layer when baked. Don't worry if you find that you are piping more than three layers of dough. Simply keep piping in layers until all of the dough is used. The ring of dough should not be more than about 4 inches in height.

Bake for 20 minutes. Reduce the heat to 375°F and bake until the gougère is dark brown and sounds hollow when tapped, 15 to 20 minutes. Place on a cooling rack and let it sit for 15 minutes, and serve. Or let it cool and serve at room temperature.

Serves 6 to 8 as an appetizer or as a bread accompaniment to a meal

Note: To make individual puffs, pipe or spoon the mixture into puffs 3 inches wide and 1-inch high. Bake at 425°F for 20 to 25 minutes, or until golden brown.

WILLOW HILL FARM

"I WOULD HAVE BEEN AN EIGHTH-GENERATION CATTLE RANCHER if I had stayed in Hawaii," says Willow Hill owner Willow Smart. Eighth-generation anything in Hawaii is fairly rare, but at a relatively young age, Willow's mother moved her to New York and then to Europe. After these experiences, Willow vowed that she would never return to farming.

She went on to college in Florida, where she double-majored in psychology and languages. But a visit to Vermont with her husband, David Phinney, was all it took to convince her that she still had farming in her blood. Her route to making sheep cheese is a little less clear, except that Willow thinks her exposure to sheep's milk cheeses in Italy may have gotten under her skin.

Like many Vermont sheep's milk cheesemakers, Smart apprenticed with the Majors at Vermont Shepherd Cheese (see page 178). She then went off to make her own cheeses, called Autumn Oak and Alderbrook. She also still makes a small amount of cheese for the Majors.

Autumn Oak has been likened to a Corsican cheese, but since we get only one or two Corsican cheeses in this country, that comparison is lost on most of us. It is a raw milk, semi-firm, natural washed-rind cheese that ages for seventy-five days. It's nutty, a little salty, and has a lovely, firm consistency. Alderbrook is a pasteurized, high-moisture, mold-ripened cheese akin to a soft-ripened cheese.

As to her career choice, Willow is clear. "I love making cheese. I was going to be either a chef or a veterinarian, but I am obsessed with food. It's all I think about," she says. Her cheese has a wonderful home in the brand-new cheese cave that she and Dave have built. The cave is carved into the side of a hill, and one entire wall is solid rock. It provides a constant cool temperature and humidity level, which helps to age the cheese more evenly.

Willow Hill is Vermont's only certified organic sheep dairy, and the animals are treated homeopathically. Since sheep cheesemaking is seasonal, Willow and David also sell organic free-range eggs, vegetables, berries, sheep stock, meat, and wool fibers.

In existence only since 1998, the Willow Hill cheeses are a mere promise of what might be in store from this innovative farm. For now, they are simply further proof that cheesemaking in America is breaking new ground every day.

WHAT THEY MAKE
Alderbrook
Autumn Oak

HOW TO REACH THEM
Milton, Vermont
802-893-2963
802-893-1954 (fax)
website: www.sheepcheese.com

Crescia
(Italian Easter Cheese Bread)

❧ ◆ ❧

There are three facts that are indisputable when it comes to crescia: *first, it is a bread made at Eastertime in Italy; second, it contains cheese; and third, it's one of the richest, best breads you'll ever taste. After that all bets are off. My San Francisco friend Lori Viti, whose family comes from the Marches section of Italy, where crescia is said to have originated, insists that real crescia contains only aged Pecorino (sheep's milk) cheese. Other recipes I've seen call for a variety of cheeses, including Swiss cheese. Even though I'm not Italian, I'm with Lori. I think this bread is best with a strong, aged sheep's milk cheese. Although she uses Italian cheese, I, of course, think the fantastic aged sheep's milk cheeses made in this country, such as Willow Hill's Autumn Oak, work as well or better.*

What is fun about this recipe is that it is really quite easy and, unlike most breads, very forgiving. Still, there are a few things you need to know. First, it's important that you taste your cheese to determine its saltiness. If it's quite salty, add less salt to the flour mixture. The opposite holds true as well: a milder cheese will mean the need for more salt. Lori says her grandfather liked crescia best when it was loaded with pepper. He would toast the bread and then eat it with his coffee. The amount of pepper you use, however, is up to you. I say make it zing.

This recipe makes four large loaves of bread. Feel free to cut the recipe in half. Likewise, you can double it, but you'll have to mix it in batches since that quantity of dough will be too heavy and stiff to work with.

>·↦·○·↤·I·↞

3 envelopes active dry yeast (¾ ounce total)
½ teaspoon sugar
About 2⅓ cups warm water
10 cups (2½ pounds) bread flour or all-purpose flour
1¼ teaspoons salt
2 tablespoons freshly cracked pepper, or more to taste
1 pound aged sheep's milk cheese, medium grated
½ cup (1 stick) unsalted butter, softened
5 eggs, beaten
Olive oil

Dissolve the yeast and sugar in ⅓ cup of the warm water. Stir gently and let sit for about 5 minutes, or until mixture becomes foamy.

In the large bowl of a stand mixer, mix together the flour, salt, and pepper. Add the cheese, butter, beaten eggs, and dissolved yeast mixture. Mix until smooth. (The dough will be sticky but dry.) Little by little, add the remaining warm water just until the dough holds together and becomes stiff (you probably won't need to use the full 2 cups). You can also do this all by hand if you don't have a stand mixer. You might want to do it in two batches, though, since it will require a good deal of muscle power.

Place the dough on a floured board and knead until fairly smooth and elastic, about 10 minutes. (The dough will never be entirely smooth because of the cheese in it.) Form into a ball. Grease a large bowl with olive oil and place the dough in the bowl. Turn the dough to coat it evenly. Cover with a towel and let rise in a warm place for 2 hours. (The dough will not quite double in size, but it will rise substantially.)

Remove the dough from the bowl and divide it into four equal pieces. Shape them into round balls, and place them on two large greased cookie sheets. Do not let them touch. (Alternatively, you can put them in four 9-inch round cake pans.) Cover and let rise for 1 to 2 hours, or until almost doubled in size.

Preheat the oven to 350°F.

Bake the bread for 25 minutes. Reverse the pans in the oven to ensure even baking, and bake for 20 to 30 minutes more, or until the bread is a deep golden color.

Let cool for at least 1 hour to let the flavors settle in. Slice and serve.

Makes four 1½-pound loaves

Note: This bread freezes very well for up to 6 months.

Sweet and Sour Panini

Pickled onions are almost certainly one of the world's best condiments. They are sweet and sour, and once they are refrigerated, they remain crunchy no matter how long they are immersed in their cooking liquid. There is no end of uses for these tangy onions, including eating them with no accompaniments at all. It is preferable to make the onions the day before, as this will give them time to develop their flavor.

In the case of this panini, a smattering of pickled onions is the perfect foil for the slices of soft, fruity but pronounced Fontina cheese. The smoky ham and spicy mustard bring up the rear, creating a sweet, sour, and moderately spicy combination with an assortment of textures, from the soft cheese and ham to the crisp onions.

FOR THE ONIONS

4 small red onions (about ⅔ pound total), peeled, cut into wedges, and thinly sliced

¾ cup red wine vinegar

¾ cup balsamic vinegar

1 cup sugar

2 bay leaves

FOR THE PANINI

1 fresh regular or sourdough baguette (about 24 inches long by 3 inches wide), cut in half lengthwise and then quartered to make 4 sandwiches

2 tablespoons spicy brown mustard, preferably German-style

8 paper-thin slices (¼ pound) cooked smoked ham

8 ounces Fontina cheese, cut into 16 equal-size slices

To prepare the onions: Bring a large pot of water to a boil. Add the onions and cook for 2 minutes. Drain immediately in a colander. Let sit for 15 minutes. Shake the colander occasionally to remove excess water and to help the onions cool. Put the onions in a large bowl. Set aside.

In a nonreactive saucepan, combine the vinegars, sugar, and bay leaves. Bring to a boil, reduce to a simmer, and cook for 3 minutes. Remove from

the heat and pour over the onions. Let sit for an hour, or until the onions are about room temperature. You may use the onions now, or for more flavor, refrigerate them overnight. Bring them to room temperature before using. The sandwiches use up ¾ cup of the onions; you'll have over 4 cups to use elsewhere.

To make the panini: Set the bread in front of you, cut side up. Spread the mustard evenly on all 8 pieces. On the 4 bottom halves, put 3 tablespoons of the pickled onions. Follow with 2 slices of ham and 4 slices of cheese. Place the top half over the bottom half, and serve. Or wrap well in plastic wrap (the pickled onions might leak a little) and take on a picnic or to work.

Makes about 5 cups onions; 4 panini

Mozzarella and Roasted Mushroom Panini

Because of its simplicity and texture, mozzarella is far more than a melting cheese. Fresh mozzarella goes nicely on sandwiches with other ingredients because it acts as a neutral bridge between those ingredients. In this case, the roasted mushrooms and the olive spread known as tapenade are rather rich, but the cheese softens them both. Prepared tapenade can be found at many supermarkets and gourmet food stores. Or you can make your own; see the note at the end of this recipe.

This is a great sandwich to bring along on a picnic or hike. It doesn't get as soggy as most sandwiches or panini, and it's far more interesting than normal sandwich fare. Bring along some fruit and you'll have an energizing, well-balanced meal.

½ pound white mushrooms, stems removed, caps cut into 3 or 4 slices

2 tablespoons olive oil

Kosher salt

½ cup purchased tapenade (see Note)

1 baguette (24 inches long), cut in half lengthwise and then quartered to make 4 sandwiches

1 pound fresh mozzarella cheese, cut into ¼-inch-thick slices

½ bunch watercress, large stems removed, rinsed and separated into individual sprigs

Preheat the oven to 475°F.

In a baking pan, drizzle the oil over the mushrooms. Add salt to taste, and shake the mushrooms around to coat them. Roast in the oven until they are soft and the edges have turned brown, 10 to 12 minutes. Remove from the oven and let cool.

Spread about 2 tablespoons tapenade on the bottom halves of the bread. Lay the cheese slices over the tapenade. Distribute the mushrooms over the cheese, and then add the watercress. Top with the remaining bread, and wrap or eat right away.

Makes 4 panini

Note: If tapenade is unavailable, make a version of it yourself by coarsely chopping 20 pitted kalamata olives. Add 1 tablespoon rinsed, drained, and chopped capers, 1 teaspoon fresh lemon juice, and 2 teaspoons olive oil. Add ½ teaspoon anchovy paste (optional) and a little cracked pepper. Mix well and use as directed.

SALADS

JUNIPER GROVE FARM

WITH A NAME LIKE PIERRE, it may seem that making a fresh chèvre would be second nature. But Pierre Kolisch, owner of Juniper Grove Farm in central Oregon, has his early professional roots in the law, and he learned to make cheese with cows' milk, not goats' milk. Now, after fulfilling his dream of buying a farm, the lawyer-cum-cheesemaker is churning out some of Oregon's—and the nation's—best cheese.

Like several American cheesemakers, Kolisch went to France for his training. Although not French himself, he does speak the language, which helped him gain entry into one of France's two exclusive Camembert operations in Normandy. He ended up spending two years at a few different cheesemaking operations before returning to Oregon to start his own venture. Since Camembert is made with cows' milk, Kolisch had figured that he would also make cheese from cows' milk. But in his particular area of Oregon, milk from cows was hard to come by. That's when he decided on goats.

In 1991 Kolisch began selling cheese to the public. His farm, located in Redmond, in the heart of the state, is in an area of about 100,000 people. The local restaurants and retail operations, which were always interested in procuring local products, began buying the Juniper Grove cheese. Kolisch then set his sights on Portland restaurants, which swept up his cheese as well.

For good reason. His Tumalo *tomme*, or wheel-shaped cheese, an aged raw milk mountain-style washed-rind cheese, has many sensational dimensions. It starts off tasting a little sweet, then it moves to earthy, even musty, then it comes around to being a delicate balance of all of these flavors with a hint of salt thrown in. It has a light-yellow interior and is firm but silky in texture. It is truly magnificent and stands beautifully alone or side by side with some olive oil-drizzled raw fennel. His pyramid-shaped cheese is also 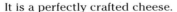 commendable. Aged just a few weeks, it is a little lemony, a little rustic, and lush. It is a perfectly crafted cheese.

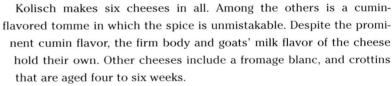

Kolisch makes six cheeses in all. Among the others is a cumin-flavored tomme in which the spice is unmistakable. Despite the prominent cumin flavor, the firm body and goats' milk flavor of the cheese hold their own. Other cheeses include a fromage blanc, and crottins that are aged four to six weeks.

Anyone who appreciates great cheese can be grateful that Kolisch replaced his "esquire" title with that of cheesemaker. His cheeses are tangible proof that the highest-quality cheeses can be and are being made in America.

WHAT THEY MAKE
Buche
Crottin
Fromage blanc
Pyramid
Tumalo Tomme: plain, cumin-flavored

HOW TO REACH THEM
Redmond, Oregon
888-FROMAGE
541-923-8353
website: www.junipergrovefarm.com

OPPOSITE: Melon and Prosciutto with Goat Cheese and Mint (see page 108).

Mixed Beet and Crottin Salad with Walnut Oil and Lemon

❧◆❧

A crottin is a cylindrical goat cheese with a yellowish rind. It is aged ten days to three weeks, is a little dry, and is packed with flavor. In this salad its pronounced flavors play off the earthiness of the beets and the walnuts, while its tanginess melds with the tart lemon juice. The slightly sour component brings a refreshing quality to the salad, making it equally good before or after a meal. Although this calls for both orange and red beets, you can use any combination you'd like.

It is very important that a good-quality walnut oil is used. Otherwise this salad will be flavorless. Gourmet and specialty shops, along with many supermarkets, now carry very good nut oils. If you cannot find walnut oil, substitute a good extra-virgin olive oil. It won't be the same, but it is better than using a flavorless oil.

> ❧ ❖ ❧ ❧

½ **pound (about 4 small) orange beets**
½ **pound (about 4 small) red beets**
1 **head frisée (curly endive), torn into**
   3-inch-long pieces
¼ **cup fresh lemon juice**
Scant ⅓ **cup high-quality walnut oil, extra for**
   drizzling
Salt, to taste
4 **small crottins, such as Juniper Grove**
   crottins (about 1 ounce each; or use 4
   ounces slightly aged sheep's milk cheese,
   such as Old Chatham's Mutton Buttons,
   or 4 ounces fresh goat cheese, sliced)
⅓ **cup walnut halves, toasted**
Freshly ground pepper

Preheat the oven to 400°F.

Wrap the orange beets in a large square of foil. Place the red beets in another piece of foil. Seal both packets well. Place them in the oven and roast for 1 hour. Remove the packets from the oven and let cool. When cool enough to handle, unwrap the packets, peel the beets, cut them into ½-inch cubes, and place them in a large nonreactive bowl. Let them cool completely.

Add the frisée to the beets. Add the lemon juice, scant ⅓ cup walnut oil, and salt, and gently toss together. Distribute the frisée-beet mixture around the edges of four salad plates. Place a disk of cheese in the center of each plate. Sprinkle each salad with the walnuts, and drizzle a very small amount of walnut oil over the cheese. Give one twist of the peppermill to each disk of cheese. Serve immediately.

Serves 4

Dill-Lemon Greek Salad

Greek salad recipes vary widely, but because the emphasis is on the fresh ingredients, simple is best. That way, all of the flavors are pronounced, yet none is more important than the other. Naturally, it is best to make this salad when tomatoes are at the height of their season, since the dish celebrates the sweetness of the tomato. It happens to look prettiest then, too.

Be sure to add the oil, lemon juice, and cheese just before serving. Otherwise, the tomatoes will become mushy and the assertive flavors from the feta will be replaced by oil and lemon. Red onion is an ingredient that many people like in a Greek salad, although it can be overpowering compared with its fellow salad constituents. It is a purely personal decision—the salad tastes good either way.

4 large ripe tomatoes (about 2 pounds) cut
   into ½-inch wedges
1 English (hothouse) cucumber, halved
   lengthwise and cut into 1-inch slices, or 2
   medium cucumbers, peeled, halved lengthwise, seeded, and cut into 1-inch slices
¼ large red onion, very thinly sliced
   (optional)
¾ cup kalamata olives, pitted
1 tablespoon chopped fresh dill, or ¾
   teaspoon dried dill
Freshly ground pepper

3 tablespoons fresh lemon juice
¼ cup extra-virgin olive oil
3 ounces feta cheese (preferably sheep or
   goat or a combination), crumbled

In a large bowl, mix together the tomatoes, cucumber, onion, olives, and dill. Add pepper to taste. Just before serving, add the lemon juice and oil. Mix well. Top with cheese and serve immediately.

Serves 4

Blood Orange, Fennel, and Feta Salad

The combination of fennel with blood orange juice is remarkably invigorating. It offers a little sweetness, a tinge of bitterness, and most of all, bright flavors.

Although this salad calls for feta, in fact a number of different types of cheese work well. The only criterion is that the cheese has a good amount of salt to help flavor the overall dish. A blue cheese works very well and brings a more pronounced flavor to the salad, while a lighter touch would be to top the salad with shavings of a salty hard cheese such as Parmesan. Any way you go, the dish will taste refreshing and light. It will also impress because of the deep, exotic color of the blood oranges. If you cannot find blood oranges, use regular juice oranges.

SALADS

5 blood oranges
2 teaspoons cider vinegar
¼ cup extra-virgin olive oil
Salt and freshly ground pepper
2 large fennel bulbs (about 1 pound each),
    with fronds
3 ounces feta cheese, crumbled (or use crum-
    bled cotija, blue cheese, or 2 ounces salty
    hard cow, goat, or sheep cheese, shaved)
½ cup chopped almonds (skin-on), toasted
    until lightly browned

Cut 1 orange in half and squeeze the juice into a small bowl or glass. Add the vinegar. Slowly whisk in the oil. Add salt and pepper to taste. Set aside.

Cut the fronds from the fennel bulbs. Finely chop the fronds and set aside; you should have 3 tablespoons.

Using a mandoline, cut the fennel bulbs into paper-thin slices (or use a sharp knife to slice as thin as possible). Place in a large serving bowl.

Cut off about ½ inch from the tops and bottoms of the remaining 4 oranges, or enough until the orange pulp is showing. Place 1 orange on its end. Using a serrated knife and working from top to bottom, carefully shave away the skin and pith to reveal just the orange. Try not to cut away too much of the orange, but do remove all of the white spots. Gently slice the orange horizontally into ¼-inch-thick slices. Repeat with the remaining oranges, and set aside.

Add the cheese and dressing to the sliced fennel. Add a small amount of salt and pepper, and mix well. Distribute the salad on individual plates or in bowls. Place the orange slices around the salad, and sprinkle with the almonds and the reserved fennel fronds. Top with a little more freshly ground pepper, and serve immediately.

Serves 4 to 6

BLYTHEDALE FARM

TWO PEOPLE, TWENTY COWS, AND TWENTY ACRES come together to form one of America's finest farmstead cheesemaking operations. Blythedale Farm in Corinth, Vermont, has been putting out Brie and Camembert since its beginning in 1992, and now their Green Mountain Gruyère and Jersey Blue are becoming well known—and much sought after. Unfortunately, a small operation can keep up with only so much demand, and as a consumer, catching up with a Blythedale cheese can be tricky.

Karen Galayda and Tom Gilbert got their start at a farm in Massachusetts where Tom was managing a herd of cows and Karen was brought in to be an assistant cheesemaker, despite the fact she had no experience. They both ended up making cheese where on-the-job was the primary form of training. Since Tom's parents were in Vermont, Karen and Tom eventually moved there to help them with their farm. Soon after, they moved to Blythedale Farm to begin their own operation.

What they might not have anticipated is that they would become cheesemakers who would work fifteen hours a day, seven days a week. For Karen and Tom it is obviously hard work; for cheese-lovers, it is a luxury. The reason lies in the extraordinarily skillfully made cheeses. The Jersey Blue is a raw milk cheese that is spicy, balanced, yellowish in color with blue veins—reminiscent of English Stilton, but creamier and less crumbly. It has a deep earthy flavor and is lovely on its own with the classic glass of port or, as in the following recipe, on top of a salad.

About 500 pounds of Brie and Camembert emerge from Blythedale weekly, while the award-winning Jersey Blue spills out at the rate of about 175 pounds a week. The Blythedale cows are all Jerseys, which contributes to the richness, golden color, and flavor of all of their cheeses. Top-notch restaurants and cheese shops clamor to carry Blythedale products because every step of the way is tended to by Karen and Tom alone.

This includes feeding and milking the cows in the predawn hours, making the cheese, and handling the business affairs in between. It is a feat that many American cheesemakers are familiar with but one that still makes any city-dweller's jaw drop.

Websites, mail order, and other modern-day forms of commerce are not on the Blythedale agenda. This results in a hard-to-find cheese, though it's not impossible. Several specialty cheese shops around the country carry Blythedale cheeses and fortunately are set up for mail order. These cheeses are unquestionably worth the extra effort it takes to find them. Indeed, perhaps it's only fair, given the remarkable effort that goes into making them.

WHAT THEY MAKE
Brie
Camembert
Cookeville Parmesan (limited production)
Green Mountain Gruyère
Jersey Blue

HOW TO REACH THEM
Corinth, Vermont
802-439-6575

Endive, Pear, and Blue Cheese Salad with Candied Walnuts

This dish requires more steps than most salads do, and it involves two different dressings, but everything can be done as much as a week in advance, except for cutting the endive and assembling the salad. Besides, the effort is well worth it, especially since you'll inevitably end up with extra candied walnuts. These positively addictive nuts can also be found accompanying the Summer Fruit Salad on page 113 and the honeyed goat cheese dessert on page 209.

This recipe is an adaptation of one given to me by a popular Napa Valley chef named Philippe Jeanty. His eponymous restaurant, Bistro Jeanty in Yountville, has been the talk of the valley ever since it opened in 1997. And for good reason. Close your eyes and you're on the wine roads of France at a small family-run restaurant in a century-old building where all of the local patrons know one another and share stories well into the night. Bistro Jeanty is that place, and it provides a wonderful respite—and repast—after a day of touring among the vineyards.

SALADS

FOR THE MUSTARD DRESSING
¼ cup sherry vinegar
1½ tablespoons red wine vinegar
1 tablespoon Dijon mustard
¾ cup olive oil
Salt and freshly ground pepper

FOR THE CITRUS DRESSING
3 juice oranges
2 lemons
1 lime
2 tablespoons sherry vinegar
1 piece fresh ginger (about 1 × 1½ inches), peeled
¾ cup olive oil
Salt and freshly ground pepper

FOR THE WALNUTS
¼ cup confectioners' sugar
⅛ teaspoon cayenne pepper
⅛ teaspoon salt
4 ounces (about 1 heaping cup) walnut halves

FOR THE SALAD
8 Belgian endives, cut in half lengthwise and then cut crosswise, at a slight angle, into ½-inch slices
2 pears, such as Comice or French Butter, cored, seeded, quartered, and cut into half-inch pieces
4 ounces blue cheese, such as Blythedale's Jersey Blue, crumbled
Finely chopped fresh chives, for garnish

To make the mustard dressing: In a small non-reactive bowl, combine both vinegars and the mustard, and whisk until well blended. Slowly add the olive oil in a steady stream, whisking vigorously until it is fully incorporated. Season with salt and pepper to taste. Set aside, or refrigerate if not using right away.

To make the citrus dressing: Extract the juice from all of the citrus and place in a small saucepan. Add the vinegar. Bring the citrus-vinegar mixture to a boil and reduce until it's about one-third its original volume, about 10 minutes. (It should reduce to about ¼ cup.) Remove from the heat and immediately add the ginger. Let the ginger steep for about 2 minutes; then discard it. Slowly add the oil in a steady stream, whisking until the mixture becomes thick and creamy. Add salt and pepper to taste. Set aside, or refrigerate if not using right away.

To prepare the walnuts: Preheat the oven to 350°F.

In a medium-size bowl, mix together the sugar, cayenne, and salt.

Bring a small saucepan of water to a boil. Add the walnuts and blanch for 3 minutes. Drain well, and immediately roll the walnuts in the sugar mixture until thoroughly coated. The sugar will melt slightly. Transfer the walnuts to a baking sheet or pan, and bake until they are a deep golden brown, about 10 minutes. Watch carefully because the sugar can burn easily.

To assemble: Put the endive, pears, and cheese in a large bowl. Add ½ cup of the mustard dressing and ¼ cup of the citrus dressing, and toss.

Divide the salad among four plates. Scatter 6 to 8 candied walnuts over each serving. Sprinkle chives on top of the salad and around the edges of the plate, and serve.

Serves 4

Note: This recipe makes more dressing than you need for the salad. The mustard dressing can also be used on a simple butter lettuce salad or even as a substitute for the truffle vinaigrette on page 110. The citrus dressing could be mixed with some cooked Asian soba or udon noodles, and topped with scallions and red pepper for a refreshing Far Eastern salad.

SALADS

COACH FARM

COACH FARM, IN THE HUDSON VALLEY town of Pine Plains, New York, earned its reputation for excellent cheese almost the day it opened for business. What people may not know is that the name is directly related to the Coach Leather Company, famous for their Coach handbags and other leather accessories. Miles and Lillian Cahn were the owners of Coach when they sold it to the Sara Lee Corporation and took off for the country. Not long after, they turned the defunct cow dairy farm they had purchased into the site of a herd of frolicking goats. The Cahns also planted some hay and unknowingly embarked on a journey that would eventually put them in a position to take advantage of the decided lack of goat cheese on New York restaurant menus.

That was in 1984. Now, 1,000 goats later, the operation is thriving, but in many ways it is as traditional as most small operations in its farming and cheesemaking methods. Coach Farm's head cheesemaker, Rose Parsons, has been with the company since the beginning. She apprenticed under a French cheesemaker whom the Cahns brought in during the early stages of the operation. Although Coach Farm makes several different types and shapes of goat cheese, it is all still done by hand. The curds are hand-ladled into the molds where they are left to drain, and the aged cheeses are carefully tended.

The clean flavor of Coach Farm goat cheese may be its most distinguishing characteristic. It is a no-frills yet rich and balanced cheese. The cheese is made in a variety of shapes, including sticks, cones, pyramids, tomes (small wheels), bricks, and even hearts. The green peppercorn brick is particularly noteworthy: the spice from the pepper is immediately soothed by the soft, tangy cheese. Try bathing it in a pool of fruity olive oil, as in the following recipe.

Coach Farm is also one of the few farmstead operations that makes a low-fat version of its regular cheese. More than half of the fat is removed, and the resulting cheese is a reasonable substitute for the regular Coach Farms goat cheese, and infinitely better than most of the pre-packaged low-fat cheeses available.

Although Coach Farm goat cheese can be found in many specialty stores and in numerous restaurants, it is not available by mail order directly from the farm. Not to worry, though, since many retail outlets that carry Coach Farm cheese are happy to mail cheese (see Resources).

WHAT THEY MAKE
Fresh goat cheeses
Plain or rolled in herbs, black pepper, or dill
Brick, button, disk, fresh curd, log, low-fat sticks, low-fat bricks, medallion

Aged goat cheeses
Cone, grating sticks, Green Peppercorn Brick, heart, pyramid, round, stick, tome, wheel

HOW TO REACH THEM
Pine Plains, New York
518-398-5325
518-398-5329 (fax)

Marinated Peppered Goat Cheese and Roasted Tomatoes

The brightness of the tomatoes, the freshness of the herbs, and the pepper-flecked cheese floating in a light sea of fruity olive oil in this dish are enough to make you want to book the next flight to the South of France. Fortunately you don't have to, since all of the wonderful ingredients, including the cheese, are found right here.

You can make your own peppered goat cheese by rolling a log of fresh goat cheese in some freshly cracked pepper or whole peppercorns. You can use any type of goat cheese you like, including those that have a soft rind. Just be sure it is slightly firm so that it will not break down in the oil. You can use individual disks, or you can slice a log into equal-size pieces. Allow 1 to 1½ ounces of cheese per person.

8 medium Roma (plum) tomatoes (about 1¼ pounds total), peeled, cut in half lengthwise, and seeded
About ¾ cup high-quality fruity extra-virgin olive oil
1 tablespoon balsamic vinegar
Salt and freshly ground pepper
4 (1 to 1½ ounces each) pieces of peppered goat cheese, such as Coach Farm's Green Peppercorn Brick
2 teaspoons chopped fresh oregano leaves
¼ pound (about 20) kalamata or Niçoise olives
4 sprigs oregano

Preheat the oven to 300°F.

In a baking pan, place the tomatoes cut side down on a rack. Roast in the oven until the tomatoes have shriveled to about half their original size, 1 to 1½ hours. Remove the pan from the oven and let the tomatoes cool.

In a medium-size nonreactive bowl, combine the tomatoes, ¼ cup of the olive oil, the vinegar, and salt and pepper to taste. Set aside but do not refrigerate.

In a large shallow bowl or gratin dish, pour ½-cup olive oil over the cheese. Add more oil if this does not cover the cheese. Sprinkle with the chopped oregano and let sit for at least 2 hours, or up to 4 hours, at room temperature. (If you wish to make it a day in advance, then refrigerate the cheese in the oil. Remove from the refrigerator at least 2 hours before serving.)

To assemble, carefully remove the cheese from the olive oil and place each piece on an individual plate. Drizzle with some of the olive oil in which the cheese was marinating. Viewing each plate as a clock with the cheese being at the "12," place 4 pieces of tomato at 4 o'clock, and put 5 or 6 olives at 8 o'clock. Place an oregano sprig in the center, and serve. You may assemble the plates up to 1 hour before serving and cover them tightly with plastic wrap.

Serves 4

Note: To make your own peppered goat cheese, scatter 2 tablespoons very coarsely cracked green, black, or pink peppercorns, or 1 tablespoon whole peppercorns, in a shallow dish. Dip the cheese in the pepper, pressing lightly on both sides so the pepper sticks to the cheese.

CAPRIOLE

JUDY SCHAD SUBSCRIBES TO THE NOTION that small is beautiful. She is part of a special breed of goat cheese makers who began their craft two decades ago, who sell their cheese in relatively small pockets across the nation, and whose overall production is comparatively small. For this group, the end result is cheeses that are specialized and highly prized. Schad is a member of this elite group, and her Capriole cheeses could be considered the role models.

It is hard to tell whether Schad's perseverance or her southern brand of humor played a bigger role in developing and marketing her award-winning goat cheeses. Whichever the case, cheese consumers are all the better for it.

Capriole's Mont St. Francis, named after a nearby monastery, is unquestionably one of the best cheeses made in this country. It is a washed-rind aged raw milk cheese (until recently it was made with pasteurized milk), and excels in that unmatched aged goat cheese flavor that encompasses gaminess, earthiness, a little salt, a little butter, a few hints of fruit, and a firm but supple texture. The rind straddles the line between brown and gold-colored, and the texture falls between smooth and slightly rough. It is made in the shape of a wheel, or tomme.

Another similar cheese, though aged for a shorter period, is the Old Kentucky Tomme. A little Schad humor in its name, the wheel-shaped cheese is mellower than the Mont St. Francis, less salty, and its buttery qualities are more dominant. Both are cheeses that Schad says she loves to make. They are especially noteworthy because of the depth of flavor. Therein lies the challenge.

"The mark of really great cheese," says Schad, "is that it keeps unfolding." With that as the criterion, her cheeses could unequivocally be called "really great."

The Capriole operation is located in Greenville, Indiana, just over the border from Louisville, Kentucky. Although a city-bred girl herself, Schad settled in this rural part of the country after spending summers on her grandparents' farm. There her grandfather "grew everything," and her grandmother was a superior cook. As an adult, she says, it seemed natural to her to return to life in the country. Her husband, Larry, agreed, and they have been building their farm ever since.

WHAT THEY MAKE

American Alpine
Banon
Buttons
Crocodile Tear
Fresh goat cheeses
Mont St. Francis

Old Kentucky Tomme
Sofia
That's Amore (heart-shaped slightly aged cheese)
Wabash Cannonball

HOW TO REACH THEM
Greenville, Indiana
812-923-9408 (phone and fax)

Contrary to the direction most cheesemakers go as they build their business, the Schads' farm has gone from one in which outside sources of milk and feed were used, to a farmstead operation, including growing much of their own hay for feed. The goal, Schad says, is to be able to manage every stage of the cheesemaking process instead of being dependent on others for supplies.

When she began making goat cheese in the early 1980s, she was among the first to do so. This meant few role models and a big learning curve. She eventually turned to Ricki Carroll at New England Cheesemaking Supply (see page 87) to help her improve her technique. That launched her into the next phase of cheesemaking, which would eventually take her and her cheese to restaurants in and around Louisville.

In the meantime, Schad had to find a place to make her cheese (other than her kitchen). A nearby farmer had a cheesemaking facility, and every "morning," at 2:00 A.M., she would travel the two miles over bumpy country roads to make cheese, often losing a milk tank or two along the way. Not until 1990 did the Schads build their own cheesemaking facility on their own farm.

Those hardworking beginnings have led to some of the most respected cheese made in this country today. Schad's goat cheeses range from fresh to aged, from raw milk to pasteurized, and from natural-rind to chestnut leaf-wrapped. The latter shares the name of its French counterpart, Banon. The names of some of the other cheeses are chosen for their shapes: the Wabash Cannonball is, naturally, round with a light coating of ash, and the Crocodile Tear, as might be imagined, is tear-shaped. It is dusted with paprika. These are both firm but smooth, mild yet flavorful cheeses that can be spread on a thin piece of toasted walnut bread, eaten alongside a few briny olives, or served as a counterpoint to some slices of ripe avocado. The rich avocado and tangy goat cheese flavors marry surprisingly well.

Fortunately for cheese aficionados, many of the Capriole cheeses can be found in the finer cheese shops around the nation. (They are also available by mail order directly from Capriole and from other retailers.) They are well worth seeking out, since it is rare to find cheesemakers in the U.S. who have been at their craft for two decades, as Judy has. Schad is truly an American cheesemaking pioneer as well as talent. The proof is in her cheese, which stands out as some of the most exceptional found anywhere within our borders.

Melon and Prosciutto with Goat Cheese and Mint

Sometimes simple is best, and when it comes to good cheese, that is almost always the rule. In this combination, the sweet melon and the fresh mint really highlight the earthy, salty flavors of the cheese.

This dish is a wonderful way to start a meal because the flavors are clean and the melon is refreshing. But for these same reasons, it is also a nice dish with which to end a meal. Another alternative is to have it as a light meal by itself, adding a few other cheeses and an assortment of melons. You can arrange the ingredients any way you like.

1 large cantaloupe (about 3 pounds), or other ripe melon
8 paper-thin slices prosciutto (about 4 ounces)
1 piece (8 ounces) hard cheese, preferably goat, such as Capriole's Mont St. Francis, divided into 8 equal chunks (or use an aged Provolone or dry Jack)
2 tablespoons chopped fresh mint
Whole mint leaves, for garnish

Cut the melon in half lengthwise and remove the seeds. Cut each half into 8 slices, and then cut each slice from the rind. Divide the melon among four plates.

Drape 2 slices of prosciutto over the melon, leaving some melon exposed. Place 2 chunks of cheese in the middle of each plate. Sprinkle with chopped mint, and garnish with whole mint leaves. Serve immediately.

Serves 4

Note: You can have all of the ingredients ready in advance. Bring them to room temperature before assembling.

OLD CHATHAM SHEEPHERDING COMPANY

WHEN A BOY HAS A DREAM of becoming the nation's largest sheep farmer, chances are it will remain a dream. But for Tom Clark it became a reality. He and his wife, Nancy, own Old Chatham Sheepherding Company in New York's Hudson Valley and have built their flock to a startling 1,000 sheep. So far. That is, indeed, this country's largest flock of dairy sheep.

The farm that is now Old Chatham had been a sheep milking operation that was set up to supply a nearby cheesemaking facility called Hollow Road Farms. The owner of Hollow Road Farms, Joan Snyder, was one of America's first sheep's milk cheesemakers, and her cheeses are still remembered for their exceptional quality. Snyder eventually stopped making cheese, and the Clarks purchased Hollow Road Farms' assets. They also rented the Hollow Road Farms creamery facility until their own cheese plant could be completed.

The Clarks bought their farm in 1995, attracted by the prospect of building a sheep operation and also by the beauty of its location, about 2½ hours from New York City. The property had a Georgian-style home that gave Nancy Clark her own dream project, since she is an interior designer.

But the real story at Old Chatham is the cheese. The Clarks recruited Benoit Maillol and Alison Appleby, both from Hollow Road, to be their cheesemakers. It didn't take long for the cheesemaking duo to come up with award-winning cheeses.

Among those is the Hudson Valley Camembert, which is a combination of sheep's milk, cows' milk, and a little bit of cream, but it may as well be soft butter, given its flavor. One cut into a ripe wheel reveals a cream-like interior that is best captured with a spoon. Old Chatham also makes a Shepherd's Wheel, which is made from pure sheep's milk and is aged a little longer. A prize for the cleverest name could be given to their Mutton Button, a small round soft-ripened sheep's milk cheese that also has a strong buttery flavor but is not quite as rich as the Hudson Valley Camembert.

Making sheep's milk cheese is difficult due to the fact that sheep give relatively little milk. Compounding that is the short milking season, generally from May to September. But Old Chatham Sheepherding Company has found ways to boost their sheep's milk production by encouraging off-season breeding. This allows them to make cheese in the fall, when demand is high and milk production is low. With a flock as large as Old Chatham's, they have the luxury of working with nature to devise new and safe ways to increase their animals' milk production.

WHAT THEY MAKE

Sheep's milk cheeses
Feta (limited production)
Fresh Sheep's Milk Cheese
Fresh Garlic & Herb Cheese
Mini Wheel
Mutton Button
Peppered Pyramid
Shepherd's Wheel
Sheep's Milk Yogurt

Cows'/Sheep's milk cheeses
Fresh Ricotta
Hudson Valley Camembert
Nancy's Hudson Valley
    Camembert

HOW TO REACH THEM
Old Chatham, New York
888-SHEEP-60
518-794-7641 (fax)
website: www.blacksheepcheese.com

Mushroom and Camembert Crostini on Butter Lettuce with Truffle Vinaigrette

Sautéed mushrooms and Camembert are an unparalleled food marriage. The buttery mushroom flavor intertwines perfectly with those same qualities in the Camembert. The rich crouton that is created from these ingredients, along with the bed of truffle-dressed butter lettuce, is so satisfying that it could easily make a main course salad for light eaters. It's also ideal as an impressive first course.

If you like, you can cook the mushrooms in advance and reheat them just before serving. Feel free to use a variety of mushrooms, or use easy-to-find white mushrooms instead. However, if you use white mushrooms, be aware that they release a lot of liquid. Be sure to cook most of this liquid away before topping the crostini, or the crostini will become soggy.

One note about melting Camembert or other soft-ripened cheeses: Once it is put under the broiler, the cheese, except for the rind, virtually disappears. Don't worry—the creamy, rich taste definitely lingers.

Finally, you will see that the dressing calls for truffle paste, which is available at some gourmet food stores. If you cannot find it, or don't wish to use it, then use 1 tablespoon truffle oil, or simply make the dressing without it. It will naturally have a different flavor, but it will be delicious nonetheless.

FOR THE DRESSING
3 tablespoons sherry vinegar
1 tablespoon Dijon mustard
3 tablespoons black truffle paste in oil
½ cup plus 2 tablespoons extra-virgin olive oil
Salt and white pepper (or black pepper)

FOR THE CROSTINI
1 regular or sourdough baguette, about 3
    inches in diameter, cut into 32 ¼-inch-thick
    slices
2 to 3 tablespoons olive oil for brushing the
    bread
1 tablespoon unsalted butter
3 portobello mushrooms (about ¾ pound
    total), stems removed, caps sliced ¼ inch
    thick, then cut crosswise into quarters

½ pound shiitake mushrooms, stems removed,
    caps sliced ¼ inch thick, then cut crosswise
    into thirds
Salt and freshly ground pepper
3 ounces Camembert cheese, such as Old
    Chatham's Hudson Valley Camembert, at
    room temperature (or use Brie or another
    soft-ripened cheese)

FOR THE SALAD
3 heads butter lettuce, washed and torn into
    large pieces
4 hard-boiled eggs, finely grated or pressed
    through a sieve
2 tablespoons chopped flat-leaf parsley, for
    garnish

To make the dressing: In a small bowl, whisk together the vinegar, mustard, truffle paste, olive oil, and salt and pepper to taste. Set aside.

To make the crostini: Preheat the broiler.

Brush the cut sides of the baguette slices with olive oil, and place under the broiler just until the bread is toasted on both sides. Set aside.

In a medium saucepan, heat 1 tablespoon of the olive oil and the butter over medium heat. Add the mushrooms and sauté until they are tender and the juices, if any, have cooked away. (Wild mushrooms release almost no juices.) If the mushrooms seem dry, add a few drops of chicken stock or water and continue to cook until they're nice and tender and any remaining liquid has boiled away. (You want the mushrooms to be dry, almost crisp on the outside.) Add salt and a generous amount of pepper, and set aside.

Spread or spoon about 1½ teaspoons Camembert on each slice of toast. Broil for 1 to 2 minutes, or until the cheese has melted (or maybe even disappeared).

To assemble: Reheat the mushrooms if they have cooled, or, if you prefer, keep them at room temperature.

Toss the lettuce and eggs with the dressing. Distribute on individual salad plates. Place four crostini on each plate, and top each one with about 1 tablespoon of the mushrooms. Sprinkle with a little parsley, and serve.

Serves 8

Note: It is not necessary to remove the rind from the cheese, but if you do not like the taste and/or the consistency, cut it off. For minimum waste, cut off the rind when the cheese is cold. After the rind has been removed, bring the cheese to room temperature before using.

SALADS

KU`OKO`A FARM

ON THE EASTERN SIDE OF THE BIG ISLAND of Hawaii, about seventy goats wander amongst wild orchids and neon-colored bromeliads. Rain in the Puna District is the norm, falling at a rate of about 200 inches a year, but the goats don't mind. It is their only source of water, as it is for the goats' owners, Karin and Steve Sayre, and their teenaged son. Living on an old lava flow, where until recently no electricity flowed, the Sayres catch all of their water from their roof and divert it to holding tanks. Otherwise, no formal water supply exists. This, along with their dependence on a rudimentary power source, are just two of the astonishing facts that come together to form the story of Ku`oko`a Farm.

According to Karin, Ku`oko`a in Hawaiian means "independence, liberty, and freedom." She and Steve chose that name because it embodied their mission when they moved from Lake Tahoe on the California-Nevada border to a remote area 3,000 miles across the Pacific. She says she and Steve had a dream of living in a rural place and raising a child who would learn what it was like to grow up without power and other core urban fixtures.

Like Captain Cook, they arrived on the island of Hawaii, the newest island in the Hawaiian chain, and did anything they could to make a living. Coincidentally, Karin worked for a specialized library that offered information on how to live in areas where modern conveniences did not exist, while Steve worked as a zookeeper in a rain forest facility.

That was in 1980. At that time they bought a few goats, and in 1982 a problem with contaminated cows' milk in Hawaii convinced the Sayres to sell some of their goats' milk. They later traveled to Colorado to a convention of dairy goat producers, and while there took a short course in cheesemaking. That, plus a French cheesemaking recipe and ten more years of preparation, was "all" it took to become full-fledged cheesemakers.

ORCHID ISLAND
Chèvre
GOAT MILK CHEESE
Made in Hawaii
Ingredients: pasteurized cultured goat milk, salt, and rennet (vegetable).
Ku'oko'a Farm
Kurtistown, HI
96760

It didn't take much to convince local chefs that a fresh goat cheese made in the Islands was a good idea. The high quality of the cheese cemented that, and soon the Sayres were selling their cheese as fast as they could make it.

Fresh foods are the hallmark of the Hawaiian Islands, and Ku`oko`a Farm's goat cheeses exemplify that. Perhaps the tropical climate contributes to the exceedingly fresh taste of their chèvre, which is creamy and straightforward. It is not quite as tangy as some other fresh goat cheeses, yet it leaves a pleasant fresh milk taste behind. It glides down particularly easily because of its smooth consistency.

WHAT THEY MAKE
Feta
Fresh goat cheese
Oil-marinated goat cheese

HOW TO REACH THEM
Kurtistown, Hawaii
808-966-7791

The cheese is still sold primarily to restaurants and some stores in the five-island chain, but as travelers get a taste of it, they are starting to demand it as well. A restaurateur in Austin, Texas, uses it, as does an individual in Hong Kong who sampled it while in Hawaii. While their main product is fresh goat cheese, Karin also makes a small amount of feta as well as an oil- and- herb-marinated goat cheese.

Summer Fruit Salad with Goat Cheese

"Fruit salad" conjures up all kinds of images, including the type that comes in a can. Fortunately, this is one fruit salad that is as fresh as a summer day is long. At first glance, the ingredients might seem like a hodgepodge, but the salad comes together when the ripe summer fruit mingles with the herbaceous dressing. The crunchy candied walnuts have a sweet-salt taste that mirrors the rest of the flavors, and the bright color of the fresh goat cheese further enhances the fresh impression of this salad.

FOR THE SALAD
24 fresh cherries, pitted and cut in half
2 medium-size peaches, peeled and sliced ½ inch thick
3 plums, cut into ½-inch slices
8 cups baby spinach, rinsed and dried
1 head frisée (curly endive), torn into bite-size pieces

FOR THE DRESSING
¼ cup extra-virgin olive oil
1 large shallot, thinly sliced
1 tablespoon chopped fresh sage leaves
1 tablespoon Dijon mustard
2 tablespoons sherry vinegar
Salt and freshly ground pepper
2 to 3 ounces fresh goat cheese, such as Ku`oko`a Farms or Laura Chenel Chèvre, cut into small pieces
½ cup candied walnuts (see Endive, Pear, and Blue Cheese Salad, page 102)

To make the salad: In a large bowl, mix together the fruits, spinach, and frisée. Set aside.

To make the dressing: In a medium-size sauté pan, heat the olive oil over medium heat until warm but not hot. Add the shallots and cook, stirring occasionally, until they being to soften, about 5 minutes. Add the sage and cook for 1 minute. Turn off the heat and add the mustard and vinegar, stirring until the mustard is dissolved and the ingredients are thoroughly mixed. Remove from the heat and let cool to lukewarm. Season with salt and pepper to taste.

To assemble: Pour the dressing over the fruit and greens. Add the cheese and walnuts, and toss well. Adjust the seasoning, if necessary, and serve. Top with a little extra cheese, if desired.

Serves 4

SKUNK HOLLOW FARM

YET ANOTHER AMERICAN CHEESEMAKING family is earning accolades just a few years after learning their craft. Frankie and Mary Beth Whitten are makers of two highly regarded sheep's milk cheeses under the Northeast Kingdom Sheep Milk Cheese label. Although they manage Skunk Hollow Farm for another family, the mark of distinction belongs to the Whittens.

They began as the first sheep milkers at Old Chatham Sheepherding Company in New York in 1995 (see page 109). They then moved to Vermont, where they apprenticed under Cynthia and David Major at Vermont Shepherd Cheese (see page 178). Then, in 1996, they went to their current location in Greensboro, Vermont, where they continued making cheese for Vermont Shepherd. Eventually they began to make their own cheese as well.

Demand was nearly immediate for the Whittens' cheeses, which include raw milk, washed-rind, and aged cheeses. Their Greek-style cheese, called Graviera, is aged as long as twelve months. It is washed with a local hard cider that imparts an apple flavor to the rind. They do this so that people who don't normally eat natural rinds will be courageous enough to try them. The cheese itself is naturally apple-like, a little mushroomy, rustic, and herbaceous. The apple notes balance the cheese particularly nicely.

Skunk Hollow's best-seller is the Abbey, named for a monastery in Belgium. The Whittens' cheesemaking teacher is Belgian, as is the style of this cheese. The complex flavor makes it no wonder that Abbey is popular. It starts out with hints of melon but quickly moves into the buttery, earthy phase. Its interior is a pale yellow; it has small eyes and is semi-firm in texture. The natural rind can be eaten, though most people probably choose not to. The rind does, however, carry flavor components that are crucial to the flavor of the cheese. The Abbey is aged for two to six months.

The sheep at Skunk Hollow Farm are milked only when they are eating fresh grass, from May to October. During the cold winter months when there is no grass, the sheep must eat hay, which translates to milk that is not as good for cheesemaking. In fact, no sheep dairy farmers in Vermont make cheese when the sheep are not on (eating) grass.

Most of the Skunk Hollow Northeast Kingdom cheese is sold in Vermont and other small pockets on the East Coast. But some cheese shops in New York and Connecticut will mail-order the cheese. Skunk Hollow Farm is open to the public during the milking season for the evening milking, and private group tours are offered as well.

WHAT THEY MAKE
Abbey
Graviera

HOW TO REACH THEM
Greensboro, Vermont
802-533-2360
802-533-9916
website: www.skunkhollowroad.com

Minted Fava Bean and Prosciutto Salad
with Sheep's Milk Cheese

This composed salad captures the bright colors of springtime perfectly. The fava beans, which are the true harbingers of spring, are bright green, and the relatively pale fennel and broccoli serve as the vegetable bridges between winter and summer. It is really a picnic on a plate, and with the mint, tastes as fresh as the spring air. The salad needs very little dressing since the ingredients stand well enough on their own, and the cheese brings another dimension of flavor that minimizes the need for much dressing.

¾ **pound fava beans**
½ **pound broccoli**
**1 large fennel bulb very thinly sliced
  (about 2 cups)**
**2 tablespoons plus 1 teaspoon chopped
  fresh mint**
1 tablespoon fresh lemon juice
1 tablespoon champagne vinegar
3 tablespoons quality extra-virgin olive oil
Salt and freshly ground pepper, to taste
16 paper-thin slices prosciutto (4 ounces)
**1 ounce aged sheep's milk cheese, such as
  Skunk Hollow Farm's Abbey, shaved into
  thin slices**

Remove the beans from their pods and place them in a small bowl. Bring a small pot of water to a boil, add the fava beans, and blanch for 1½ minutes. Drain immediately and run cold water over the beans. Do not wash the pot.

Now peel the beans: Find the root end of a bean, the slightly darker green little point that protrudes from the bean. Hold the root end between your thumb and index finger. With a fingernail of your other hand, tear a small slit in the thin skin at the opposite end of the bean. Gently squeeze the root end and the bean will come out through the slit. It might squirt out, so press gently on the root end. Set the beans aside.

Separate the broccoli tops into florets. (Save the stems for another use). Using the same pot as for the fava beans, fill the pot two-thirds full with water and bring to a boil. Add the florets and blanch until they are bright green, about 1 minute. Drain and immediately run cold water over them. Pat dry. Cut the florets into tiny pieces, about ½ inch long and ⅛ inch wide.

In a medium-size serving bowl, combine the broccoli, fennel, and 2 tablespoons fresh mint. Add the lemon juice and vinegar and mix gently, being careful not to break up the broccoli pieces. Add the olive oil, salt, and pepper, and mix. Add all but 2 tablespoons of the fava beans. Toss just until the beans are mixed in. Do not overmix because the vegetables are quite delicate.

Divide the salad among four serving plates, placing a mound in the middle of each plate. Surround each salad with 4 slices of prosciutto. Scatter a few shavings of cheese over the salad and the prosciutto. Sprinkle with the remaining beans and mint. Grind a little fresh pepper over the salads and serve immediately.

Serves 4

LAURA CHENEL CHÈVRE

IT IS NEARLY IMPOSSIBLE to utter the name Laura Chenel without using adjectives like "pioneer," "first," and "champion." For Chenel did something no one had done before: She introduced goat cheese to the national palate.

In the 1970s, Chenel was looking for a way to combine her love of goats with her affection for the rural lifestyle. She was also looking for a means to channel her creativity. She had always liked food and cooking, and given the excess milk coming from her goats, making goat cheese was the natural choice. Early attempts at cheesemaking were mostly unsuccessful, until she spent three months making goat cheese in France. That was the turning point.

Chenel returned to the United States educated in the proper method of making goat cheese and began making cheese in Sonoma County, in northern California. One of her earliest customers was Alice Waters, proprietor of Berkeley's famed Chez Panisse restaurant. With that exposure alone, goat cheese entered the vocabulary of American diners.

Since few Americans had ever heard of chèvre, or goat cheese, when Chenel first began making it, there was naturally little appetite for it. There was also no equipment with which to make it. That meant that Chenel was not only honing her cheesemaking skills, she was also instructing stainless-steel fabricators and others how to make the equipment necessary to make the cheese.

Little by little, she began to sell her chèvre to small cheese shops around northern California, as well as to Chez Panisse, and gradually word caught on. Today, 450 goats and 600,000 pounds of cheese per year later, Chenel still keeps a tight rein on the company she runs. Officially carrying the title of president of Laura Chenel Chèvre, Inc., Chenel's duties run the gamut from tending the goats (her first love), to the cheese, to the financial end of the business, to the company's future.

WHAT THEY MAKE

Cabecou   Fromage blanc
Chabis   Logs
Chef's Chèvre   Taupinière
Crottin   Tome

HOW TO REACH THEM
Sonoma, California
707-996-4477
707-996-1816 (fax)

Part of that future has already happened—in Norway. Because of declining demand for Norwegian goat cheeses, Norway was finding itself with an excess of goat milk. Hoping to maintain the Norwegian tradition of raising goats, and looking for a home for the milk produced by that country's 60,000 or so goats, a Norwegian cheese seller in the U.S. approached Chenel about the possibility of making her goat cheese in Norway. A factory was set up, and years and innumerable experiments later, Laura Chenel Chèvre is now on the shelves of Norwegian markets, having been as well received in that country as in the U.S. The different breeds of goats and the different feed on which they live yield a slightly different-tasting product, but there is no mistaking the label, "Laura Chenel Select, Norwegian Chèvre." It is not sold in this country.

Domestically, Chenel makes seven cheeses, including her well-known fresh cheeses in both log and barrel shapes, an olive-oil marinated Cabecou "button," and three aged cheeses, the oldest of which is the Tome, which is aged for six months.

There is no limit to the uses of Chenel's cheeses since they span the spectrum from fresh to aged. The fresh log can be sliced, warmed, and placed on a piece of oil-brushed crostini, or nut-crusted as in the accompanying recipe. The crottin, a slightly aged small cylindrical goat cheese, can be cut and served with dried fruit and nuts. The aged Taupinière, with its bloomy rind and layer of ash beneath it, is highlighted when paired with room-temperature roasted beets that have been drizzled with a little fresh lemon juice and olive oil.

Any way you slice it, Laura Chenel Chèvre provides a window into the pioneering spirit that has brought about some of the greatest cheeses we now have in this country. Chenel claims little credit for her contribution to American cheesemaking, but goat cheese aficionados know that her early endeavors are largely responsible for the cheeses they enjoy now.

Pistachio-Coated Goat Cheese Rounds on Mixed Greens with Nut Oil Vinaigrette

❧✦☙

There is something about warm goat cheese that I find very soothing. It coats the mouth, though it isn't chalky; it's silky and smooth, yet slightly tangy. In this salad, the coating of bread crumbs and pistachio nuts elevates the cheese to an elegance matched by the rich nut oil on the mixed greens. Because of its richness, I use only one cheese disk per person, but you may decide to serve more. The goat cheese rounds should be only slightly chilled when you coat them, but they should be thoroughly chilled before baking. That will help prevent the cheese from overbaking. Also, because the rounds do not take very long to bake, you should have the greens already prepared and distributed on salad plates before you put the cheese in the oven.

¼ cup sherry vinegar
¼ cup highest-quality pistachio, walnut, or pecan oil
4 tablespoons olive oil
Salt and freshly ground pepper
5 tablespoons raw unsalted pistachio nuts, coarsely chopped
¼ cup toasted bread crumbs, preferably sourdough
4 ounces log-style goat cheese, such as Laura Chenel Chèvre, cut into 4 equal-size disks
6 cups mixed greens, such as arugula, mizuna, radicchio, and frisée

Preheat the oven to 325°F.

In a small bowl, whisk together the vinegar, nut oil, and 2 tablespoons of the olive oil. Add salt and pepper to taste, and set aside.

In a small shallow pan, bake the nuts until they are lightly browned and emit a slight nutty aroma, 8 to 10 minutes. Set aside 1 tablespoon of the nuts, and leave the rest in the pan.

Put the remaining 2 tablespoons olive oil in a small flat dish, and put the bread crumbs in a second small dish. Coat each cheese disk thoroughly with the olive oil. Next, dip the disks in the bread crumbs, again coating well. Gently press one side of each disk in the nuts until the nuts adhere to the cheese. (If the nuts do not stick, let the cheese warm up slightly, and using your fingers, press the nuts onto the tops of the cheese rounds.) Put the goat cheese rounds, nut side up, on a small baking pan. Refrigerate for at least 15 minutes and up to 24 hours.

In a large bowl, toss the greens with the vinaigrette, and distribute the salad on four salad plates.

Bake the cheese rounds for 6 to 8 minutes, or just until the cheese begins to feel soft to the touch. It is better to underbake these than to overbake them, since the latter will result in a sea of melted cheese.

Remove cheese from the oven and immediately place one cheese round on the side of each plate of greens. Sprinkle with the remaining 1 tablespoon nuts, top with a little coarsely ground pepper, and serve.

Serves 4

CYPRESS GROVE CHÈVRE

MARY KEEHN DIDN'T KNOW ENOUGH to avoid cheesemaking. What she did know, however, was how to work with goats. Her goats were national champions and, most important, big milk producers, largely because of her knowledge of biology and interest in genetics. This milk surplus led Keehn and her four daughters to making cheese. They had no intention of selling it—only of making it for themselves and a few friends in the northern California community of McKinleyville.

"I had no clue," Mary says, when she recalls what she *didn't* know about the business and craft of cheesemaking when she first set out. Nonetheless, she pushed ahead at the urging of a friend and café owner who was interested in using Mary's goat cheese at her restaurant. Keehn then bought a nearby egg production facility and turned it into a small cheesemaking facility.

The word "struggle" characterizes Cypress Grove's early days, since most Americans then balked at the suggestion of a nibble of goat cheese. (One French couple, however, then in their seventies, became faithful buyers and remain so to this day.)

Now Keehn's cheeses, sold under her Cypress Grove label, are considered among the finest goats' milk cheeses made in the United States. Among them is Humboldt Fog, which brings to mind superlatives like "unparalleled," "unrivaled," "superb," and "elegant." It is a two-layer pillow of two-month-old cheese separated by a thin layer of vegetable ash and rolled in vegetable ash before developing its soft white rind. (Vegetable ash is just that: vegetables that are dried and then rendered into ash. It is flavorless.) As the Humboldt Fog ages, the soft-ripened cheese oozes around the edges while the center paste stays firm, yet gentle in flavor. Even non-goat-cheese-eaters revel in the wonder of Humboldt Fog. But that cheese does not stand alone. Keehn's other cheeses, including her fresh chèvre and Bermuda Triangle, a long triangular "log" that also develops a lovely rind, are equally superior in their genres.

The fresh chèvre, in particular, is noteworthy. It is smooth and creamy, having none of the granular texture that some other fresh goat cheeses have. It also has a hint of sweetness that is rarely found in chèvre, but it still has the signature tangy goat cheese flavor as well. It is truly among the superior cheeses found anywhere in the world.

That superior quality has brought Cypress Grove Chèvre innumerable blue ribbons, including "Best of Show" in the goat cheese category at

WHAT THEY MAKE

Bermuda Triangle
Chèvre
Chèvre logs
Fromage blanc
Fromage à Trois (pesto, dried tomato, and pine nut torta)
Goat milk cheddar
Humboldt Fog
Marble Mountain
Mt. McKinley (aged cheese)
Pee Wee Pyramid
Sempervirens

HOW TO REACH THEM

McKinleyville, California
707-839-3168
707-839-2322 (fax)
website: www.cypressgrovechevre.com

the 1998 American Cheese Society (ACS) awards. In that same competition, they received first place in the American Original Goat Milk Cheese category for their Humboldt Fog, first place for their fresh chèvre, first place in the American Made International Style Goat Milk Cheese for their Bermuda Triangle, and second place in the unripened goat cheese category for their fromage blanc. In 1999, the ACS bestowed no less than five awards on Cypress Grove—four of them blue ribbons. One of those was for their Marble Mountain, which is a pyramid-shaped cheese that, when sliced, looks like a slab of marble. Its flavor matches its beauty.

Cypress Grove has grown from its roots as a family operation, now employing about fourteen people. But Mary's daughter, Malorie McCurdy, plays a key role in the business as well as the cheesemaking. The cheesemaking is, in fact, very labor-intensive at Cypress Grove because of the hands-on nature of their process. The cheese is hand-ladled, which means that the coagulated milk is scooped up and ladled into individual molds that are outfitted with tiny holes. These holes allow for whey drainage. Some other goat cheese producers have taken to machines to mold their cheese. Cypress Grove is also fastidious about the milk they use, and Mary's background and extensive knowledge of goats' milk adds another layer of quality assurance.

Cypress Grove's Humboldt Fog.

The Cypress Grove cheeses have numerous cooking applications, though they are also outstanding on their own. In fact, a cheese course devoted to goat cheese could easily feature an array of these cheeses because they are all different and outstanding in their own right.

It is fitting that Keehn would produce such superior cheese, because of her intelligence and commitment to her product. She has been very active in the community of cheesemakers who have worked diligently to promote their cheeses and their craft as a whole. She and Malorie are also very approachable, which adds a gratifying human element to these first-rate cheeses.

Warm Cabbage and Goat Cheese Salad

My husband made this salad for me shortly after I met him, and I was duly impressed. I loved how a seemingly simple salad could take on so much color and flavor. I felt like a kid in a candy store, picking out the lush pieces of goat cheese here, the crunchy nuts there, the salty pancetta neutralized by the sweet balsamic, and the strings of cabbage that I could sort of twist around my fork. Being a salad fanatic anyway, I knew that this salad would soar to the top of my "favorites" list. And there it remains.

This salad is slightly unusual in its proportions. Salad dressings don't often have the same amount of oil and vinegar, but since this needs very little oil and the cabbage can hold up to a little more vinegar, the amounts work well.

Cypress Grove's silken Humboldt Fog is so lovely on its own that I normally would not recommend cooking with it. But since this salad doesn't alter the taste of the cheese, the use of Humboldt Fog brings it a wonderful depth and richness. Other fresh goat cheeses, including Cypress Grove's fresh chèvre, will also work.

½ **medium-size red cabbage (about 1½ pounds)**
½ **cup pecan halves, toasted**
3½ **ounces Humboldt Fog or other fresh goat cheese, cut or pinched into small pieces (depending on the softness of the cheese)**
½ **cup coarsely chopped pancetta, or 4 to 6 slices bacon, coarsely chopped**
¼ **cup olive oil**
¼ **cup balsamic vinegar**
Salt and freshly ground pepper

Slice the cabbage ¼-inch thick. Cut each slice in quarters and then separate the layers of cabbage. You'll end up with individual strands of cabbage about 1½ to 2 inches long. In a large bowl, toss the cabbage with the pecans and cheese.

In a medium-size sauté pan, cook the pancetta over medium-high heat, until crispy and dark brown. Drain on a paper towel. Discard the pancetta fat, but do not wash the pan. Return the pan to the stove, and over medium heat, add the olive oil. Heat the oil until it's very warm but not hot or smoking. Turn off the heat and add the vinegar. Mix well and immediately pour over the cabbage mixture. Add the pancetta, and salt and pepper to taste. Toss and serve.

Serves 4

LOVETREE FARM

SIXTY MILES NORTH OF THE TWIN CITIES and just over the border into Wisconsin lies a group of lakes surrounded by acres of grassland and wild pastures. It is a place where Canada geese and osprey fly overhead and where the Trade Lakes shimmer in the summer sun and stand frozen in the blustery winter. This is where California native Mary Falk knew she belonged.

Mary explains that she found her hundred-year-old farmhouse on a winter day when below-zero temperatures prevailed and snow blanketed most of the eighty-acre property. She bought it instantly and sold her beachfront cottage in Santa Cruz within two days. Grantsburg, Wisconsin, would become her home.

Mary moved to Wisconsin and met her future husband, Dave Falk. Together they set up an organic farm on their property and accumulated sheep to graze the rich grasslands. They also bred the sheep since there was a market for good lamb. In 1994, after receiving an offer from a Twin Cities business to buy 150 lambs, Mary and Dave sought the advice of a Wisconsin sheep milker, Hal Koller. He convinced them to milk their sheep and raise the lambs for milking rather than selling them for meat.

The Falks then devised a plan to make cheese. Mary began by experimenting with goats' milk cheese, using an old fireplace in her farmhouse kitchen as the "aging room." She put rounds of cheese in water-soaked bamboo steamers and then placed them in the 55°F fireplace to ripen, tasting them along the way. In the spring, when the evening temperatures were still cool and the daytime temperatures were moderate, she moved the cheese to her front porch to finish ripening.

By 1997 Mary had gotten her cheesemaker's license and had apprenticed in a cheese factory, while Dave had constructed their cheesemaking and aging facility. They began turning out sheep's milk cheese. Almost instantly, their Trade Lake Cedar, an aged raw milk cheese, became a hit. By the summer of 1998, that cheese won "Best of Show" at the American Cheese Society's annual conference. The organization bestows no higher award. In 1999, the American Cheese Society once again honored the Trade Lake Cedar as well as another LoveTree Farm cheese called Sumac Holmes.

WHAT THEY MAKE

Big Bears
Big Holmes
Lil' Bears
Little Holmes

Pasta Potion #9
Sumac Holmes
Trade Lake Cedar

HOW TO REACH THEM
Grantsburg, Wisconsin
715-488-2966
715-488-3957 (fax)

LoveTree Farm's Sumac Holmes.

Trade Lake Cedar is a 5-pound wheel that is wrapped in cedar fronds. It is aged, but in its younger stage it is a little fruity, a little buttery, and slightly grassy. When it is older, it takes on a faint musty flavor but maintains a hint of fruit and a stronger milk flavor. Young and old, it is a model cheese. Mary makes other sheep cheeses, including the herbaceous hand-ladled "Big Holmes," named after another of the nearby lakes. It is coated with rosemary, mint, and cedar and becomes aromatherapy and a taste delicacy in one bite. Their Big and Lil' Bears are ash-coated, while the aged Sumac Holmes is bathed in an exotic combination of sumac berries and ground peppercorns that lend a deep, spicy flavor to the soft, earthy cheese.

The Falks' dedication extends beyond their cheese. They are committed to establishing a flock of sheep that will produce high-quality milk for their operation. In fact, they have bred a sheep they call Trade Lake Sheep, and that sheep's milk is the only type that can be used for the Trade Lake Cedar cheese. They are also passionate about helping other sheep farmers in their area. "My agenda is to save the local family farms," says Mary. It is a grand agenda, but she and Dave are helping to do that by buying other people's milk in addition to using the milk from their own 250-sheep flock to make cheese (other than the Trade Lake Cedar). They are advising farmers on how to boost sheep milk production and how to manage their pastures, and they act as a go-between for equipment dealers and farmers to negotiate good prices for the farmers. They provide all of these services for free.

The Falks' story is one of devotion. They are committed to keeping their farm organic, to helping others in the area, to maintaining a healthy flock, and to putting out unique and truly excellent cheese. No strangers to hard work, most of their efforts are motivated by the desire to pursue a dream of making sheep dairying viable in their part of the country. If they are successful, they will end up with more than great cheese. They will have written yet another chapter in the book of America's cheesemaking—and agricultural—history.

Marjoram-Scented Panzanella
with Aged Cheese

Panzanella, or Italian bread salad, could well be the supreme showcase for summer tomatoes. A little bread, a little vinegar, and a few other ingredients exaggerate the sweetness of the tomatoes even more than if they were eaten alone. In this case, panzanella is taken one step further by the addition of a rich, luscious sheep's milk cheese. The slight saltiness and gaminess of an aged sheep's or goats' milk cheese meld seamlessly with the sweet tomatoes and the earthy licorice flavor of the marjoram.

FOR THE VINAIGRETTE
¼ cup red wine vinegar
1 tablespoon balsamic vinegar
1 teaspoon Dijon mustard
Salt and freshly ground pepper
½ cup olive oil

FOR THE SALAD
½ loaf (½ pound) day-old Italian or
　French bread, cut into 1-inch cubes
　(4 cups)
2 tablespoons olive oil
6 ripe tomatoes (about 1¾ pounds total),
　gently seeded and coarsely chopped
　(about 2½ cups)
½ cup finely chopped red onion
1 tablespoon finely chopped fresh marjoram
　leaves
2 ounces very cold aged sheep's milk cheese,
　such as Trade Lake Cedar, shaved (or use
　any hard, flavorful grating cheese such as
　aged goat cheese, aged Provolone, or
　Parmesan)

To make the vinaigrette: In a small bowl, combine the vinegars, mustard, and salt and pepper to taste. Let stand about 5 minutes. Then slowly add the olive oil in a steady stream, whisking until thoroughly blended. Set aside.

To make the salad: Preheat the oven to 375°F.

Place the bread cubes on a baking sheet. Drizzle the olive oil over them, stirring to distribute the oil. Bake until the bread cubes are lightly browned and crisp, 10 to 15 minutes. Remove from the oven and let cool. (Or, you can heat the oil in a large sauté pan over medium heat. Add the bread cubes and stir until they become brown and crisp.)

In a medium bowl, mix the tomatoes, onion, and marjoram with ¼ cup of the vinaigrette. Let sit for 10 minutes. Add the bread cubes and another ¼ cup of the vinaigrette; mix well. Let sit for about 15 minutes to allow the vinaigrette to infuse the bread and the other ingredients. Add the remainder of the vinaigrette, if needed (the ingredients should be well coated but not bathing in dressing). Distribute the mixture among four salad plates, and top each with some of the cheese and a little freshly ground pepper.

Serves 4

SALADS

PIZZAS, POLENTAS,
PASTAS, and RISOTTI

Pizza Dough

This is a dough for a very thin pizza, which I think is the best host for flavorful, colorful pizza toppings and sweet, creamy cheeses. Because it is thin and rather fragile, it is best to stretch the dough by hand rather than roll it. Simply place the prepared dough ball directly on a cornmeal-sprinkled pizza pan and stretch it out by hand, making sure that your hands are well floured. It takes a little bit of finesse, but after you've done it once or twice, you will see that it isn't difficult. The flat part of the crust will be paper-thin, while the edges will be slightly thicker. This is exactly what you want for a perfect pizza crust.

Another nice thing about this dough: If you don't have time to gather pizza toppings, you can just stretch out the dough, brush it with olive oil, sprinkle on some crushed red pepper, fennel seeds, salt and pepper, and a grated dry cheese, pop it in a 500°F oven for 15 minutes, and come out with a light and flavorful flatbread.

1 envelope active dry yeast (2¼ teaspoons)
1½ cups warm (110°F) water
2 tablespoons olive oil
1 tablespoon kosher salt
About 3½ cups unbleached all-purpose flour

Dissolve the yeast in the warm water. Let it sit for about 10 minutes, until it becomes foamy.

In a large bowl, mix together the oil and the salt. Add the yeast mixture and stir well. Slowly add 3 cups of the flour and mix until the dough sticks together but isn't too dry. Turn the dough onto a floured surface and knead in the remaining ½ cup flour, or as much as you need until the dough becomes smooth and elastic. (For a thinner crust, use slightly less flour. The dough will be a little stickier, however.)

Form the dough into a ball and place it in an oiled bowl, turning once to coat the dough with

oil. Cover with plastic wrap or a towel and set in a warm place. Let rise until doubled in bulk, 1½ to 2½ hours.

Divide the dough into two balls. Let rest, covered, for 15 minutes. Proceed according to individual recipe.

Makes two 14-inch pizzas

Note: This dough can be made 24 hours in advance and placed in the refrigerator in the bowl and covered with plastic wrap after the first rising stage. Bring it to room temperature before stretching it out to form a crust. It can also be frozen after the first rising stage. Defrost it overnight in the refrigerator. The next day, place the defrosted dough in an oiled bowl and leave it at room temperature for at least 3 hours. It should almost double in size.

OPPOSITE: Spaghetti with Spring Vegetables and Goat Cheese (see page 154).

Summertime Pizza

This pizza is a catchall for the best of summer: corn, tomatoes, and basil. But instead of butter running down your fingers from corn on the cob, it's the cheese on the pizza, along with the other ingredients, that necessitates a few extra napkins. This colorful dish can be served as a main course, along with a green salad, or on its own as an appetizer.

PIZZAS AND POLENTAS

1 ear corn, preferably yellow, cut from the cob (about ¾ cup)
1 tablespoon plus 1 teaspoon olive oil
1 large clove garlic, minced
1½ pounds tomatoes (about 4), peeled (see Note), seeded, and coarsely chopped
2 tablespoons chopped fresh basil leaves
Salt and freshly ground pepper
Dough for one 14-inch pizza (see page 127)
1 to 2 tablespoons cornmeal
Coarse sea salt or kosher salt
½ pound mozzarella cheese, coarsely grated

Preheat the oven to 500°F. If using, place a pizza stone in the oven.

Bring a small saucepan of water to a boil. Add the corn and cook for 1 minute. Drain in a colander or strainer, and immediately run cold water over it to halt the cooking process. Set aside.

In a medium-size sauté pan, heat 1 tablespoon of the olive oil over medium heat. Add the garlic and sauté for 2 minutes. Let cool. Add the tomatoes, basil, and salt and pepper to taste, and set aside.

Dust the pizza pan with cornmeal. Stretch the dough out on the pan, using your fingers to stretch it from the center toward the edges. (Since the dough is very loose and pliable, this takes a little patience.) The middle of the dough will be paper-thin. Sprinkle coarse salt over the dough. Using a slotted spoon, distribute the tomato mixture evenly over the dough, leaving a ½-inch border. (You do not want the juices from the tomatoes.) Sprinkle the corn over the tomatoes, and top with the cheese. Bake until the crust is browned and the cheese is bubbling, 15 to 20 minutes.

Serves 2 to 4 as a main course, 6 to 8 as an appetizer

Note: Here's an easy method for peeling tomatoes: Bring water to a boil in a medium-size pot. Add the tomatoes and blanch for 1 minute. Remove from the water and drain. The skin will peel right off. (Do not blanch tomatoes if they are very ripe—they will become mushy. Instead, use a knife or vegetable peeler to peel them.)

GREAT HILL DAIRY

UNLIKE MOST CHEESEMAKERS, Tim Stone of Marion, Massachusetts, embarked on cheesemaking by researching the market *first*. Having no experience in cheesemaking (he was an engineer in Washington, D.C.), all he knew was that he had a farm and that he had access to good cows' milk. But the question for him was how he could best use these resources. After a lot of interviews with cheese sellers and buyers, he hit on blue. Although some very good domestic blue cheeses were being made, a blue cheese that was made with both unpasteurized and unhomogenized milk was unheard of within our borders. Stone took advantage of the opportunity and with his wife, Tina, and a couple of employees created Great Hill Blue.

The name Great Hill refers to the farm's hilly geologic profile. It is located just west of the gateway to Cape Cod. Stone's great-grandfather had bought the land, which Tim returned to about ten years before deciding to make cheese. At the time, he ran the dairy, which consisted of a herd of about seventy Guernseys. But once the local veterinarian left the area, Tim says he had no choice but to sell them.

This left him with a dilemma: How to stay on the farm and still make a living. Since Great Hill already had a well-established history of dairying, he hit upon cheesemaking as the answer. (He had considered fish farming and raising buffalo as other possibilities.) Tim embarked on a fast education in cheesemaking, and in 1996 made his first cheese.

Great Hill Blue is aged longer than most domestic blue cheese, about one year, and is injected with the same mold used to make the famous Roquefort in France. (One big difference, however, is that Roquefort is made with ewe's milk.) In the first few hours of the cheesemaking process, "hands-on" only partially describes the labor involved. After the curds are scooped into the molds, they must be flipped every forty-five minutes, and a little later in the day, every three hours. This means that someone has to get up in the middle of the night to turn the cheese.

The result of Stone's cheesemaking process is a creamy, salty, lovely looking six-pound wheel of blue cheese. It is relatively smooth on the outside, and the bluish-green streaks and pinholes of mold on the inside create a striking mosaic pattern. This pattern sits against an ivory background whose texture falls mostly on the side of creamy with a slight crumbly quality thrown in. This cheese strikes a masterful balance between salt and cream, as well as between spice and fruit. It is a beautiful cheese.

It is also an award winner, taking first place in its category at the 1999 American Cheese Society's annual competition. For being just three years "out of the gate," that's an impressive honor. In turn, that has led to greater recognition and wider distribution. Finding Great Hill Blue is now easier than it was just a short time ago, giving blue cheese fans something to really celebrate (maybe along with a glass of champagne).

WHAT THEY MAKE
Great Hill Blue

HOW TO REACH THEM
Marion, Massachusetts
888-748-2208
508-748-2208
508-748-2282 (fax)
website: www.greathillblue.com

Pizza with Blue Cheese, Butternut Squash, and Fried Sage Leaves

❧ ❦

Although squash's sweetness varies according to variety (and within the same variety as well), odds are that with a butternut squash, you'll get a nice sugary flavor. In this recipe, that sweetness is enhanced by roasting the squash first, and further by pairing it with salty blue cheese. Serve this with a butter lettuce salad topped with a few pomegranate seeds, and you've got a simple autumn dinner.

1 small butternut squash (1 pound)
4 tablespoons olive oil
Salt and freshly ground pepper
1 clove garlic, minced
2 tablespoons unsalted butter
15 fresh sage leaves
5 ounces Gruyère cheese, such as Roth Käse, coarsely grated (about 1¼ cups; or use Fontina, Gouda, or Emmentaler)
4 ounces blue cheese, such as Great Hill Blue, crumbled
Dough for one 14-inch pizza (see page 127)
1 to 2 tablespoons cornmeal

Preheat the oven to 350°F. If using, place a pizza stone in the oven.

Cut the squash in half lengthwise. Hold one half on its end, and with a sharp knife, shave the tough peel. Remove the seeds and pith. Set the squash flat side down and cut it into ¼-inch-thick slices. Repeat with the other half, or until you have 2 cups of sliced squash.

Spread the squash out on an oiled baking sheet. Brush it liberally with 2 tablespoons of the olive oil, and sprinkle with salt and pepper to taste. Bake for about 20 minutes, or until soft. It is okay if the squash is slightly underdone since it will continue to cook on top of the pizza.

Remove from the oven and increase the oven temperature to 500°F.

In a small sauté pan, heat the remaining 2 tablespoons olive oil over medium-high heat. Once the oil begins to darken, remove the pan from the stove and toss in the garlic, swirling it around to caramelize it. Set aside.

In another small sauté pan, heat the butter over high heat. When it begins to bubble, add the sage leaves and cook for 30 seconds. Watch carefully, the leaves can easily burn. Remove from the butter and drain on a paper towel.

Dust the pizza pan with cornmeal. Stretch the dough out on the pan, using your fingers to stretch it from the center toward the edges. (Since the dough is very loose and pliable, this takes a little patience.) The middle of the dough will be paper-thin. Brush it liberally with the garlic oil. Sprinkle the Gruyère cheese over the dough. Arrange the squash slices in concentric circles over the cheese, spacing them about ½ inch apart. Bake for 15 minutes. Remove from the oven and top with the blue cheese and sage leaves, placing the leaves decoratively on the pizza. Continue baking until the cheese is bubbling and the edges of the crust have browned, 5 to 10 minutes more. Remove from the oven and serve immediately.

Serves 2 to 4 as a main course, 6 to 8 as an appetizer

PURE LUCK GRADE A GOAT DAIRY

IT MAY BE CALLED THE LONGHORN STATE, but Texas is also home to some smaller-horned animals—namely, goats. Just a few miles outside of Austin is the Pure Luck Grade A Goat Dairy, residence of fifty goats and great goat cheese. Pure Luck Organics, a certified organic farm, also sells cut flowers, vegetables, and herbs to anyone who happens to be driving by.

The story here, though, is the cheese, which is made by Sara Bolton, her daughter, Amelia Sweethardt, and occasionally other family members as well. Bolton started making cheese several years ago, though her love affair with goats began twenty years ago following a stint babysitting her friend's goats. She got hooked on the spunky animals and soon acquired a few of her own. Five years ago, she began making cheese in earnest; Amelia joined her mother in the cheesemaking venture in 1997.

The Pure Luck Grade A Goat Dairy cheese is as memorable as a Texas summer day is long. It has an unqualified richness and balance, though its goats' milk origin informs its signature tangy tones. One of the best cheeses is their Queso del Cielo, literally "cheese of the sky." It is indeed heavenly with its white, bloomy rind and the slightly soft interior. The hand-ladled, round-shaped cheese is akin to Camembert and has been a blue-ribbon winner at the American Cheese Society. Another award winner is Pure Luck's Sainte Maure, which is a log-shaped cheese that straddles the line between firm and creamy on the inside and has a faint flavor of blue cheese. It sports a slightly wrinkly exterior. Unlike many Sainte Maures, this one is not coated with ash.

Their cash cow is their fresh chèvre, which, like their Queso del Cielo, features a lovely balance of tanginess and earthiness. They also offer a line of flavored chèvres and spreads, including a basil pesto spread that was yet another American Cheese Society winner. Of course, great milk is essential to making great cheese, and the Pure Luck goats feast on a diet of five different grains and seeds, hay, and green oak leaves. According to Sweethardt, the milk is better-tasting when the goats eat these foods rather than "dine" on pasture. In fact, she says, the goats don't really care for pasture. In an area which is slowly being encroached upon by the inevitable urban sprawl, it's probably just as well that the goats gravitate toward grain and hay.

How just two women and two helpers make such great cheese is no small wonder. Their small size belies their big plans, however, which

WHAT THEY MAKE

Claire de Lune
Feta
Fresh chèvre and
  chèvre spreads: plain and flavored

Queso del Cielo
Sainte Maure

HOW TO REACH THEM

Dripping Springs, Texas
512-858-1041
website: www.purelucktexas.com

include a blue cheese and possibly a raw milk cheese as well. Texas may not seem like an obvious location for a goat cheese operation, but one taste of the cheese made here will convert any skeptics. In the hands of the right people, great cheese can be made just about anywhere in this country.

Four-Cheese Pizza

❧◆☙

One of the great things about a four-cheese pizza is that you can use just about any type of cheese you want. The only guideline is that the cheeses should work well together. Just as you probably wouldn't serve a blue cheese and a Limburger together, neither would you put them on the same pizza. The cheeses in this recipe harmonize nicely and are easy to find. Because this pizza has no herbs and no meat, it is sure to please everyone. Leftover pizza can be wrapped in foil and refrigerated; reheat it on a pan in a 375°F oven for about 15 minutes.

1 to 2 tablespoons cornmeal
Dough for one 14-inch pizza (see page 127)
Kosher salt
½ pound mozzarella cheese, grated
6 ounces Havarti or Fontina cheese
2 ounces fresh goat cheese, such as Pure Luck, divided into pieces about the size of a small gumball
3 ounces dry Jack, finely grated (or use any hard grating cheese—cow, sheep, or goat)

Preheat the oven to 500°F. If using, place a pizza stone in the oven.

Dust the pizza pan with cornmeal. Stretch the dough out on the pan, using your fingers to stretch it from the center toward the edges. (Since the dough is very loose and pliable, this takes a little patience.) The middle of the dough will be paper-thin. Sprinkle a little coarse salt over the dough. Distribute the mozzarella over the dough, leaving a 1-inch border. Top with the Havarti or Fontina cheese. Bake for 10 minutes. Distribute the goat cheese on the pizza and top with the dry Jack. Bake until the crust is golden and the cheese is brown and bubbly, 5 to 10 minutes more. Serve immediately.

Serves 2 to 4 as a main course, 6 to 8 as an appetizer

VERMONT BUTTER & CHEESE COMPANY

IMAGINE THE ROAD SIGNS: Vermont: the Napa Valley of Cheese. But that is just what Allison Hooper, co-owner of Vermont Butter & Cheese in Websterville, Vermont, and co-founder of the Vermont Cheese Council has in mind for her adopted state. And for good reason. Vermont is a small state that produces some of the most highly regarded goat, sheep, and cow milk cheeses in the country. Now, Allison believes that it's time that the rest of the country knew about it.

Hooper and her partner, Bob Reese, formed Vermont Butter & Cheese in 1985. Back then, their cash cow was butter, but goat cheese was Allison's love and area of expertise. She had spent two summers in Europe learning how to make cheese and returned to New Jersey to make cheese on her own. She subsequently moved to Vermont, but found no goats until she found Don Hooper. He had a small herd, and between him and his goats, she found an enduring relationship.

At that time, Allison was working for the Vermont Department of Agriculture. Enter Bob Reese, whose job was to match up chefs with Vermont-made products. A chef in Stowe, Vermont, was in need of goat cheese, and Allison came to the rescue. A batch was made and a partnership between her and Bob was formed.

Like many cheesemakers, they had an inauspicious beginning, having to spend their time and money repairing old equipment and generally losing money faster than they could earn it. But they managed to keep the business afloat by producing a small amount of goat cheese and a larger amount of butter. It was hard work. Twice a week, Allison would hop in a truck and traverse the state, picking up goats' milk along the way.

Over time the company began to grow, to the point where it now has sixteen full-time employees as well as about twenty farms from which it gets its milk. These resources  come together to form about twenty different fresh and aged cheeses. The aged goat Fontina is exceptional. The natural rind cheese, aged about seven months, took no less than three years to perfect. It cannot really be likened to a cows' milk Fontina since it has its own unique flavor, but it is clean, a little lemony, and has that unmistakable goat cheese flavor. The texture is silky and smooth, and as the cheese ages, it gets stronger but manages to stay in balance with its contrasting sweet and tart flavors.

WHAT THEY MAKE

Cow milk:
Cultured butter
Crème fraîche
Mascarpone
Fromage blanc
Torta Basil
Torta Salmon
Quark

Goat milk:
Bonne-Bouche
Feta
Fontina
Goats' Milk Cheddar
Vermont Chèvre
Goats' Milk Impastata
Vermont Chevrier

HOW TO REACH THEM
Websterville, Vermont
800-884-6287
802-479-9371 (phone)
802-479-3674 (fax)
website: www.vtbutterandcheeseco.com

Their Chevrier is a cylindrical soft-ripened cheese that also sings out "balance." At its perfect ripeness, it develops the soft-ripened signature creaminess just inside the rind that offsets the tangy, fresh curd-like paste. Perhaps most exciting, though, is their newest cheese called Bonne-Bouche, literally "good mouth." It is a four-ounce ash covered silken disk that, because of its high moisture content, is creamy and positively delicious. After a little bit of time, it develops a thin "skin" which, when cut, reveals the practically liquified and immensely flavorful interior. Hooper is rightfully proud of this cheese which she has been "fussing around with" for about a year. It is hand-ladled, which adds to the delicate nature of the cheese, and it is aged for one week. It will then last for up to one month.

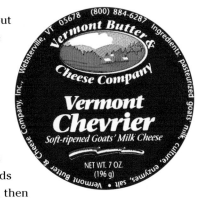

As the name of this company suggests, cheese isn't all they make. Their cultured butter is showing up in tony New York restaurants because of its superior taste as well as its versatility in cooking. The reason this butter is notable begins with the Jersey cream that is used. It has a high fat content. A bacterial culture is added to the rich cream to ferment it, and the resulting butter emerges with a low pH level which creates a softer consistency. This type of texture is particularly useful in pastry-making since the butter is more easily incorporated into the rest of the ingredients. The result is a flakier pastry. Also, the butter is called a demi-sel which means that it is very lightly salted. This small amount of salt helps bring out the flavor of the butter, which emerges from the churn at a flavorful 86-percent butterfat, but it is not so much salt that the butter can't be used in recipes that call for unsalted butter. The company produces about 3,000 pounds of butter a day.

As for their goal of Vermont becoming to cheese what the Napa Valley is to wine, Allison, Bob, and the Vermont Cheese Council are well on their way to making this effort a reality. Once a month, Vermont cheesemakers gather to share issues, problems, successes, and anything else they wish to talk about in an effort to continually improve their cheesemaking efforts. With this kind of communal support, it is almost a given that not only America but the rest of the world will stand up and take note of the outstanding cheesemakers in this one small eastern state. Among those, naturally, is Vermont Butter & Cheese, which continually sets new standards of excellence and can hardly keep the blue ribbons from adorning their walls.

Red and White Pizza

Why not put the best of Italy on top of a pizza? That's just what these ingredients do, but even more, they transform the bitterness of the radicchio into a sweet topping that was preordained to sit side by side with garlic and pancetta. These assertive ingredients are soothed by the creaminess of the Fontina cheese but brought out again by the slight zip from the ricotta. This pizza is rustic in both taste and appearance, and should be served with little more than a mixed green salad or the salad of fennel and oranges on page 100.

PIZZAS AND POLENTAS

1 tablespoon olive oil

2 cloves garlic, minced

1 small head radicchio (about ¾ pound), cored and separated into about 15 leaves

2 tablespoons fresh lemon juice

Salt and freshly ground pepper

1 to 2 tablespoons cornmeal

8 ounces Fontina cheese, coarsely grated (about 2 cups; or use Havarti or Gruyère)

2 ounces pancetta, sliced paper-thin (about 3 slices)

¼ cup ricotta cheese, room temperature

Dough for one 14-inch pizza (see page 127)

Preheat the oven to 500°F. If using, place a pizza stone in the oven.

In a large sauté pan, heat the olive oil over medium-high heat. Reduce the heat to medium and add the garlic, stirring vigorously, about 2 minutes. Do not let it brown. Add the radicchio, lemon juice, and salt and pepper to taste, and sauté just until the radicchio begins to wilt,

about 3 minutes. The radicchio will lose some of its red color, becoming a sort of brownish-mauve. Remove from the heat.

Dust the pizza pan with cornmeal. Stretch the dough out on the pan, using your fingers to stretch it from the center toward the edges. (Since the dough is very loose and pliable, this takes a little patience.) The middle of the dough will be paper-thin. Sprinkle the dough with the Fontina cheese. Place the radicchio leaves on top, leaving about ½ inch between the leaves. Unwind the pancetta slices and cut each one into four pieces. Arrange the pancetta between the radicchio leaves. Brush the edges of the pizza dough with olive oil.

Bake for 20 minutes, or until the edges of the pizza are dark brown and the pancetta and radicchio are brown on the edges. Remove from the oven and dot the pizza with dollops of the ricotta cheese. Cut and serve immediately.

Serves 2 to 4 as a main course, 6 to 8 as an appetizer

EVERONA DAIRY

A COUNTRY DOCTOR AND A SHEEP CHEESE MAKER don't often come together in the same person. But Pat Elliott of Everona Dairy in Rapidan, Virginia, finds it enjoyable to tend to her twenty-five ewes in the morning and then report for her duties as a general practitioner for the rest of the day.

Elliott has been a licensed cheesemaker only since 1998, but the one cheese she makes, called Everona, is an exceedingly impressive first launch. It is a raw milk, aged, natural-rind cheese that is yellowish-gold in color with tiny eyes in the body of the cheese. The flavors are like those of butter, grass, earth, and fruit all rolled up into one. It is a semi-hard cheese that, while rich, is the type of cheese that one can imagine eating chunk after chunk, accompanied by a fruity but spicy wine in a meadow on a sunny day. It conjures up such images the way exciting cheeses often do.

Elliott says she had worked with sheep when she was in college, but getting a border collie a few years ago was the event that reunited her with sheep. "The dog needed something to do," she says in her affable southern way. (Border collies are traditionally herding dogs.) And now her dogs are probably among the best-fed in the state of Virginia because Elliott makes sheep's milk ricotta for them.

As the only sheep's milk cheesemaker in Virginia, Elliott's accomplishments are all the more impressive. Nonetheless, she couldn't appear less impressed with herself. Instead, she goes about her duties tending to the needs of the sick in her rural section of Virginia while quietly making some of America's best cheese. Imagine what it will be five years from now.

WHAT THEY MAKE
Everona Sheep's Milk Cheese

HOW TO REACH THEM
Rapidan, Virginia
540-854-4159
540-854-6443 (fax)

Polenta Sampler

One night when I was testing these polenta recipes, I decided to test all three at once. Then I decided that there was no reason why I couldn't actually serve three polentas at one time, for a first course or even as a main course, along with a nice salad. All three are certainly very flavorful and distinct from one another. If you decide to do this, simply cook the polenta and then divide it among three bowls. Into each bowl stir one-third of each cheese mixture, as described in the recipes. (You should have all of your ingredients measured and ready to go before starting the polenta.) Whether you are making one recipe or all three, the toppings should be prepared while the polenta is cooking.

One other note: I have found that no matter how much liquid I add to the polenta or how much I stir it, I invariably need to add a little more liquid to keep the polenta nice and moist.

PIZZAS AND POLENTAS

BASIC POLENTA
2 cups good-quality unsalted chicken stock
2 cups water
1 cup yellow cornmeal (polenta)
1 teaspoon kosher salt

In a large pot, bring the chicken stock and water slowly to a boil. Add the polenta, pouring it in a steady stream into the middle of the boiling liquids. Stir vigorously for 3 minutes. Add the salt, stir again, lower the heat, and cover. Cook, stirring every 5 minutes, until most of the liquid has evaporated and the polenta is smooth, about 20 minutes. If it seems dry, add more chicken stock a little at a time. You don't really need to worry about adding too much liquid. Cover and keep warm over low heat.

If the polenta seems dry when you're ready to add the topping ingredients, mix in more stock or water.

Serves 4

Polenta with Wild Mushrooms, Fontina, and Aged Cheese

The earthiness and richness of the mushrooms in this dish make for a satisfying meal in itself. A crisp spinach salad or a tangle of watercress adorned with a few slices of blood orange and some olive oil is all you need to complete the picture.

1 tablespoon olive oil

1 clove garlic, minced

½ pound fresh wild mushrooms, such as chanterelle and shiitake, stems removed, caps cut into ¼-inch-thick slices

2 cups unsalted chicken stock

2 teaspoons fresh thyme leaves

¼ teaspoon finely chopped fresh rosemary leaves

Dash of salt

Freshly ground pepper

1 recipe polenta (see page 138)

3 ounces Fontina cheese, coarsely grated (or use Gruyère or a raw milk Gouda)

¼ cup milk

¼ cup finely grated hard cheese, such as Everona (or use another aged cheese)

In a medium-size sauté pan, heat the oil over medium heat. Add the garlic and swirl it in the oil, trying not to brown the garlic, about 1 minute. Add the mushrooms and cook until they are tender, about 10 minutes. Add the chicken stock, thyme, rosemary, salt, and pepper to taste, and boil until the liquid has reduced to 1 cup, about 10 minutes. Reduce the heat to low.

Add the Fontina and milk. Stir vigorously until the cheese is melted and well incorporated. Divide the polenta among four bowls. Pour the mushroom mixture over the polenta and top with the Everona cheese. Serve immediately.

Polenta with Teleme, Asiago, and Truffle Oil

Butter, cheese, and truffle oil are my "holy trinity." I'll use any excuse to combine the three. However, a little goes a long way, and if you're serving this with other food, make sure the other dishes are not too rich or too bland. If they are bland, they will definitely get lost with this polenta; if they are too rich, your dinner companions will curse you the next day. A nice in-between offering might be a roasted pork tenderloin cooked with a little rosemary and garlic.

1 recipe polenta (see page 138)
1½ tablespoons butter
¼ cup finely grated Asiago cheese (or use
    domestic Parmesan or dry Jack)
Salt and freshly ground pepper
2 ounces Teleme cheese, cut or spooned into
    teaspoon-size pieces (or use Crescenza or
    high-moisture Jack cheese, coarsely grated)
About 1 teaspoon white truffle oil

When the polenta is done, add the butter, Asiago cheese, salt and pepper to taste, and half of the Teleme. Mix well and divide among four bowls. Lay slices of the remaining Teleme over each bowl and drizzle each with a little truffle oil. (If the Teleme is in its soft stage, then spoon about a tablespoon of the cheese onto each serving.) Give one twist of the peppermill to each portion, and serve immediately.

Polenta with Swiss Chard and Parmesan

This preparation is similar to one used in Italy, where it is sometimes served as an accompaniment to osso buco. You can also use it as a bed for braised lamb shanks or simply as a side dish to almost any roasted or braised meat or chicken. You may substitute red chard or kale for the Swiss chard, or use a combination of all three.

3 quarts water
1½ teaspoons salt
1 bunch Swiss chard (about 1 pound), stems
    removed, leaves cut into 3-inch-long strips
½ cup plus 2 tablespoons finely grated
    Parmesan cheese (about 2¼ ounces)
    (or use Asiago, dry Jack, or Romano)
Salt and freshly ground pepper
1 recipe polenta (see page 138)

Bring a large pot of water to a boil. Add the salt and let the water return to a boil. Add the chard and boil until tender, 10 to 15 minutes. Drain thoroughly, reserving ½ cup of the cooking liquid. Add the chard and reserved cooking liquid to the polenta, and stir until the liquid has been absorbed. Add ½ cup of the cheese, and salt and pepper to taste, and mix well. Divide among four serving bowls, and top each with ½ tablespoon of the remaining cheese and a little more pepper. Serve immediately.

SALLY JACKSON CHEESES

SALLY JACKSON CHEESES ARE LIKE NO OTHER. They are complex, they are diverse, they are supple, and they are beautiful. Sally Jackson's signature aged raw milk sheep's milk cheese wrapped in chestnut leaves, and her aged raw milk goats' milk cheese wrapped in grape leaves, are tied with twine and look like precious bundles. Untying and cutting them to reveal the white rounds inside is as delicate and rewarding a procedure as any cheese "unveiling" could possibly be.

Tasting them is no less gratifying. Each has its own qualities, but they share such characteristics as depth of flavor, earthiness, and sometimes gaminess. The goat cheese has a floral yet gamy quality, while the sheep cheese is herbaceous and buttery. These magnificent cheeses, along with her flavored and mixed-milk cheeses, are made with milk from the Jacksons' twenty goats, forty sheep (only twenty are milked at a time), and one Brown Swiss cow.

That such noteworthy cheeses are being made might be enough. But the fact that these cheeses are still made over a woodstove in a facility that got electricity only five years ago is a marvel. Sally and her husband, Roger, who does the milking and farming, moved to Washington State twenty-five years ago. They live in the Okanogan Highlands, 4,200 feet above the Okanogan Valley, six miles south of the Canadian border. Sally started making cheese and discovered that rather than following a recipe, she had to work with her animals and with what they were giving her, based on their particular location and what they were eating. That led to her superior cheese.

To make the cheese, Jackson heats the milk over the stove, adds a starter and rennet, and when the curds begin to form, she breaks them up by hand and ladles them into molds to let the whey drain out. The next day they are salted, and the day after that they are wrapped in their precious leaves. Contributing to the farmstead nature of this cheesemaking operation, the Jacksons harvest the leaves themselves—and they try to grow all of their own animal feed.

Sally started making sheep's milk cheese fifteen years ago and was among the first to do so in this country. When she and Roger took off for the "middle of cowboy country," they intended to live off the land. They have done that. But they have also raised the bar for American cheesemaking through hard work and, just as important, an intuitive sense about flavor. They have never named the individual cheeses; instead they all share the name, "Sally Jackson Cheeses." In this case, it's a name that says it all.

WHAT THEY MAKE

Goats' milk cheeses
Flavored: dried tomato, oregano, basil, garlic and dill, garlic and chives
Grapeleaf-wrapped aged cheese
Mixed goat and cow with herbs
Mixed goat and cow with jalapeño and garlic
Plain aged (at least five months)

Sheep's milk cheeses
Chestnut leaf-wrapped aged cheese
Hard, well-aged cheese (at least nine months), rubbed with cocoa

Cows' milk cheeses
Flavored: sweet red peppers, chives
Hard, well-aged cheese (at least five months)

HOW TO REACH THEM
Oroville, Washington
No mail order except through retail stores (See Resources)

Green Garlic Risotto with Cauliflower, Pancetta, and Fromage Blanc

Green garlic has a very short season, usually mid-May to early June. It looks like a large scallion, but its flavor is unmistakably garlic. Still, it is milder than its cloved counterpart. Because it has such a short season, however, it isn't always a practical ingredient. In the case of this risotto, regular garlic works just fine, although it should be cooked slightly differently. Instructions follow below.

Fromage blanc is a fresh cows' or goats' milk cheese with a bit of a tang. Here it is added at the end to lend further creaminess to the risotto as well as a slightly sharper flavor. It ties all of the ingredients together beautifully, cooling the zip from the red pepper flakes and coating the caramelized cauliflower. You can prepare the cauliflower mixture as much as two hours in advance, making the last-minute nature of risotto a little easier.

1 very large cauliflower or 2 small
    cauliflowers (about 2¼ pounds total),
    cored and broken into medium-size florets

3 thick slices pancetta (about ⅓ pound),
    cut into ½-inch pieces

1 tablespoon plus 2 teaspoons olive oil

3 stalks green garlic, bulb and lighter green
    parts finely chopped (or use 3 small cloves
    garlic, finely chopped)

½ teaspoon red pepper flakes

Kosher salt

About 8 cups unsalted chicken stock

3 shallots, finely chopped

2 cups Arborio or Carnaroli rice

⅔ cup fromage blanc (or use fresh goat
    cheese)

2 ounces aged cheese, such as Sally Jackson's
    aged goats' or sheep's milk cheese, finely
    grated (about ¼ cup; or use dry Jack)

Bring a large pot of salted water to a boil. Add the cauliflower and boil until crisp-tender, about 5 minutes. (It's better to undercook than to overcook the cauliflower.) Drain in a colander, and run cold water over it to stop the cooking process. When the cauliflower is cool enough to handle, break it into tiny florets, about 1 inch long, cutting the stems if necessary. Set aside.

In a large sauté pan, cook the pancetta until brown and crisp, about 10 minutes. Using a slotted spoon, transfer the pancetta to a paper towel-lined plate. Remove all but 2 tablespoons fat from the pan, and add the 2 teaspoons olive oil to the pan. Heat over medium heat. Add the cauliflower florets and the garlic. Cook until the cauliflower becomes browned and caramelized on the edges and the garlic starts to brown slightly as well, about 7 minutes. (If using regular garlic, cook the cauliflower for 5 minutes and then add the garlic.) Add the red pepper flakes and plenty of coarse salt to taste. Keep warm. (Or if not using right away, set aside in a single layer and then warm slowly before using.)

Warm shallow bowls or plates in a low oven.

Pour the chicken stock into a pot and heat until hot but not boiling. Have a ladle or a glass measuring cup with a handle nearby. Keep the stock at a very low simmer.

In a large saucepan, heat the remaining 1 tablespoon olive oil over medium-high heat. Add the shallots and sauté until soft, about 5 minutes. Add the rice and stir constantly until it begins to look slightly translucent around the edges, about 5 minutes. Using the ladle or measuring cup, add about 1 cup of the hot stock to the rice and stir vigorously. Once the rice has absorbed the liquid, repeat with another cupful of stock. Continue this process for about 15 to 20 minutes, or until the rice is tender but still retains a little firmness. You may have a little extra stock. Or, if you need more liquid, add near-boiling water. To achieve a creamy risotto, cook away all but about $\frac{1}{4}$ cup of the liquid after the last addition. Add the cauliflower mixture and the pancetta to the risotto, and stir to distribute the ingredients. Add the fromage blanc and stir. It will melt as it gets distributed. Spoon into the warm bowls and top each one with a little grated cheese. Serve immediately.

Serves 8 as a first course, 4 as a main course

THE MOZZARELLA COMPANY

PAULA LAMBERT IS ANOTHER ON THE LIST of cheese pioneers in this country. Unlike many of the other cheesemakers, who started on their own farms, Paula started a company in the middle of Dallas, Texas. No animals there—just a passion for cheese.

The Mozzarella Company got its start in 1982, but it had its beginnings much earlier, when Paula was living in Perugia, Italy. She fell in love with all things Italian, especially the food. After five years she returned to the U.S., but she made frequent trips back to Italy with her husband. During one such trip, around 1980, Paula once again tasted mozzarella cheese, or what is also known there as *fior di latte*, usually referring to mozzarella made with cows' milk. She decided that a good-quality mozzarella was needed in Dallas. A cheese factory in Italy became the training ground where she was introduced to cheesemaking. She then returned to Dallas to start her company.

Although Lambert had never run a business, she had worked with her husband in his business and had done a significant amount of volunteer work. Those experiences contributed to her ability to start and operate her own company. What she started was an operation that now employs between fifteen and twenty people who continue to make the cheese almost entirely by hand.

The signature cheeses are, naturally, the *pasta filata*, or stretched-curd cheeses, such as the mozzarella. But the Mozzarella Company makes twenty-four other cheeses as well. Most of them are made with cows' milk, but two years after starting the company, Paula added goat cheese to the assortment—"because I loved it," she explains.

At one point along the way, Paula did make *mozzarella di bufala* (mozzarella made from the milk of water buffalos), but getting the milk was problematic, and not enough people appreciated the difference to make it worth the trouble. Paula points out that most people think fresh mozzarella *is* made from water buffalo milk, "and they think that water buffalo is American bison," she explains. It is not, although it is an understandable confusion since we do not have water buffalo in this country and are not familiar with them. (Water buffalo originally came from India, but today they are found primarily in Italy and in Bulgaria.)

Cheeses like caciotta (a semi-soft cheese), crescenza, and ricotta are regulars on the line at the Mozzarella Company, but Paula's ebullient personality really comes through in her flavored cheeses, many of which are spicy and are customized for Southwest cuisine. Among those is a queso blanco with serrano chiles and epazote, an herb widely used in Mexico. Another is a hard grating goats' milk cheese she calls Montasio. It is based on the Italian cows' milk cheese of the same name and is made plain or with an ancho chile rub. For an Italian twist on southern cuisine, Paula adds pecan praline to her mascarpone, while her Hoja Santa Goat Cheese Bundles are similar to the French banon, only with a Latin twist. *Hoja santa* is an edible leaf used widely in cooking throughout Mexico. (Banons are wrapped in chestnut leaves.)

The Mozzarella Company continues to be successful, in

large part due to Paula's unflagging energy. She is just as likely to be called on to help out with the cheese as she is to fix a broken-down piece of equipment. At the same time, she is fastidious about the cheese, choosing to distribute it directly, rather than through distributors, to restaurants, retailers, and consumers.

The Mozzarella Company's cheeses circle the globe, from Mexican to Southwestern to Italian. While they are good eating cheeses, most of them are equally suited to cooking. They have good melting ability, and the herbs and spices that flavor the cheeses add distinct and unusual accents.

WHAT THEY MAKE

Cows' milk cheeses
Caciotta: plain and
    flavored
Cream cheese
Crème fraîche
Crescenza
Feta
Fromage blanc
Mascarpone: regular and
    flavored
Mozzarella: regular and
    smoked
Queso blanco: plain and
    flavored
Queso Oaxaca
Ricotta
Smoked scamorza
Taleggio

Goats' milk cheeses
Capriella (mixed goats'
    and cows' milk
    mozzarella)
Feta
Fromage blanc
Fresh Texas Goat Cheese:
    soft, pieces, herb logs
Goat caciotta: plain and
    flavored
Hoja Santa Goat Cheese
    Bundles
Jocoque
Montasio
Montasio Festivo
Ricotta

HOW TO REACH THEM
Dallas, Texas
800-798-2954 or 214-741-4072
214-741-4076 (fax)
website: www.mozzco.com

Risotto with Yam Puree, Kale, and Smoked Mozzarella

This risotto measures a "10" on the comfort scale, drawing on the flavors of the Deep South and resting them comfortably on a bed of creamy rice. The smoked mozzarella naturally lends a very smoky taste, which might be too strong for some. To reduce and yet retain some of that smokiness, you can cut the smoked mozzarella portion in half and use regular mozzarella to make up the difference. Because mozzarella is by definition stringy, it's important that the cheese be grated rather than added in chunks. That way, the cheese will be evenly distributed throughout the risotto.

---

4 yams (about 2½ pounds total)
About 8 cups unsalted chicken stock
2 tablespoons butter
1 tablespoon plus 2 teaspoons olive oil
1 clove garlic, minced
1 bunch kale, rinsed but not dried, stems removed, leaves cut crosswise into 1-inch-wide strips
1 yellow onion, chopped
2 cups Arborio or Carnaroli rice
4 ounces Mozzarella Company or other smoked mozzarella, coarsely grated (about 1¼ cups)
1 ounce aged Asiago cheese, finely grated (about ¼ cup)
Freshly ground pepper

Preheat the oven to 400°F.

Using the tines of a fork, poke a few holes in the yams to let steam escape. Place them in a baking pan and bake until very tender, 45 to 60 minutes. Remove them from the oven and let sit just until cool enough to handle, about 10 minutes. Scoop the flesh out of the skins and put it in a blender. Add ½ cup of the chicken stock and puree until smooth. Add more stock if necessary to achieve a creamy consistency. Transfer the puree to a small saucepan and heat it slowly. When it is hot, whisk in the butter and set aside. Keep warm.

In a medium sauté pan, heat the 2 teaspoons oil over medium heat. Add the garlic and stir for 1 minute. Add the kale, cover, and cook, stirring occasionally, until it is tender and bright green, 6 to 8 minutes. Remove the cover, salt lightly, and keep warm over very low heat.

In a medium saucepan, heat the remaining stock until it is steaming but not boiling. Keep hot.

In a large saucepan heat the remaining 1 tablespoon oil over medium-high heat. Add the onions and cook until they are translucent, about 5 minutes. Add the rice, stirring vigorously, and cook until it begins to turn a milky white, about 5 minutes. Add 1 ladleful (or cup) of the hot stock. Stir the rice until all of the stock is absorbed. Continue this procedure with the stock, adding 1 ladleful at a time and stirring, until the rice is plump, tender, and creamy, 15 to 20 minutes. It should take about 6 to 7 more cups of stock. (If you run out of stock, add near-boiling water.) Next add the yam puree, stirring until it has coated all of the rice. Add the kale and the mozzarella. Stir until the cheese has melted. Divide the risotto among individual bowls or plates, and top each one with grated Asiago and a little freshly ground pepper. Serve immediately.

Serves 8 as a first course, 4 as a main course

THE ANTIGO CHEESE COMPANY

AT A PRODUCTION LEVEL OF 1 MILLION POUNDS A WEEK, and with an employee roster of about a hundred, The Antigo Cheese Company is sizable by any standard. But size notwithstanding, the story of this company in Antigo, Wisconsin, can be seen as symbolic of the cheesemaker's passion.

The company, a producer of cows' milk Italian hard cheeses, was one of the first plants established by J. L. Kraft in 1922. In 1993 Kraft's parent company, Phillip Morris, decided to close the plant. Employees were not about to go quietly, so they bought the plant with the help of investors and funding from the state. The result was a seamless switch—not a day of production was missed in the process. Nonetheless, the new owners had to weather many changes and refocus their energies. Several of their milk suppliers dropped out during the transition, and many employees left as well. Perhaps more challenging was that Kraft, which still contracted to buy much of Antigo's cheese, also held the rights to their cheese "recipes." This meant that Antigo had to develop their own if they were going to sell to others besides Kraft.

To further differentiate themselves from their former owner, the employees came up with a brand name for their cheeses: Wisantigo, as in Wisconsin + Antigo. They began to develop premium specialty cheeses, and that's where they have made their mark.

The Antigo Cheese Company makes only four cheeses right now, but when one of them is as good as the Stravecchio, why look for more? Stravecchio is the trademarked name for Antigo's aged Parmesan. Instead of the ten months of aging that the Wisantigo brand Parmesan gets, the Stravecchio, which means "very old," is aged for twenty months. It is as close to true Parmigiano-Reggiano as any American-made Parmesan has gotten. It's nutty, buttery, salty, granular, and so flavorful as is that it's hard to imagine grating it for pasta or risotto. On the other hand, it lifts those dishes into a much more flavorful orbit.

Like most hard grating cheeses, Stravecchio is made with a fair amount of salt. The curds are salted on the draining tables, and when the wheels are formed, they are placed in a saltwater brine for several days. They are then brought into the aging room and are turned frequently during the first thirty days to distribute the moisture evenly. They will sit for another nineteen months before they are packaged and sold.

Since it is fairly new in its current incarnation, the company is hoping to expand, and is looking into making more Italian-style hard cheeses. The employees who bought the plant, though originally not well versed in the vagaries of cheesemaking, have already created some winning cheeses. It will be interesting to watch them progress.

WHAT THEY MAKE
Asiago
Parmesan
Romano
Stravecchio

HOW TO REACH THEM
Antigo, Wisconsin
800-356-5655
715-623-2301
715-623-4501 (fax)
website: www.antigocheese.com

Lemon Parmesan Risotto with Asparagus

One night, when I didn't have time to go to the store, I took inventory of what I had at home. From that list I came up with this simple and refreshing risotto. Since I always have more than one type of cheese on hand, I tried this risotto with three different types of grating cheeses. Two were made from goats' milk and one was a Parmesan. Although I liked them all, I found that the more assertive Parmesan was the best complement to the sour lemon. If asparagus is out of season, simply eliminate it. The risotto is equally good without it.

PASTAS AND RISOTTI

½ **pound asparagus (preferably thin stalks), ends cut off**
About 8 cups unsalted chicken stock
1 tablespoon olive oil
1 large yellow onion (about ¾ pound), coarsely chopped
2 cups Arborio or Carnaroli rice
½ cup dry white wine
⅓ cup fresh lemon juice (from about 1½ lemons)
3 tablespoons butter
Salt and freshly ground pepper
4 ounces Antigo Stravecchio, finely grated (or use domestic Parmesan or Asiago)

In a small sauté pan, bring lightly salted water to a boil. (You should have enough water to cover the asparagus.) Add the asparagus and cook for 2 minutes. Remove from the heat and drain immediately. Rinse with cold water. Pat dry and cut into 2-inch pieces. Set aside.

Pour the chicken stock into a large pot and bring to a boil. Reduce the heat to medium-low and maintain a low simmer.

In another large saucepan, heat the oil over medium-high heat. Add the onions and stir until they are translucent, about 5 minutes. Do not let them brown. Add the rice and stir constantly until it begins to look slightly translucent around the edges, about 5 minutes. Add the wine and stir until it boils away.

Using a ladle or a glass measuring cup, add about 1 cup of the hot stock to the rice and stir vigorously. Once the rice has absorbed the liquid, add another cupful. Stir the risotto vigorously after each addition of stock. Continue adding stock just until the rice grains are translucent and are firm but tender to the bite, 15 to 20 minutes. It may not take all of the stock or it could take more—it all depends on the rice. If you need more liquid, add near-boiling water.

After the last ladleful of stock has been added, add the asparagus and lemon juice. Stir vigorously until most of the lemon juice has been absorbed. Add the butter and stir just until melted. Add half of the cheese along with plenty of salt and a generous amount of pepper.

Divide the risotto among individual bowls or plates, and sprinkle with the remaining cheese. Serve immediately.

Serves 8 as a first course, 4 as a main course

THREE SHEPHERDS OF
THE MAD RIVER VALLEY

ONE COULD EASILY MISTAKE THE NAME of this cheese operation for the name of a village church. But in this case, the three shepherds are the three children of Linda and Larry Faillace, all of whom are integral to the family's sheep cheese operation in the area known as the Mad River Valley in Warren, Vermont.

At age thirteen, the Faillaces' youngest child, Jackie, is most certainly one of America's youngest cheesemakers. The word "prodigy" comes to mind upon learning that Jackie began cooking at age seven, made up her own recipes when she was eight, and by the time she was nine, regularly made dinner for the family. Her older sister, Heather, age fourteen, milks the family's flock of 101 sheep. At four feet eleven, that's no easy feat, but Linda says the sheep display no ambiguity as to who is boss. They are compliant milk-givers. Older brother Francis, age fifteen, is in charge of the dog and pasture management. Since the Faillaces manage other people's pastures besides their own, Francis has a lot of ground to cover.

Since most of the work in sheep cheese making and pasture management is done during the summer, the children's other primary responsibility—school—does not interfere. However, when cheesemaking and the school calendar coincide, the sheep milking and cheesemaking duties begin early in the morning, before school, and resume after school. It is a pioneer life in a modern-day world. And the kids love it.

The Faillaces decided to enter the field of sheep dairying while they were living in England. Larry Faillace was finishing his Ph.D. in animal science at the University of Nottingham, and they were looking  for an agriculture-based business that would make money as well as be an interesting project in which all of the kids could be involved. They settled on Vermont as the location, and they settled on sheep dairying because their research showed that 48 million pounds of sheep's milk cheese was being imported into the United States. This confirmed for them that there was a market here.

The Faillaces then accumulated cheesemaking equipment and hired a cheesemaker from Belgium, named Alfred "Freddie" Michiels, to teach them the art. This is the same cheesemaker who taught the Whittens at Skunk Hollow Farm (See page 114) how to make their cheese. In the summer of 1999, the Faillaces were finally under way with

---

WHAT THEY MAKE

Sheep's Milk Cheeses
Feta
Montagne
Summer Solstice
Warren Meadows

Cows' Milk Cheeses
Aurora
Vermont Brabander

HOW TO REACH THEM
Warren, Vermont
802-496-3998
802-496-4096 (fax)

their cheese production. Jackie and Larry make the cheese together, although he eventually expects to turn those duties over to his daughter.

The result of this collaboration is stunning cheese. One of the most exciting is a Brin d'Amour-style cheese called Warren Meadows. Brin d'Amour is a Corsican sheep's milk pyramid-shaped cheese that is cloaked in herbs. The Faillaces' is similar, including the fact that it is made with raw milk, but it is covered with their local herbs, including rosemary, thyme, and savory. The Montagne is a hard aged cheese similar to a Spanish Manchego but with a little more moisture, and their Summer Solstice is a beer-washed cheese. Jackie also makes a small amount feta cheese, which hasn't made it past the country store about fifty yards away. The locals snatch it up.

In addition to sheep cheese making, the Faillace's also make cows' milk cheese. A neighbor, a member of the Von Trapp family (of *Sound of Music* fame), who settled in the Mad River Valley decades ago, had Jersey cow milk to offer. The result: Werner and Erika Von Trapp now have something to sing about. The brined, washed rind cheese called Aurora is similar to Alsatian Muenster cheese, though not as soft, and the Vermont Brabander, a mild, natural rind cheese takes on the flavor of an aged Gouda over time.

Three Shepherds of the Mad River Valley is a newcomer to the world of American-made cheese. But given their current operation as well as their future plans, they plan to be around awhile. They intend to accumulate more sheep; they have a portable milking parlor that allows them to go to the grazing sheep rather than beckoning them to a stationary milking facility; and they already offer cheese-making courses throughout the year. In addition, they have a vegetable garden that is run by a local nonprofit group that also sells the produce. More than anything, they have youth, or the "three shepherds."

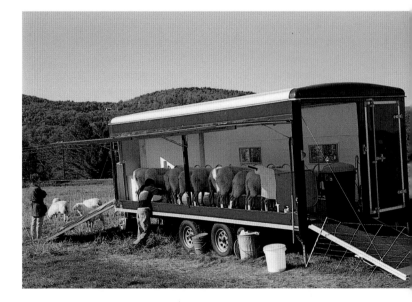

Heather Faillace prepares to milk the sheep in the portable milking parlor that allows the sheep to stay in the pasture instead of being brought to a barn for milking.

As a cheesemaker, Jackie Faillace shows great promise. But her sixth-grade graduation statement hints at still further ambition: "I want to attend the Culinary Institute of America, become a world famous chef, and own my own restaurant next to the Eiffel Tower." She added that she also wants to have a few sheep on the side.

Linguine with Pesto, Potatoes, Green Beans, and Cheese

The original version of this dish comes from Liguria, a large region on the west coast of Italy, of which Genoa is the capital. Liguria is the birthplace of pesto, and the best way to make the basil-garlic sauce is the subject of great debate there. They say a mortar and pestle work best to grind the ingredients but I think a blender works fine.

PASTAS AND RISOTTI

FOR THE PESTO
1 bunch basil, leaves only (about 2½ cups)
3 small cloves garlic, peeled
2 tablespoons pine nuts
½ cup finely grated aged sheep's milk cheese (about 2 ounces), such as Three Shepherds' Montagne
1 tablespoon unsalted butter, softened
⅓ cup olive oil, plus extra for covering the pesto
½ teaspoon salt (or less, depending on the saltiness of the cheese)

FOR THE PASTA
1 teaspoon kosher salt
¼ pound fresh green beans, such as Blue Lake, ends trimmed
1½ tablespoons olive oil
½ pound small red potatoes, unpeeled, cut into ⅛-inch-thick slices
Salt and freshly ground pepper
12 ounces dried linguine
1 ounce aged sheep's milk cheese, shaved into paper-thin slices

To make the pesto: In a blender or food processor, combine the basil, garlic, pine nuts, grated cheese, and butter. Whirl for about 30 seconds, or until the basil is finely chopped. Add the oil and whirl just until the pesto is somewhat creamy but still has bits of basil showing. Add salt to taste. (Since you will be putting the pesto on pasta, it is okay to be generous with the salt.) Put the pesto in a small bowl, drizzle a little olive oil over the top, and cover with plastic wrap. Set aside or refrigerate for up to 3 days. (Pesto can be frozen for 3 months.)

To prepare the pasta: Bring a small saucepan of water to a boil, and add the kosher salt. Add the beans and cook for 4 minutes. Drain, and immediately rinse with very cold water. Set aside.

Bring a large pot of water to a boil, and salt it well.

In a large sauté pan, heat the olive oil over medium heat. Add the potatoes and cook for about 5 minutes without turning. The potatoes should begin to get tender and the undersides should turn golden brown. Turn the potatoes and cook for 2 more minutes. Add the beans, stir, and continue cooking for 2 minutes. Stir carefully so the potatoes don't break apart. Add salt and pepper to taste. Set aside.

Add the linguine to the boiling water and cook according to the package directions, 10 to 12 minutes. When the pasta is tender but firm, drain it, reserving ¼ cup of the cooking water. Put the pasta back in the pot and place it on the stove over medium heat. Mix 1 tablespoon of the cooking water into the pesto, and pour the pesto over the pasta. Mix well. Add more liquid, if necessary, along with the potatoes and green beans, stirring carefully until all of the ingredients are heated through. Add a little cracked pepper and top with the cheese. Serve immediately.

Serves 4

QUILLISASCUT CHEESE COMPANY

RICK AND LORA LEA MISTERLY HAVE BEEN MILKING their thirty-eight goats and turning that milk into about 6,000 pounds of cheese every year since 1987. They've taken all of one month off, give or take a couple of weeks, since their cheesemaking began.

Lora Lea is the cheesemaker for the Quillisascut Cheese Company, which is located along the Columbia River, about equidistant from the Canadian and Idaho borders. Quillisascut is a Native American term meaning "Place of Scattered Bushes." The mixed vegetation in the area—low bushes and tall trees—was said to be good for hunting. But the Misterleys stick mainly to cheesemaking, turning out rounds of an earthy aged goats' milk cheese they call Curado. They base their cheese on a Spanish recipe for the sheep's milk cheese known as Manchego, but this is pure goat. It is gamy and buttery, very firm, and makes a lovely table cheese or an exceedingly flavorful grating cheese. It is also a soothing light yellow color with tiny eyes. Although herb-flavored aged cheeses can sometimes be a dicey proposition, in the case of Quillisascut's lavender-fennel Curado, it is a successful marriage. The hints of perfumy lavender and the more pronounced fennel are brought into balance by the strength of flavor in the goats' milk cheese. Together they form a vibrant cheese that is satisfying on its own and, surprisingly, when it is accompanied by a fruity white wine. Somehow the flavors in the cheese and the wine don't compete; they simply flow. The Misterleys also make a goats' milk cheese wrapped in chestnut leaves, a smoked Curado, and an herbed cows' milk cheese from the milk of their Jerseys.

The cows' milk cheese, called Selkirk, contains black pepper and garlic. As a result, this cheese elevates a basic bread or biscuit recipe to one of distinction. The smoked Curado lends itself to a spinach and apple salad or to enjoying in its simplest form, with nothing at all.

Rick and Lora Lea are Quillisascut's only employees, which for their customers means personal service. Rick still makes the 700-mile round-trip trek to Seattle once a month to deliver his cheese to restaurants and retail stores. Lora Lea stays back to milk the goats and make the cheese. They both run the farm and, Rick says, they love it. "You couldn't do it if you didn't enjoy it."

Their love is apparent in their product, and while they don't make a lot of cheese, what they do make is exciting, cutting edge, and dynamic. Their cheese also provides a glimpse into the hidden talents that often lie unseen in rural America.

WHAT THEY MAKE
Goats' milk cheeses
Curado (plain and smoked)
Lavender-Fennel Curado
Chestnut Leaf Aged Goat

Cows' milk cheese
Selkirk (black pepper and
  garlic cow)

HOW TO REACH THEM
Rice, Washington
509-738-2011

Spaghetti with Spring Vegetables and Aged Goat Cheese

When fava beans, peas, artichokes, and morel mushrooms start appearing together in the produce section of the grocery store and at farmers' markets, it is an epiphanous moment. Spring is here; summer is coming; and this in-between stage produces some of nature's best offerings. This recipe may seem to squeeze a lot of vegetables onto one plate, but just wait. It's kid-in-the-candy-store time, since laying under every strand of pasta is a different yet wonderful representation of spring. Any type of grating cheese will do, but one like Quillisascut's Curado or Juniper Grove's Tomme creates a more assertive flavor and a nice balance for the vegetables.

Morel mushrooms have a fairly short season and are usually rather expensive. Consider two alternatives: You can use dried morels or assorted dried mushrooms. Reconstitute them in just enough hot water to cover for about 20 minutes. (Strain and reserve the mushroom water for use in the pasta in place of the chicken stock, then slice the mushrooms.) Or you can buy another type of wild mushroom to substitute for the morels.

PASTAS AND RISOTTI

---

2 tablespoons kosher salt
1¼ pounds fava beans
1 pound fresh peas, shelled
¼ cup fresh lemon juice or white wine
    vinegar
1 pound baby artichokes
7 tablespoons butter
½ cup unsalted chicken stock or mushroom
    broth
¼ pound morel mushrooms, washed and cut
    crosswise into ¼-inch slices (or 1 ounce
    dried mushrooms, reconstituted and sliced)
Salt and freshly ground pepper
3 ounces hard goats' milk cheese, such as
    Quillisascut, shaved into paper-thin slices
    (or use another hard goats', sheep's, or
    cows' milk cheese)
12 ounces dried spaghetti

Bring a large pot of water to a boil and add the salt.

While the pasta water is heating, peel and discard the tough outer shells, or pods, of the fava beans. Place the beans in a small bowl. Bring a medium-size pot of water to a boil, add the fava beans, and blanch for 2 minutes. Keeping the water at a boil, remove the beans with a slotted spoon. Immediately run cold water over the beans to stop the cooking. Set aside.

Using the same boiling water, add the peas and blanch for 2 minutes. Drain, and run cold water over them to stop the cooking.

Peel the fava beans: Find the root end of the bean. This is the slightly darker green little point that protrudes from the bean. Hold the root end between your thumb and index finger.

and add them to the pan. Cook, stirring constantly, until the artichokes begin to turn brown, about 4 minutes. Reduce the heat to medium-low and add the chicken stock. (If you are using the mushroom soaking liquid, strain it into a small pot and heat it to almost boiling.) Cover and cook, stirring occasionally, until tender, about 10 minutes. If the liquid cooks away too quickly, add a little more stock, water, or strained mushroom liquid to the pan.

In the same pan with the artichokes, melt 3 tablespoons of the butter. Add the sliced morels and sauté until cooked through, 2 to 3 minutes. Add the beans and peas to the pan. Stir to coat with any remaining butter. Add salt and pepper to taste. Set aside.

Have warm pasta bowls or a platter ready.

Cook the pasta in the pot of boiling salted water until it is tender but still firm, 10 to 12 minutes.

When the pasta is cooked, reserve about 1 cup of the pasta water and drain the pasta. Add the pasta to the pan with the vegetables, along with ½ cup pasta water and the remaining 2 tablespoons butter. Turn the heat to medium-high and stir until the vegetables are dispersed throughout the pasta and the butter has melted. Add more pasta liquid if the mixture seems dry. Taste, and add more salt if necessary. Distribute among the bowls or place on a the platter. Top with the cheese shavings and a little freshly ground pepper. Serve immediately.

Serves 4

With the thumb and index fingernails of your other hand, tear a small slit in the thin skin at the opposite end of the bean. Gently squeeze the root end and the bean will come out the slit. It might squirt out, so press gently on the root end. Set the beans aside.

Fill a large nonreactive bowl with water and add the lemon juice. (This is for the artichokes after you've trimmed them, to prevent them from turning brown.)

Cut ½ inch off the top of one artichoke. Cut off the stem. Next, peel off and discard most of the outer leaves until you reach the tender, light green inner leaves. (You will be removing more than half of the artichoke leaves.) Cut the artichoke in half lengthwise, and then cut each half lengthwise again to make quarters. Put in the bowl of acidulated water. Repeat with the remaining artichokes.

In a large sauté pan, melt 2 tablespoons of the butter over medium heat. Drain the artichokes

Three-Cheese Green and Red Lasagna

The title of this recipe sounds like the colors of the Italian flag. As well it should. The layers of noodles, greens, radicchio, and cheese conjure up images of lasagna's birthplace. But this rendition is purely American, thanks to the three cheeses that make it such a standout. The recipe calls for the standard ricotta (if you can find sheep's milk ricotta, use it) and mozzarella cheeses, but the use of American aged Asiago brings a pleasant sharpness to the overall dish. The layer of garlic mushrooms comes as a rich surprise between the layers of greens and cheeses. Topping it all off is a rich béchamel sauce that provides the necessary creaminess. You can assemble this dish three hours ahead and refrigerate it. Or, you can assemble it and freeze it for up to one month. Bring it to room temperature before baking.

FOR THE NOODLES
4 quarts water
12 to 16 ounces dried lasagna noodles (see Note)
2 tablespoons salt

FOR THE MUSHROOMS
1 tablespoon olive oil
1 large yellow onion (about 1 pound), coarsely chopped
4 cloves garlic, minced
1 tablespoon butter
1 pound white mushrooms, quartered (if large, cut into 6 pieces)

FOR THE GREENS
2 heads radicchio, rinsed but not dried, each cut into 6 lengthwise pieces, leaves separated
2 bunches dandelion greens, kale, or green Swiss chard (about 1½ pounds), washed but not drained, stems trimmed and leaves cut crosswise into 2-inch-wide strips
2 bunches spinach (about 1½ pounds), rinsed and patted partially dry, stems removed, leaves cut crosswise into 2-inch-wide strips
Salt

FOR THE CHEESES
1 pound ricotta cheese, drained if wet
8 ounces mozzarella cheese, coarsely grated (about 2 cups)
4 ounces aged Asiago, rind removed, finely grated (about 1 cup) (or use any hard grating cheese—cow, sheep, or goat)
2 eggs, lightly beaten
2 tablespoons chopped flat-leaf parsley
Freshly ground pepper, to taste

FOR THE BÉCHAMEL
2 cups milk
¼ cup butter (½ stick)
3 tablespoons all-purpose flour
Dash of grated nutmeg
Salt and freshly ground pepper

⅔ cup tomato puree

Preheat the oven to 350°F.

To prepare the noodles: Place a thin dry dish towel over a jelly roll pan or baking sheet. In a large pot, bring the water to a boil, and add the salt. Bring the water back to a boil and add a few of the noodles. Cook for 5 minutes. (They will not be cooked through.) Using tongs or a large flat skimmer, remove them from the water and place them on the towel to drain. Continue until all of the noodles are partially cooked and set aside.

To prepare the mushrooms: In a wok or a deep sauté pan, heat the olive oil over medium heat. (You will be using this pan for the greens, which is why it should be oversized.) Add the onions and garlic and cook until the onions are translucent, 5 to 7 minutes. Stir constantly so the garlic doesn't burn. Melt the butter in the same pan with the onions, and add the mushrooms. Cook until the mushrooms are tender and the liquid has evaporated, about 15 minutes. Remove the mixture from the pan and set aside.

To prepare the greens: Heat the same wok or deep sauté pan over medium-high heat. When it is hot, add the radicchio, dandelion greens, and spinach. Cover. The water still clinging to the leaves will cook the greens. Add water a few drops at a time if more is needed. When the greens are wilted and cooked through (5 to 7 minutes), remove the cover and salt them to taste. If they are still watery, either cook away the water or drain them in a colander. Set aside.

To make the cheese mixture: In a small bowl, mix together the ricotta, mozzarella, ½ cup of the Asiago, eggs, parsley, and pepper. Set aside.

To make the béchamel: In a small saucepan, slowly heat the milk just until it begins to steam but not boil. Remove from the heat. In a medium-size saucepan, melt the ¼ cup butter. Whisk in the flour, stirring vigorously to make sure the mixture doesn't burn. Keeping the heat on low, add 1 tablespoon of the heated milk and mix well. Gradually, whisk in the rest of the milk. When the sauce thickens, add the nutmeg and salt and pepper to taste. Keep warm over very low heat, stirring occasionally; or even better, place in a double boiler to cook a little further. You don't want the sauce to thicken too much.

To assemble: Coat the bottom of a 9 × 13-inch baking dish (preferably glass) with the tomato puree. Top with a layer of noodles, making sure that the noodles are touching but not overlapping. Scatter one third of the greens on top of the noodles. Place one third of the mushrooms over the greens, and one third of the cheese mixture on top of the mushrooms. Repeat the layers, starting with the noodles, and pour one third of the béchamel over the cheese mixture. Add the third layer of noodles, greens, mushrooms, and cheeses. Pour the remaining béchamel over the top of the lasagna, and sprinkle with the remaining ½ cup of Asiago. Bake for 40 minutes, or until the cheese is bubbling and the lasagna is a dark golden color. Let cool for about 10 minutes and serve.

Serves 8 to 10

Note: Lasagna noodles vary in size. Some are long and some are short. As a result, you will need to use your best judgment in determining how many noodles are needed to fit a 9 × 13-inch pan. It is better to have too many noodles than not enough.

DOELING DAIRY GOAT FARM

GOAT CHEESE MAKING MAY HAVE BEEN a fait accompli for Donna Doel. Her last name ensured that. The Maine native moved to Fayetteville, Arkansas, to take an agriculture-related job, but the lure of the land and a stint making Caerphilly cheese in Ireland convinced her to acquire some goats, including a few young female goats called doelings. She eventually started making cheese, and Doeling Dairy Goat Farm was born.

Licensed in 1995, Doel has already been honored for her goat cheese, having garnered awards from the American Cheese Society in 1998 and 1999. Considerable talent notwithstanding, she marvels at the immense challenge in maintaining a cheesemaking business. With little help and a growing demand, she, like so many American cheesemakers, has had to struggle to set priorities, get capital, and do what she does best: make cheese.

Fortunately she has managed well enough to meet the demand in and around her city, in the northwest part of Arkansas. Home of Wal-Mart and Tyson's Chicken, Fayetteville is not some small southern town. It boasts well-traveled, worldly residents who have palates to match. That the Doeling Dairy cheeses are sought after is no small feat.

Although the fresh chèvre and Camembert have won awards, it is the feta that her restaurant customers ask for just as often. The raw milk cheese is aged in brine from nine months to a year, and lends itself to cooking, crumbling, cutting, you name it. It isn't goaty and it isn't meek. It is, as Goldilocks said, just right.

Doel is also making crottins, which are slightly aged small cylindrical cheeses with a yellowish rind. They are earthy and a little dry because of their small size, but they pack a lot of flavor. By definition, crottins age quickly, becoming hard in just a few weeks, or even less. They can often be turned into a fine grating cheese at this stage, though. This is one of her favorite cheeses, though she admits it has yet to catch on in her area.

What has caught on is her raw milk goat Gouda. Aged only sixty days ("I'd love to age it longer, but I can't keep enough of it around"), it has a black wax rind and is fairly mild but well-rounded. Since not many goat Goudas are made in this country, hers is particularly noteworthy. But of all of her cheeses, Donna is proudest of her Camembert. It is a soft-ripening, creamy specimen of rich milk flavor and hints of lemon.

Doel describes her corner of Arkansas as flush with rivers, creeks, magnolias, and dogwoods. But for all of its beauty and rural appeal, she is the only goat cheese maker in the entire state. Arkansas residents are fortunate to have a cheesemaking star in their midst.

WHAT THEY MAKE
Camembert
Crottin
Feta
Fresh chèvre: plain and herbed
Gouda

HOW TO REACH THEM
Fayetteville, Arkansas
888-524-4571
501-582-4571
501-582-1213 (fax)
website: www.doelingdairy.com

OPPOSITE: Goat Cheese, Apricot, and Sage-Stuffed Chicken Breasts (see page 168).

Leg of Lamb Stuffed with Roasted Garlic, Feta, and Basil Leaves

Lamb is a food that heralds the springtime almost more than any other. For some it has biblical connotations, and for others it is symbolic of the ending of a harsh season and the beginning of a warmer one, a time for renewal. That is why a leg of lamb, while plenty flavorful on its own, lends itself to embellishments that create an entirely festive dish. In this case, a filling of vibrant-colored herbs, vegetables, sweet roasted garlic, and salty feta cheese result in a true representation of the essence of spring in both its beauty and its flavor. The sauce, made from pan drippings, and the potatoes help round it out, but the spring theme might also be completed by the addition of a few oven-roasted asparagus spears served on the side.

A note about the lamb: Rolling a leg of lamb can be a bit unwieldy. To make it easier, even it out by trimming the very thick parts, and score, or make shallow cuts, on the inside surface of the meat before stuffing it.

---

1 leg of lamb, boned and butterflied
  (3½ pounds)
1½ cups good-quality full-bodied red wine,
  such as a syrah, petite sirah, or cabernet
  sauvignon
2 tablespoons olive oil
2 cloves garlic, minced
1 tablespoon chopped fresh oregano leaves
1 tablespoon chopped fresh basil leaves
Salt and freshly ground pepper
1 whole head garlic
4 ounces feta cheese, such as Doeling Dairy,
  crumbled
1 tablespoon milk
1 red bell pepper, roasted, skinned, and cut
  lengthwise into ¼-inch strips
12 to 15 whole basil leaves
1½ pounds small creamer potatoes
  (about 18), cut in half (or use larger red
  potatoes and cut into quarters)

1 tablespoon all-purpose flour
½ cup unsalted lamb, chicken, or beef stock

Place the lamb in a large nonreactive roasting pan or baking dish. In a small bowl, mix together 1 cup of the wine, the olive oil, garlic, oregano and chopped basil, and salt and pepper to taste. Pour this over the lamb, cover with foil, and let sit at room temperature for up to 2 hours or in the refrigerator for as long as 24 hours.

Meanwhile, preheat the oven to 400°F.

Slice about ¼ inch off the top of the garlic bulb. Brush the exposed top with a little olive oil. Wrap the garlic in a piece of foil and bake for 1 hour. Let cool to room temperature. (You can do this step up to 6 hours in advance. Keep at room temperature.)

Holding the root end of the garlic head, squeeze the now-soft garlic into a bowl. Add the feta, milk, and a little freshly ground pepper. Mix until creamy. (This can be done up to 2 hours in advance and refrigerated. Bring to room temperature before proceeding.)

Bring the lamb to room temperature if it has been refrigerated. This should take 45 minutes to 1 hour.

Preheat the oven to 500°F.

Discard all but ¼ cup of the marinade. Lay the lamb out on a work surface. Score, or make several shallow cuts, in the meat to help it roll more easily. Place the red pepper strips side by side down the middle of the lamb, leaving a 1-inch border around the edges. Place the whole basil leaves on top of the pepper strips. Gently spread the feta-garlic mixture on top of the basil leaves. Beginning with one long side, roll the lamb up jelly-roll fashion. It might be a little difficult to roll, but kitchen string will ultimately hold it together. (You can also try a diagonal roll. To do this, hold the left bottom corner of the lamb with one hand and the top right corner with the other hand. Gently twist the lamb, as if wringing out a towel, until the filling is encased. Proceed as follows.)

Secure the lamb by tying string around both ends as well as one or two places in the middle. Place the lamb in a roasting pan or baking dish.

Distribute the potatoes around the sides of the pan, and pour the reserved ¼ cup marinade over the lamb and potatoes. Stir the potatoes around to make sure they're well coated with the marinade. Lightly salt and pepper the surface of the lamb and the potatoes. Roast in the oven for 10 minutes. Turn the oven temperature down to 425°F and roast until a meat thermometer registers 160°F at the thickest part for medium rare, 35 to 40 minutes. (Roast 5 to 10 minutes longer for more well-done meat.)

Remove the pan from the oven, place the lamb and potatoes on a serving platter or carving board, and cover loosely with foil. Let sit for 15 minutes to allow the juices to flow through the meat.

To make the sauce, remove all but about 2 tablespoons of the fat from the roasting pan. Place the pan on the stove over one or two burners, and turn the heat to medium-high. Add the flour and stir quickly so it won't burn. Add the remaining ½ cup red wine and bring to a boil. Let it reduce by half, about 5 minutes. Add the stock and bring to boil. Reduce again by half, about 5 minutes, and add salt and pepper to taste.

Cut the kitchen string from the lamb. Slice the meat crosswise. Place a few potatoes on each plate, and drizzle with sauce.

Serves 6

CROWLEY CHEESE COMPANY

THE COMBINATION OF CRACKERS AND CHEESE is one that most people are introduced to early in life. It stands to reason, therefore, that the cheesemaker at Crowley Cheese Company, Michael Ward, had cracker-making on his resumé. First crackers, then cheese.

Ward came to Crowley in January 1998 and is carrying on the tradition that began there in the 1880s. Crowley is the oldest continuously operated cheese factory in America. Located in Healdville, Vermont, a tiny town in the south central part of the state, Crowley Cheese Company got its official start in 1882. Winfield Crowley began the company, and it passed on through his family until the late 1960s, when a retired school principal named Randolph Smith bought it. Smith grew the company, and after he died in 1984, his son took over. He left in 1997 when it was sold to an investor group.

The people who work for Crowley Cheese are quick to point out that their cheese is an American original. It is neither a Colby nor a cheddar, though it has been likened to both. Director of marketing Mark Brebach says that although it is technically classified as a Colby, it couldn't possibly be, because the Crowley cheese was created before the Wisconsin Colby was invented. Its characterization matters not as much as its taste, which is superb. The hands-on treatment from start to finish, the raw ingredients, and of course the cheesemaker, all guide Crowley cheese to its remarkable flavor.

After the basic steps of cheesemaking are followed, the making of the Crowley cheese starts to part ways from other cheese. First, the curds and whey are stirred for 1½ hours, until the curds are at the proper acid level. Three-quarters of the whey is then drained and the curds and the remaining whey are put in a curd tank. Once again the acid quotient rises to the desired level and the residual whey is drained. The curds are then washed with cool spring water, which Crowley says helps keep them moist. (By contrast, at this stage in cheddar-making, the curds are very small and most of their moisture has been pressed out.) The curds are then put into molds and pressed, and twenty-four hours later, it is cheese. Because it is made with raw cows' milk, the cheese is not sold for at least sixty days. The result of the Crowley cheesemaking method is a semi-soft cheese that has tiny "eyes," or holes, in it. It is perfect for eating on its own and equally good for cooking.

Once Crowley begins to age, it follows the path of a cheddar, though it retains a different flavor and a little more moisture. The mild Crowley is aged

---

WHAT THEY MAKE
Crowley: mild, medium, sharp, extra-sharp
Crowley flavored: caraway, dill, garlic, hot pepper,
  "muffalletta" (olive and garlic), onion, sage

HOW TO REACH THEM
Healdville, Vermont
800-683-2606
802-259-2340
802-259-2347 (fax)
website:
www.vtcheese.com/crowleystory.htm

from two to four months. The medium cheese is aged for four to eight months, the sharp is aged from nine to twelve months, and the extra-sharp is aged for over a year. They also have a host of flavored cheeses.

Steeped in tradition and handmade, Crowley cheese is produced on a small scale. In the course of a year, only about 100,000 pounds of cheese are made. That is the *daily* output of some larger cheesemakers. The seeming simplicity of the operation and its small-town roots run counter to the relative complexity of the cheese. This American original, as Crowley proudly proclaims, embodies much of what specialty cheesemaking is about: balanced yet assertive flavor, quality control, uniqueness, and an end product that manages to be entirely satisfying and never boring.

Cheese Enchiladas with Lime-Tomatillo Sauce

Cheese and Mexican food are inextricably linked. When you add American cheeses, you've got a bicultural affair, and in this case, a deeply satisfying dish. Tomatillos, sometimes called tomates vertes, *can be found in many mainstream and Latin markets. If you cannot find them, you can substitute the red tomato sauce used for the chiles rellenos on page 167, or use a purchased salsa. The sauce can be made in advance and kept at room temperature for four hours or overnight in the refrigerator. Bring it to room temperature before proceeding.*

FOR THE SAUCE

1 pound tomatillos, husks and stems removed

2 cloves garlic

1 to 2 serrano chiles (depending on desired spiciness)

¼ white onion, coarsely chopped

1 cup fresh cilantro leaves

¼ cup unsalted chicken stock

2 teaspoons fresh lime juice

½ teaspoon kosher salt

FOR THE ENCHILADAS

12 6-inch corn tortillas

About ¼ cup vegetable oil

12 ounces Monterey Jack cheese, coarsely grated

6 ounces Colby-style cheese, such as Crowley, coarsely grated (or use a mild cheddar)

½ cup crème fraîche or sour cream

Slivered zest of 1 lime (about 1 teaspoon), for garnish

To make the sauce: Bring a large pot of water to a boil. Add the tomatillos, garlic, and chile(s), and cook for 7 minutes. Remove ½ cup of the cooking water and drain the rest.

In a blender or food processor, combine the boiled ingredients and the reserved cooking water. Add the remaining sauce ingredients and blend until mixed but still slightly chunky. Taste, and add more salt if necessary. Set aside.

To prepare the enchiladas: Preheat the oven to 375°F.

Place the stack of tortillas next to the stove. Next to those, put 1 cup of the sauce in a shallow bowl, and next to that, a large plate or platter.

In a large sauté pan, heat the oil over medium heat. The oil should be ¼ to ½-inch deep. When the oil is hot but not smoking (about 325°F), put in 1 tortilla (tongs work well for this) and cook for about 10 seconds. You want the tortilla to become limp but not brown, so that you'll be able to roll it. Using the same tongs, run the tortilla through the bowl of sauce to give it a thin coating. Place it on the platter. Repeat with remaining tortillas, adding more oil to the pan if necessary.

Working with 1 tortilla at a time, spoon about ¼ cup of the Jack cheese down the center of the tortilla and roll it up. Place it in a baking pan that is large enough to hold all of the enchiladas, preferably in one layer. Repeat with the remaining tortillas and cheese, lining them up in the pan so that they are touching. Pour the remaining sauce over the enchiladas, and scatter the Colby cheese over the sauce. Cover with foil and bake for 20 minutes. Remove foil and bake for 5 more minutes. Drizzle with a little crème fraîche and top with the lime zest. Serve immediately.

Serves 4 to 6

JOE MATOS CHEESE FACTORY

THE CHANCES OF A CHEESE BEING ORDINARY are extremely low when that cheese arrives hand-stamped with a "thank you," and when it has been sent on the honor system rather than with the security of a credit card number. But that is exactly how the Matos family has been doing business since they began selling cheese, and it is a reflection of the honesty, simplicity, and purity that they bring to cheesemaking itself. Simply put, St. George cheese is one of the most distinguished cheeses in America today.

Like a lot of American cheese, St. George cheese has its roots in Europe. José ("Joe") and Mary Matos grew up on the island of São Jorge in the Azores, a group of islands off the coast of Portugal. (The cheese took on the English spelling once it was made here.) Three generations of cheesemakers preceded Joe Matos, but he wasn't terribly interested in the business himself. In 1965 the Matoses emigrated to the U.S., and in 1979, Mary (along with the local Portuguese community) convinced Joe that they should start making their beloved island cheese.

That "island cheese" is made in the middle of one of California's wine regions, in Sonoma County, near the city of Santa Rosa. It is a raw milk cheese made with the milk of the Matoses' Holsteins. Despite the fact that the cheese is aged a minimum of two months, it has an intoxicating fresh milk flavor and aroma. The tiny eyes, the yellowish color of the paste, the melting qualities when it's young, and the nuttiness when it is aged make St. George one of the most versatile and fulfilling cheeses around.

The Matoses make only St. George cheese, and recently their daughter, Sylvia Tucker, has been the cheesemaker, learning her craft exclusively through on-the-job training. She has never taken a class. Although their cheese has become immensely popular, the Matos operation remains small, since, Sylvia says, "My parents are very old-fashioned." That means that phone orders are taken but credit card numbers aren't. They send you the cheese; you send them the check. Paradoxically, before becoming a cheesemaker, Sylvia worked in a bank helping business customers set up credit card accounts.

MATOS CHEESE FACTORY
QUEIJO TIPO SAO JORGE

This type of honest hard work can't help but be reflected in the cheese itself. Joe Matos still gets up every day before dawn and milks his cows. Since St. George is its own cheese, it can only be described as the best of a fruity Jack cheese with the consistency of Havarti and a little cheddar-like flavor thrown in. As a table cheese, St. George not only brings the taste buds to life, it also awakens the sense of smell, which is involuntarily seduced by the perfumy and fresh milk aroma. Perhaps that is the fragrance of the Azores.

WHAT THEY MAKE
St. George

HOW TO REACH THEM
Santa Rosa, California
707-584-5283 (mail order available)

Cheese Chiles Rellenos

A cheese-stuffed chile, or chile relleno, is one of the finest—and most flexible—showcases for cheese. I use Joe Matos' St. George cheese, but if you cannot get it, all you need to know is that the St. George has the same melting qualities as a Monterey Jack and the slightly sharper flavor of a cheddar.

---

8 pasilla or poblano chiles
1 tablespoon olive oil
6 large ripe tomatoes (about 3 pounds total), peeled, seeded, and diced
1 white onion, coarsely chopped
2 cloves garlic, minced
Salt and freshly ground pepper, to taste
2⅔ cups coarsely grated Matos' St. George cheese (about 12 ounces), or use Monterey Jack and/or cheddar
4 eggs, separated
1 cup all-purpose flour
2 teaspoons kosher salt
Vegetable oil for frying
¼ cup crumbled cotija cheese (or use feta)

Using tongs, roast the chiles over a medium gas flame until they are blackened all over (or roast them on a low shelf under the broiler). Place them in a plastic or paper bag and close it tightly. Let sit for 15 minutes. Remove the chiles from the bag. Using a sharp paring knife, gently scrape away the charred skin, being careful not to break the flesh of the chiles. Make a small slit in each chile and remove the seeds. Set aside.

In a large sauté pan, heat the olive oil over medium-high heat. Add the tomatoes, onions, and garlic. Cover and cook until all the ingredients are very soft, 15 to 20 minutes. Turn off the heat and spoon the ingredients into a food mill fitted with the blade with the smallest holes. Puree the mixture back into the same pan, add

salt and pepper to taste, and keep warm. (Alternatively, use a blender or food processor.)

Fill each chile with about ⅓ cup cheese, being careful not to tear the chile. (If it does get torn, use a toothpick to hold the chile together.)

In a medium-size bowl, beat the egg whites until stiff peaks form. Stir in the egg yolks. Mix the flour and salt together on a plate. Coat each chile with the flour mixture and then dip it in the egg mixture.

In a large sauté pan, heat about ½ inch of vegetable oil to 325°F. Place a paper towel-lined plate or baking sheet next to the stove. Put as many chiles as will fit in the hot oil. Do not crowd them. Turn occasionally, and cook until they turn a deep golden brown, 5 to 7 minutes. Transfer them to the plate and repeat with any remaining chiles.

Put the chiles on a serving platter or on individual plates. Place a large spoonful of the tomato sauce on each chile, and sprinkle with a little cotija cheese. Serve immediately. If there is extra sauce, serve it on the side.

Serves 4 as a main course, 8 as a first course

Note: If you prefer to bake rather than fry the chiles, preheat the oven to 350°F. Prepare the chiles as instructed. Place the filled chiles in a baking dish and bake for 20 minutes or until golden brown. Assemble as described.

Goat Cheese, Apricot, and Sage-Stuffed Chicken Breasts

The Japanese panko crumbs that are used to coat these chicken breasts are much coarser and lighter than regular bread crumbs. Because of this, they create an extremely crunchy exterior. The result is a crackling bite that leads to the soothing, creamy filling. These special crumbs can be found in Japanese markets and at many supermarkets. If you cannot find them, make or buy coarse bread crumbs and lightly toast them. This dish is particularly versatile since you can serve the chicken breasts whole or you can slice them into roulades for a dressier presentation.

---

1 tablespoon olive oil
1 cup finely chopped yellow onion (about ½ large onion)
2 small cloves garlic, minced
1 tablespoon chopped fresh sage leaves
Salt and freshly ground pepper
¼ cup dried apricots (about 2 ounces), plumped in hot water, drained, and chopped into ¼-inch pieces
½ cup fresh goat cheese (2 to 3 ounces), (or use fromage blanc or softened cream cheese)
2 whole boneless, skinless chicken breasts (about 2 pounds total), each cut in half lengthwise
1 egg, lightly beaten
1 cup Japanese panko crumbs or use toasted coarse bread crumbs
5 tablespoons unsalted butter
2 tablespoons white wine
½ cup unsalted chicken stock
Whole fresh sage leaves, for garnish

Preheat the oven to 400°F.

In a medium-size sauté pan, heat the olive oil over medium-high heat. Add the onions and cook for 5 minutes. Turn the heat down to medium and add the garlic. Cook for 5 minutes, stirring frequently. Don't let the onions and garlic brown. Next, add the chopped sage and salt and pepper to taste, and cook until the onions are translucent, 5 to 10 minutes. Add the apricots and cook until heated through, 5 minutes. Remove the pan from the heat and let cool for 10 minutes. Thoroughly mix in the goat cheese and set aside. (This can be made up to 24 hours in advance and refrigerated. Bring to room temperature before stuffing the chicken breasts.)

Place each chicken breast between two pieces of plastic wrap. With a kitchen mallet, a cleaver, or a heavy tin can, such as a can of tomatoes, pound the breasts until they are between ⅛ and ¼ inch thick. (They will not roll easily if they are too thick.) Season with salt and pepper.

Spread about ¼ cup of the stuffing down the center of each chicken breast. Fold up the short ends of the chicken breast, and then roll one

long side jelly-roll-fashion to the other side. Tie the ends with string to secure them.

Place the egg in a shallow bowl and the panko crumbs in another shallow bowl. Dip the chicken in the egg, and then roll in the panko crumbs until completely coated. In an ovenproof sauté pan, melt 4 tablespoons of the butter over medium-high heat. Place the chicken in the pan and brown on all sides, about 8 minutes. Then put the pan in the oven and bake until the chicken is a deep golden color and firm when pressed, 10 to 12 minutes.

After the chicken breasts come out of the oven, remove the strings and put them on a warmed platter; tent with foil. Next, place the pan over high heat and deglaze it with the wine. Boil until reduced to about 1 tablespoon, 1 to 2 minutes, and then add the chicken stock. Boil until reduced by half, 3 to 5 minutes, and add salt and pepper to taste. Remove from the heat and swirl in the remaining 1 tablespoon butter.

Cut each breast in half crosswise and place one half on its side on the plate. Lean the second half against the first, facing down. Drizzle with the sauce, garnish with sage leaves, and serve immediately.

Serves 4

Note: For a slightly different presentation, cut the chicken breasts into ½-inch-thick slices and fan them out on each plate. Drizzle with the sauce and garnish with sage leaves before serving.

Spinach and Fromage Blanc-Stuffed Chicken Breasts

Fromage blanc is a fresh cheese similar to ricotta, though it is more tangy than ricotta. It's mild in flavor, and because of its smooth consistency, it adds a silkiness to almost any dish. This dish is no exception, since the fromage blanc acts as a binder for the spinach, yet it's lighter than the creamed spinach we remember from a couple of decades ago. You can make the stuffing in advance and refrigerate it for up to twenty-four hours. Do not, however, stuff the chicken until you're ready to cook it.

One other note: This recipe works equally well with bone-in pork loin chops. Prepare it the the same way as you would the chicken, but instead of filling and rolling the meat, simply cut a 1-inch-long slit in the chops to stuff them.

FOR THE CHICKEN
2 whole boneless, skinless chicken breasts
(about 2 pounds total), cut in half
lengthwise

FOR THE MARINADE
¼ cup apple cider or apple juice
2 tablespoons red wine vinegar
1 tablespoon balsamic vinegar
1 teaspoon dry mustard
1 teaspoon prepared horseradish
2 tablespoons olive oil
Dash of salt

FOR THE FILLING
4 strips bacon, chopped
2 cloves garlic, finely chopped
1 small shallot, finely chopped
1 bunch fresh spinach (about ½ pound),
rinsed, dried, and finely chopped
½ teaspoon kosher salt

¼ teaspoon freshly ground pepper
⅛ teaspoon grated nutmeg
4 ounces fromage blanc (or use fresh goat
cheese, ricotta cheese, or cream cheese)
beaten with 1 tablespoon milk or cream
2 egg yolks, lightly beaten
Olive oil

To prepare the chicken: Place each chicken breast between two pieces of plastic wrap. With a kitchen mallet, a cleaver, or a heavy tin can, such as a can of tomatoes, pound the breasts until they are each between ⅛ and ¼ inch thick. (They will not roll easily if they are too thick.) Season the chicken with salt and pepper.

To make the marinade: In a small nonreactive bowl, combine all the marinade ingredients and mix well. Arrange the chicken in a single layer in a large glass dish and pour the marinade over. Cover and marinate the chicken for 1 hour at room temperature or for up to 3 hours in the refrigerator. Bring to room temperature before continuing.

To make the filling: In a large sauté pan, fry the bacon until brown but still slightly flexible. Drain on paper towels. Reserve 3 tablespoons of the bacon fat in the pan. Turn the heat to medium-low and add the garlic and shallots. Cook, stirring frequently, until they are translucent but not brown, 5 to 7 minutes. Add the spinach, cover, and cook just until wilted, about 5 minutes. Add the reserved bacon and the coarse salt, pepper, and nutmeg. Set aside and allow to cool slightly.

When the filling is lukewarm, add the fromage blanc and the egg yolks, and mix well. (You can make the filling up to 24 hours in advance and refrigerate it. Bring to room temperature before proceeding.)

Preheat the oven to 400°F.

To assemble: Oil a medium-size flameproof baking pan. Remove the chicken from the marinade, pat dry, and put on a large plate. Reserve the marinade. Salt and pepper the chicken. Place about 2 tablespoons of the filling in the middle of each chicken breast. Roll the chicken breasts, starting at one long side, and place them seam side down in the baking pan. (If necessary, use a toothpick to keep the seam closed.) Drizzle with olive oil. Bake until the chicken is firm but still slightly springy to the touch and light brown in color, 20 to 25 minutes. Remove the chicken from the pan and keep warm.

Place the pan on the stove over medium-high heat. Add ¼ cup of the marinade and boil until reduced by half, about 5 minutes. Pour over the chicken and serve immediately.

Serves 4

Orzo Feta Salad with Grilled Shrimp and Mint-Scallion Chutney

"Cool" and "refreshing" come to mind when this dish comes to the table. The orzo salad (orzo is rice-shaped pasta) is served at room temperature, creating a summertime staple all on its own. The cool mint in the chutney gets a lift from the addition of scallions, and together they add exuberance and zest to the grilled shrimp. Think about making this cooling recipe during the hottest days of summer.

FOR THE SHRIMP

1 pound (about 24) medium shrimp, shelled
   and deveined
Olive oil
Salt and freshly ground pepper
4 bamboo skewers, soaked in water for 1
   hour (or use metal skewers)

FOR THE CHUTNEY

2½ cups (about 40) fresh mint leaves
5 scallions, white parts only, chopped
2 tablespoons slivered almonds, toasted
⅛ teaspoon kosher salt
3½ tablespoons olive oil

FOR THE SALAD

½ pound orzo
4 tablespoons olive oil
1 cup slivered fresh basil leaves (chiffonade)
8 ounces feta cheese, crumbled (about 1 cup)
¾ cup slivered almonds, toasted
1 cup fresh spinach leaves (about 2 ounces),
   slivered
¼ cup fresh lemon juice
Salt and freshly ground pepper

To prepare the shrimp: Place 6 shrimp on each skewer. Coat the shrimp with olive oil and salt and pepper to taste. Cover and set aside for up to 1 hour at room temperature or 2 hours refrigerated.

To make the chutney: In a food processor or blender, combine all the chutney ingredients.

Process until the ingredients are uniformly chopped into tiny pieces, about 30 seconds. The chutney will be chunky. Cover, and set aside for up to 2 hours at room temperature or overnight in the refrigerator.

To make the salad: Bring a medium-large pot of salted water to a boil. Add the orzo and cook until firm but tender, about 6 minutes. Drain, and immediately run cold water over the pasta. Drain well and place in a large bowl. Add the olive oil to the orzo and mix to coat. Then add all the remaining ingredients. Mix well. Taste, and add more salt and pepper if needed. Let sit at room temperature for about 1 hour to let the flavors meld together. (The salad can be made ahead and refrigerated overnight. Bring to room temperature before serving.)

To assemble: In the middle of four dinner plates, spoon about 1 cup of the salad.

Prepare a grill, or preheat the broiler.

Grill or broil the shrimp for 2 to 3 minutes on one side. Turn and cook for 1 to 2 minutes more, or until they feel slightly firm to the touch and have turned pink.

Place each skewer diagonally across the salad. Spoon a little chutney across the shrimp, and serve immediately. Serve any remaining chutney on the side.

Serves 4

MAIN COURSES

BASS LAKE CHEESE FACTORY

ABOUT TWENTY-FIVE MILES NORTHEAST of Minneapolis and St. Paul, the Bass Lake Cheese Factory quietly produces fifty-two different cheeses. Bass Lake is just over the Wisconsin border in Somerset, in the heart of the St. Croix Valley. Its proximity to the Twin Cities belies its rural expanse. It is this pastoral setting, as well as the cheese, that regularly beckons city-dwellers. Scott Erickson, a forestry and fish expert, is the unlikely cheesemaker and owner of this prolific cheese plant.

With a repertoire of over four dozen cheeses, and with the word "factory" in its name, it would seem that the Bass Lake Cheese Factory would be a maze of machinery and activity. It is not. Erickson still makes all of his cheeses by hand; his wife, Julie, runs the business; and their son Nick, at age fifteen, is Wisconsin's youngest certified cheesemaker. He, too, helps with the cheese.

Drawing from the milk of cows, goats, and sheep, Bass Lake makes a wide variety of cheeses. Among them are the traditional Wisconsin cheeses, such as the potent German brick and beerkaese, as well as Bass Lake's own creations, including a cinnamon-coated sheep's milk cheese they call Canasta Pardo. This is a semi-soft cheese that is pressed and formed in a basket. Once the cheese is set, it is sprinkled with a heavy dose of cinnamon, accenting the basket-weave pattern on the cheese. This cinnamon coating makes the cheese a natural complement to fruit, but it also provides an unusual twist with savory foods. A Mediterranean pasta enters the realm of the exotic when a little grated cinnamon-coated cheese is added. Bass Lake also makes a sheep's milk mozzarella-style cheese called Ewezarella.

Another unique invention is Bass Lake's Muenster Del Ray (Ray is Erickson's middle name). It is a round cheese with an orange basket-weave rind, but it is more assertive than the muenster made by most producers in the United States. It is not, however, a washed-rind cheese like those made in France. It is wildly popular among visitors to the cheese factory, many of whom reportedly walk away with two or three rounds of it at a time.

Despite the number of cheeses the Ericksons make, they still do everything by hand. This allows them to stay in control of their cheeses and to continually monitor the quality. Additionally, Scott Erickson is involved with improving overall cheese and dairy standards in the area.

Those who have never seen cheesemaking would be well advised to visit this operation because of its hands-on nature as well as the "mystery" factor: With so many cheeses, you never know what will be in the vat on that day.

WHAT THEY MAKE
Cows' milk cheeses
Beer Kaese
Blue cheese
Cheddar: mild to aged
Cheddar curds: plain and
  flavored
Creamy Gouda
Creamy smoked Gouda
Colby: fresh and aged
Farmer
German brick
Limberger
Monterey Jack: plain and
  flavored
Mozzarella
Muenster Del Ray
Oaxaca

Provolone
Swiss cheese

Goats' milk cheeses
Fresh chèvre: natural and
  flavored
Jack: plain and flavored
Colby
Gouda
Muenster: plain and flavored

Sheep's milk cheeses
Canasta Pardo
Ewezarella

Blended cheeses
Mezcla Kassari (sheep and cow)

HOW TO REACH THEM
Somerset, Wisconsin
800-368-2437 or 715-247-5586
715-549-6617 (fax)
website: www.blcheese.com

Grilled Pork Chops with Cheddar-Corn Spoon Bread and Apple-Sage Chutney

✦✦✦

Digging into a piping hot casserole of spoon bread, helping the melted cheese stretch and twist its way out of the dish, and piling the steaming yellow pudding-like mixture onto a plate along with a spicy chutney and a hearty grilled pork chop is my definition of heaven. Add to that the fact that most of the work comes the day before serving the dish, and it becomes a recipe that's a joy to make as well as eat. The pork chops are best marinated overnight, and the chutney is also better when made the day before to allow the flavors to mingle. The spoon bread, a kind of cornbread soufflé/pudding, should be eaten soon after it is baked. Serve this with some sautéed bitter greens, such as Swiss chard or spicy mustard greens.

FOR THE PORK CHOPS
4 bone-in loin pork chops (8 to 12 ounces each)
2½ tablespoons Dijon mustard
1½ tablespoons Calvados (apple brandy) or apple juice
2 teaspoons red wine vinegar
3 tablespoons olive oil
2 teaspoons chopped fresh sage leaves
Freshly ground black pepper

FOR THE CHUTNEY
1¼ cups cider vinegar
5 tablespoons packed light brown sugar
1¼ pounds Granny Smith apples (about 2½ apples), peeled, cored, and chopped into ¾-inch cubes
Juice from 1 lemon (about ¼ cup)
Grated zest of 1 lemon (about 1½ tablespoons)
Heaping ⅛ teaspoon crushed red pepper flakes
1 teaspoon mustard seeds
⅓ cup golden raisins
1 yellow onion, chopped (about 1 cup)
2 teaspoons chopped fresh sage leaves

FOR THE SPOON BREAD

¾ cup fresh corn kernels (or use ¾ cup
   drained canned or defrosted frozen corn)
¾ cup yellow cornmeal
2 teaspoons kosher salt
2 teaspoons baking powder
1½ teaspoons sugar
Freshly ground pepper
2 cups whole or low-fat milk
1 cup buttermilk
¼ cup (½ stick) unsalted butter, melted
3 large eggs, separated, yolks lightly beaten
2 teaspoons chopped fresh sage leaves
4 ounces sharp cheddar cheese, such as Bass
   Lake cheddar, coarsely grated (about 1 cup)

To marinate the pork chops: In a nonreactive dish, arrange the chops in one layer. In a small bowl, mix together the mustard, Calvados, vinegar, olive oil, sage, and pepper to taste. Pour over the chops, and coat both sides with the marinade. Cover and refrigerate at least 6 hours or overnight.

To make the chutney: In a medium-size heavy-bottomed saucepan, combine the vinegar and brown sugar and bring to a boil. Cook until the mixture is reduced by one third, 5 to 10 minutes. Add the apples, lemon juice and zest, red pepper flakes, mustard seeds, raisins, and onions. Stir the ingredients together, turn the heat to a low simmer, partially cover, and cook for 30 minutes. Stir occasionally—gently, so as not to break apart the apples.

Add the chopped sage and cook until the apples are very soft and the vinegar has mellowed, 30 to 40 minutes. You may need to add a little extra brown sugar. The mixture should be thick. If you will be serving the chutney the same day, let it sit at room temperature for 2 hours before serving. Otherwise, refrigerate it overnight and bring it to room temperature.

To make the spoon bread: About an hour before serving time, preheat the oven to 375°F. Butter a 2-quart casserole or soufflé dish.

In a small saucepan, bring about 1 cup of water to a boil. Add the corn and blanch for 1 minute. Drain, and run cold water over it to stop the cooking process. Pat dry and set aside.

Place the cornmeal in a large heatproof bowl. In another bowl, mix the salt, baking powder, sugar, and pepper together and set aside.

In a 1-quart saucepan, bring the milk to a low boil over medium heat. (Watch to be sure it doesn't boil over.) Pour over the cornmeal, stirring until all lumps are gone and the cornmeal has thickened slightly, 2 to 3 minutes. Add the buttermilk, melted butter, egg yolks, corn, and sage. Mix well. Stir in the reserved dry ingredients.

In a mixing bowl, beat 2 egg whites until stiff peaks form. (Save the third egg white for another use.) Gently fold into the cornmeal mixture, along with half of the cheese. Mix just enough to incorporate the egg whites, but try not to overmix. Pour into the prepared casserole. Sprinkle with the remaining ½ cup cheese.

Bake for 40 to 45 minutes, or until the cheese is brown and the center is still somewhat loose, jiggling slightly when touched. Let cool for 5 minutes before serving.

To cook the pork chops: While the spoon bread is baking, prepare a grill or preheat the broiler.

Remove the pork chops from the marinade and grill or broil on one side for 6 to 7 minutes. Turn and cook on the other side until the meat feels firm but still gives slightly, 5 to 7 minutes more. The meat should be light pink on the inside.

To assemble: If serving on individual plates, place one chop on each plate. Spoon some chutney over it. Dollop a generous portion of spoon bread next to the pork chop, and serve.

If serving on a platter, simply place all of the chops on the platter and spoon chutney over them. Serve the spoon bread on the side.

Serves 4

VERMONT SHEPHERD

CYNTHIA AND DAVID MAJOR are heralded as two of the best cheesemakers in the United States, despite their inauspicious beginning. For the first three years of making Vermont Shepherd Cheese, they produced what Cindy Major calls "sawdust." On top of that, the Majors could not get their farm out of the red, even though it had been a gift from David's parents.

Not willing to give up, they went to France to learn how to make the prized *brebis*, or Pyrenees sheep's milk cheese. Armed with samples of their own cheese, they met with sheep cheese producers whose uniform response to their cheese was that it was awful. But the kindness of strangers set them on a path that would catapult them to exemplary cheesemaking status in this country.

They returned to the U.S. and in 1993, five months after they had made their cheese the "new" way, they cut their first wheel. Much to their relief, it tasted just like the cheese they'd eaten in France. "It was the most amazing feeling," Cindy says. "I haven't been able to duplicate that feeling since."

That feeling comes from the taste of their gamy, nutty cheese that, depending on its age, might finish with a hint of fruit. It is a luscious golden-yellow color and evokes images of the earth because of both its taste and its tan-colored rind. This cheese is carefully aged, which adds to the earthy impression. The rusticity and complex flavors elevate the Vermont Shepherd Cheese to star status in this country.

In addition to the cheese itself, the Majors have developed a sophisticated cheesemaking and aging system. Much of the cheese is actually made by several nearby sheep dairy farmers. These farmers have had to undergo extensive education to learn how to make the cheese to the Majors' exact specifications. Along the way, the cheese and cheesemaking is subject to inspection to make sure that it is being done correctly. When it is ready, the cheese is then given to Cindy and David, who age it in their remarkable underground caves.

Vermont Shepherd Cheese

Ingredients: Sheep's Milk, Lactic Cultures, Enzymes, Salt
Vermont Shepherd
RFD #3 • Box 265 • Putney, VT 05346
vtsheprd@sover.net

The Majors have just begun to venture into cows' milk cheesemaking, using the milk from a neighbor's cows. The Putney Tomme is a golden, aged cheese that when young, has hints of apple, but acquires a deep earthiness as it develops. Timson Hill is their other new cows' milk cheese, named after a road nearby. Vermont Shepherd has set a new cheesemaking (and aging) standard for this country. As more sheep's milk cheeses begin to be made here, that standard will surely raise the quality of sheep cheese across the board—and across the country.

WHAT THEY MAKE
Sheep's milk cheese
Vermont Shepherd Cheese

Cows' milk cheeses
Putney Tomme
Timson Hill

HOW TO REACH THEM
Putney, Vermont
802-387-4473
802-387-2041 (fax)
website: www.vermontshepherd.com

Slow-Roasted Salmon with Arugula, Tomato Jam, and Cheese

One of this country's best chefs can be found in the small mountain town of Aspen, Colorado. Charles Dale, owner and chef at Aspen's Renaissance Restaurant, is a true talent, and because of that his recognition extends far beyond the Rocky Mountains. This recipe is just one example of his talent.

This dish is unquestionably a main course, although with the bruschetta, sweet tomato jam, and salmon topped with a pile of arugula and a scattering of cheese, it may seem more like a salad. For that reason, it makes a perfect summertime meal. But don't be fooled: it is elaborate, festive, and show-stopping. You can use just about any type of hard cheese you like. Just be sure it has a full-bodied flavor or it will get lost in the spicy arugula and wonderfully sweet tomato jam.

As you will see, the salmon is cooked at a very low temperature, called slow-roasting, and as a result never really browns on the outside. The idea is that the fish should be just cooked and still slightly translucent. It may look undercooked, but it will not be. If you like your fish more well done, simply cook it 10 to 15 minutes longer than the recipe says. Either way, this dish will be warm rather than piping hot, making it particularly nice in the summer.

MAIN COURSES

FOR THE SALMON
4 salmon fillets (6 to 8 ounces each), preferably with skin
1 teaspoon chopped lemon zest
2 tablespoons kosher salt
2 tablespoons raw sugar, or 1 tablespoon refined sugar
1 tablespoon chopped fresh oregano leaves
¼ cup whiskey, such as Jack Daniels

FOR THE TOMATO JAM
6 large ripe tomatoes (about 1½ pounds, total) peeled (see page 128), seeded, and coarsely chopped
2 cloves garlic, finely chopped
¼ cup red wine vinegar
¼ cup sugar (if the tomatoes are quite sweet, reduce to 3 tablespoons)
Pinch of salt

FOR THE SALAD
½ pound arugula (about 12 cups)
3 tablespoons extra-virgin olive oil
¼ cup fresh lemon juice
4 tablespoons large capers, rinsed and drained (or use dried salted capers, rinsed and soaked in water for at least 1 hour)
Salt and freshly ground pepper
2 ounces hard cheese, such as Vermont Shepherd, shaved paper-thin (or use any hard aged cow, sheep, or goat cheese)
Four ½-inch-thick slices hearty country bread

(continued on page 180)

To marinate the salmon: In a glass baking dish or a plastic container, place the fish skin side down in a single layer. Mix the remaining ingredients together in a small bowl, and spoon this marinade over the fish. Cover and refrigerate for 2 to 3 hours before cooking. Do not cure it overnight.

To make the jam: In a nonreactive saucepan, combine all the jam ingredients and set the mixture over very low heat. Gently simmer until it has a jamlike consistency, about 2 hours. If it is watery, cook it a little longer. (The jam can be made 24 hours in advance and refrigerated. Gently heat it before serving.)

To cook the salmon: Preheat the oven to 225°F. Oil an ovenproof pan or baking sheet.

Scrape a *small* amount of the marinade off the fish (it will be a little too salty otherwise). Transfer the fillets to the oiled pan, and slow-roast until the salmon splits slightly when squeezed, 20 to 25 minutes. It will look slightly underdone because it retains its bright pink color and browns very little on the outside with this cooking method. To remove the skin, hold the skin down with a small fork and gently lift the salmon off with a spatula.

To make the salad: In a medium salad bowl, toss all the salad ingredients *except* the cheese.

To assemble: Brush the bread with a small amount of oil, and toast it. Turn slices, brush with oil, and toast. Place 1 slice of toast on each plate. Spread about ¼ cup of the tomato jam and on each toast. Lay the salmon on top of the jam, and top with the arugula salad. Scatter a few cheese shavings over the salad. Twist a little fresh pepper over the cheese. Serve immediately.

Serves 4

OPPOSITE: Emmentaler Savoy Cabbage-Stuffed Potatoes (see page 196).

VEGETABLES and SIDE DISHES

Black Beans with Cotija Cheese

Although these beans make a fine dish alongside a green salad and maybe some spicy rice, I like to serve them as an accompaniment to the Pork and Oaxaca Cheese Quesadillas on page 76. They are equally wonderful with the Chili-Pecan Biscotti on page 70. In fact, I have served all three items together and have loved the combination.

Cotija is another of the several Mexican cheeses that are gaining in popularity (and cheesemaking) in the United States. It is very dry, crumbly, and salty, which means that a little goes a long way. Also, because of its dryness, it is not a melting cheese. It is mild, though, and can be served in a variety of ways, including as a substitute for salt in baked potatoes or in a salad.

You may use canned beans rather than dried, if you prefer. To do so, eliminate the soaking stage. Instead, sauté the onions and cumin as instructed, add the beans with their liquid, and cook just until heated through. Add only a small amount of salt since canned beans usually come already salted. If using dried beans, plan to start this dish a day ahead.

VEGETABLES AND SIDE DISHES

---

2 cups dried black beans (or two 16-ounce cans black beans with their liquid)
1½ tablespoons olive oil
2 white onions, chopped
1 tablespoon ground cumin
About 4 cups unsalted chicken stock or water (or use some of each)
Salt and freshly ground pepper
3 ounces cotija cheese, crumbled (or use feta)
2 medium tomatoes, chopped, for garnish
¼ cup finely chopped fresh cilantro, for garnish

The day before serving, place the beans in a large pot and add water to extend 3 inches above the beans. Soak overnight. (Or if you forget to soak the beans the night before, place them in a large pot and cover with water 3 inches above the beans. Bring to a boil and immediately turn off the heat. Cover and let sit for about 1½ hours.) Pour the beans into a colander and drain off the soaking liquid.

In the same pot, heat the olive oil over medium heat. Add the onions and cook until translucent, about 10 minutes. Add the cumin and stir to coat the onions. Let cook 2 minutes, stirring constantly so the cumin will not burn. Add the beans and cover with the stock. Bring to a boil and skim off the foam from the beans. Partially cover and reduce the heat to a simmer. Add salt and pepper to taste. Simmer gently until the beans are cooked through but not mushy, about 1 hour. For a thicker consistency, remove the cover and boil some of the liquid away. Using a slotted spoon, scoop up the beans and place them in a shallow bowl. Sprinkle with the cheese, and then garnish with the tomato and cilantro. Serve immediately.

Serves 6 to 8

YERBA SANTA DAIRY

THE WELL-WORN SAYING "necessity is the mother of invention" is almost certainly part of the explanation for one of this country's best cheeses. That cheese is called Alpine Shepherd's Cheese and is the product of Jan and Chris Twohy.

Alpine Shepherd's Cheese is a hard goats' milk cheese that the Twohys invented nearly twenty years ago, in large part through trial and error. Although they had always intended to make a hard cheese of some kind, their equipment led the way to the Shepherd's Cheese.

That equipment came from an old Camembert factory, and among the accoutrements were nylon bags. Unsure what to do with them, the Twohys filled them with the raw milk curds and laid a weighted board on them for pressing. This was successful, although Jan had to work on tying the bags in a certain way to achieve the desired shape. In addition, they had bought a converted bulk tank that heats from the bottom up. This type of tank is necessary to achieve the grana-type texture (dry and granular) in their cheese. This was the beginning of their exalted Alpine Shepherd's Cheese.

The process remains essentially the same today. Once the cheese is pressed (in the nylon bags), it is air-dried in the 48° to 51°F aging room for up to fourteen months. The surface of the cheese is kept very dry to discourage mold growth. The result is an earthy and nutty hard cheese that complements a slice of summer melon as well as it does a winter risotto. It has a deceptively smooth surface that belies the explosion of textures once it hits the tongue. It is also a beautiful golden color that is gentle and appealing.

Yerba santa is a type of chaparral that produces clusters of white trumpet-shaped flowers. It was a natural name for this dairy that sits amongst the wild growth. Alpine Shepherd's Cheese is so named because the Twohys have speculated that their cheese is probably similar to one made by mountain shepherds. "Because of the simplistic make technique, the shepherds could have made it on a hillside camp and cooked it over a fire, the same way ours is heated from below," Jan explains. The shepherds could then bring the cheese down from the hills in good shape. It lent itself to aging, which meant a long-term supply of cheese.

(continued on page 184)

WHAT THEY MAKE
Alpine Shepherd's Cheese
Chevito
Fresh chèvre

HOW TO REACH THEM
Lakeport, California
707-263-8131

Chevito is another of the Twohys' cheeses and earns its name from the Spanish *chivito*, which means "little goat." Chevito is a gravity-drained semi-soft cheese sold at farmers' markets and to some restaurants and retail stores.

The Twohys currently have about fifty goats, all of which roam the pastures around the house and dairy. In the summer they lease an additional twenty-five goats from a neighbor. Only now are they installing full power and a phone line in the cheesemaking room, proving once again that the fusion between craftsmanship and science—not technology—is the secret to great cheese.

Cheese-Coated Asparagus

It is always a welcome surprise when a dish is both easy and flavorful. This one hits both marks. It also hits the eye-pleasing mark, with the bright green asparagus bathed in patches of melted cheese. This dish is best served very hot, so don't broil the asparagus until just before you're ready to eat.

¾ pound fresh asparagus, rinsed, ends cut off
2 teaspoons olive oil
Kosher salt, to taste
2 ounces aged goats' or sheep's milk cheese, such as Alpine Shepherd or Vermont Shepherd, thinly shaved (or use an aged cows' milk cheese, such as Asiago, Stravecchio, or dry Jack)

Preheat the broiler.

Bring a medium-size sauté pan with about 3 inches of water to a boil. Add the asparagus and cook until bright green, about 2 minutes (a little less if using pencil-thin asparagus). Drain immediately, and run cold water over the asparagus. Dry between sheets of paper towels.

In a broiler pan, toss the asparagus and the olive oil, making sure the asparagus is well coated. Sprinkle a little salt on the asparagus. (You don't want to use too much because the cheese is salty.) Lay the cheese shavings over the middle of the asparagus, leaving about 1 inch of the ends and tips exposed.

Broil for 2 to 2½ minutes, or until the edges of the asparagus turn slightly brown and the cheese is melted and bubbling. Serve immediately.

Serves 4

BELLWETHER FARMS

AS THE FIRST SHEEP DAIRY IN THE STATE OF CALIFORNIA, Bellwether Farms began on a wing and a prayer. Owner Cindy Callahan, along with her husband, Ed, who was a doctor, bought their land north of San Francisco with the idea of retiring to a rural existence far from Ed's medical world. (Cindy had abandoned her legal practice a few years before.) They decided to purchase sheep to help graze the land, as well as to develop a lambing business. Their lamb is considered to be among the best, and Bay Area restaurants clamor to buy it.

Wanting to expand their business, they decided to breed their sheep for dairy purposes. But since no sheep dairies existed in California, finding local experts was akin to finding grazing land in the middle of a Minnesota winter—impossible. After much research, the Callahans embarked on cheesemaking, but not before enrolling in a few university courses and taking a couple of trips to Italy to learn from master cheesemakers there.

Since that time, Bellwether has turned into a family affair, although sadly, Ed Callahan passed away a few years ago. Now son Liam makes the cheese with his mother nearby. Cindy's other son, Brett, works on the farm and delivers cheese, and Liam's wife, Diana, helps with cheesemaking as well as some of the accounting and marketing responsibilities.

The result of this family effort is cheese that is indicative of the pioneering efforts going on in American cheesemaking today. The Bellwether sheep's milk cheeses, among them an aged Toscano, truly rival their Tuscan counterparts. Toscano is a hard cheese that sings out buttery, nutty, and fruity flavors. It can be eaten as is or grated. The black pepper-studded Pepato is a spicy version of the Toscano. Its rustic appearance alone is enough to entice anyone to dig into a wheel. The peppery, earthy flavors that follow are just as rewarding. San Andreas is an aged sheep's milk cheese named after the famous earthquake fault on which the Bellwether property sits. It is slightly younger than the Toscano, but

---

WHAT THEY MAKE

Cows' milk cheeses
Blue cheese
Carmody
Crescenza
Fromage blanc
Ricotta

Sheep's milk cheeses
Caciotta
Pepato
Ricotta
San Andreas
Toscana

HOW TO REACH THEM
Valley Ford, California
707-763-0993
888-527-8606 (mail order only)
707-763-2443 (fax)
website: www.bellwethercheese.com

Bellwether's Tuscan-style sheep's milk Pepato, so named because of the black peppercorns, will age for two to three months before being sold.

still has the mature taste of an aged sheep's milk cheese. Although excellent eaten along with some sun-dried tomatoes or even a slice of fennel, the San Andreas is also a wonderful melting cheese.

Bellwether's cows' milk cheeses, such as an Italian table cheese called Carmody (the name of the lane on which they live) and the crescenza, a silky, soft, oozing cheese that looks melted before it is ever touched by heat, are exemplary in their class. The exclusive use of rich, golden-colored Jersey cow milk ensures the full flavor of their cheeses, and the quality is maintained by relying on only one source for their milk: their neighbor.

Additionally, the fresh ricotta (they make both sheep and cow ricotta) is especially noteworthy, since it has a full, round, buttery flavor found only in truly fresh ricotta cheese, lending itself to baked and fresh dishes equally. Then again, a chunk of fresh-baked bread may be the best accompaniment of all.

The word "bellwether" is a sheepherding term, referring to the lead sheep who wears a bell to lead the flock. Bellwether Farms has clearly been a leader in sheep cheese making in California, but they have also been integral to setting higher overall cheese standards in California and the rest of the nation.

Eggplant-Crescenza Extravaganza

This Italian-inspired recipe turns a few simple vegetables into soul-satisfying comfort food. The star ingredient is the eggplant, but the sautéed onions, tomatoes, and balsamic vinegar wrap a lovely sweetness around the entire dish. Adding to the comfort is the creamy crescenza cheese, which is a cheese that looks melted even before it is cooked because it is so runny. Here it acts like a warm blanket over the eggplant-onion-tomato mixture. The big surprise comes after the first bite, when just a slight tinge of heat chimes in from the crushed red pepper flakes.

One note: This casserole has only a small amount of sauce, but it won't be dry. In fact, it is plenty moist due to the way the ingredients all sandwich together in the baking process.

Salt

1 large eggplant (about 1 pound) peeled and cut into ¼-inch-thick slices

About ¼ cup olive oil

¼ cup fresh bread crumbs, preferably sourdough

2 yellow onions, cut in half lengthwise and thinly sliced

2 cloves garlic, finely chopped

1¼ pounds tomatoes (about 4 medium), peeled (see page 128), seeded, and diced

1½ tablespoons balsamic vinegar

½ teaspoon crushed red pepper flakes

20 fresh basil leaves (about 1 bunch), finely chopped

⅓ pound Bellwether crescenza cheese, very cold and broken off into quarter-size pieces (or use another creamy cows' milk cheese such as Teleme or about 6 ounces young Jack cheese, coarsely grated)

Salt the eggplant slices on both sides and place in a single layer in a colander. Let sit over a bowl or in the sink for 1 hour.

Preheat the oven to 400°F.

In a small bowl, mix together 1 tablespoon of the olive oil and the bread crumbs. Scatter the crumbs in a baking pan and toast in the oven until they are lightly browned, about 5 minutes. Set aside. Turn the oven to the broiler setting.

In a large sauté pan, heat 1 tablespoon of the oil over medium heat. Add the onions and cook until they are limp but not brown, about 10 minutes. Reduce the heat to medium-low, add the garlic, and cook, stirring occasionally, until the onions are very soft and the edges are just beginning to turn a light brown, about 20 minutes. If the onions begin to brown too much, add a little water to the pan and scrape up the brown bits that have formed on the bottom of the pan. Transfer to a plate and reserve the pan.

Rinse eggplant and pat dry. Place the eggplant in a broiler pan and brush liberally with olive oil and salt. Broil for 4 minutes, or until the eggplant begins to brown. Turn the slices, brush with oil and salt, and broil just until the eggplant is golden brown, 3 to 4 minutes. Set aside.

Reduce the oven temperature to 375°F.

In the same sauté pan used for the onions, heat 1 tablespoon of the olive oil over medium heat. Add the tomatoes and cook until they begin to soften and their juices begin to be released, about 15 minutes. Continue cooking until the juices are reduced to about ½ cup, 8 to 10 minutes. (Cook less if the tomatoes are not very juicy to begin with.) Add the vinegar and red pepper flakes, and bring to a boil for 30 seconds. Season with plenty of salt and remove from the heat.

To assemble, place half of the onions in an 8-inch square baking dish or a gratin dish.

Arrange half of the eggplant slices over the onions. Spoon half of the tomato mixture over the eggplant. Sprinkle with half of the chopped basil leaves, and dot with one third of the cheese. Repeat the layering of onions, eggplant, tomatoes, and basil. Scatter the remaining cheese over the casserole. (You can assemble this dish up to six hours in advance. Cover and refrigerate it. Bring it to room temperature before baking.) Cover with foil and bake for 45 to 50 minutes, or until the eggplant feels very tender when pierced with a fork.

Remove the casserole from the oven and turn the oven setting to broil. Discard the foil. Sprinkle the bread crumbs over the casserole and broil until the cheese is bubbly and the bread crumbs are browned, about 5 minutes. Let cool about 10 minutes before serving.

Serves 4

REDWOOD HILL FARM

THERE ISN'T A LOT OF GOATS' MILK Camembert-style cheese being made, and that could be due to the impressively high standard set by Jennifer Bice and Steven Schack of Redwood Hill Farm. Their Camellia cheese, which is named after one of their goats, is a lush, creamy soft-ripening cheese akin to Camembert but whiter and ever-so-tangy from the goats' milk. At its perfect ripeness, there is no better soft-ripening cheese.

Redwood Hill is located in Sebastopol, California, in Sonoma County. It is one of the most scenic areas of California, defined by tall pine and redwood trees that gradually give way to the rugged coast of northern California. The lingering fog and winter rains keep the area verdant, and the hot summers make it fertile agricultural ground. Wine grapes can be seen dangling from their vines in the fall months, while the Russian River snakes its way to the ocean a little to the north. Redwood Hill's cheese plant and goat facility is aptly named "Vineyard View," as it peers over the vineyards of the Iron Horse winery.

It is an ideal setting in which to live, to have goats, and to make cheese. Perhaps it is this ambience that contributes to the excellent Redwood Hill cheeses. But it is also Jennifer and Steven's intense dedication to their environment, to their goats, and to their product that makes the cheeses excel. Having immersed themselves in goat cheese making for the better part of two decades, Bice and Schack bring a sophistication and sensibility to goat cheese that few have captured in this country.

Redwood Hill goat cheeses were actually born in a cows' milk facility that specialized in Italian cheeses. Having no plant of their own, Bice and Schack had to borrow one. Their cheeses were well received, but the plant machinery was too large for their production needs.

They decided to build their own plant, but in the meantime they used the cheesemaking room at Bellwether Farms (see pages 186-187). Anticipating they would need the Bellwether facility for only six weeks, they ended up using it for two years while the Redwood Hill plant met with innumerable construction delays. In 1993 they inaugurated the Vineyard View cheese plant.

WHAT THEY MAKE
California Crottin
Camellia
Fresh chèvre: plain and flavored
Feta: raw and pasteurized
Raw milk cheddar: sharp and smoked
Teleme

HOW TO REACH THEM
Sebastopol, California
707-823-8250
707-823-6976 (fax)
website: www.redwoodhill.com

The first cheese they made in their new plant was feta. An over-supply of summer milk led to this decision, since they could make the feta in the summer and let it age well into the fall and winter.

Their cheesemaking method is different than for most fetas: they brine it for just a short time and then wrap it (unlike other artisanal fetas, which are usually stored in brine). This way, it ages well and never becomes terribly salty. Both the raw and pasteurized milk versions of the feta are somewhat crumbly and tangy, and the raw version has a particularly nice bite. The cheese is drier than other fetas because of the lack of brine, and it has greater intensity for the same reason. A few tastes leads to the unavoidable habit of seeking out this cheese. It is wholly satisfying.

The same is true of the Redwood Hill crottin, which is a cylindrical soft-ripened cheese. Molds are added to the milk, causing the rind to become a yellowish, slightly wrinkled, delectable foil for the intense white paste on the inside. They are 1- to 2-ounce jewels that become hard grating cheeses after a couple of months.

Since Greek Teleme cheese is actually in the same family as feta, Redwood Hill has come out with their own version of this remarkable cheese. Unlike their feta, the Teleme has a high moisture content and lends itself to dishes where the cheese is melted. It, too, is a lovely cheese—not to be confused with the cows' milk Telemes made by Peluso and the Sonoma Cheese Factory.

The Redwood Hill story is one of perseverance, intelligence, and passion. Sadly, Steven succumbed to cancer in the summer of 1999, leaving Jennifer to carry on the Redwood Hill legacy. It is a huge task, but it won't change her dedication to making great cheese. What also will not change is the fact that both she and Steven have been community-involved, down-to-earth people devoted not only to what they do but to the land, its health, its offerings, and its ongoing preservation. For twenty years they have been local icons, and their cheese follows suit.

Herbed Sugar Snap Peas with Goat Cheese

Sugar snap peas are one of nature's finest treasures. As the name implies, they are naturally sweet, and their texture is crunchy. Because of that combination, they meld effortlessly with the other ingredients in this dish. The "snap" counters the creamy goat cheese, and the earthy tarragon contrasts perfectly with the vegetable's natural sugars.

Snap peas are available in the spring and fall and are especially good when they are just picked. If you can't find them, this dish works equally well and looks just as beautiful with fresh green beans. Simply cook the green beans about a minute or two longer than the snap peas.

VEGETABLES AND SIDE DISHES

2 pounds fresh sugar snap peas, stems and
   strings removed
½ cup plus 2 tablespoons olive oil
3 medium shallots, finely chopped
3 tablespoons chopped fresh tarragon leaves,
   plus additional sprigs for garnish
Salt and freshly ground pepper
12 ounces cherry tomatoes (about 1½
   cartons), cut in half lengthwise
½ pound fresh goat cheese, such as Redwood
   Hill, cut into small pieces (if the goat
   cheese is particularly creamy, spoon it onto
   the vegetables; or use fromage blanc)

Bring a large pot of salted water to a boil. Add the peas and cook until crisp-tender, 2 to 3 minutes. Drain, and run under cold water. Set aside.

In a large sauté pan, heat the 2 tablespoons olive oil over medium-low heat. Add the shallots and cook, stirring occasionally, until they are limp but not brown, 5 to 7 minutes. Add the remaining ½ cup olive oil and heat for 1 minute. Turn off the heat and add the chopped tarragon and peas, stirring to coat the peas with the oil, shallots, and tarragon. Add plenty of salt and pepper. Let cool to room temperature, about 15 minutes.

Arrange the pea mixture, tomatoes, and cheese on a serving plate; garnish with additional tarragon. Do not mix.

Serves 8 to 10

WESTFIELD FARM

AFTER YEARS IN THE SHIPPING INDUSTRY, Debbie and Bob Stetson decided they wanted to ship themselves out of the metropolitan Boston area and immerse themselves in country living. A meeting with Bob and Letty Kilmoyer, then the owners of Westfield Farm, secured that dream as well as their other goal, which was to have a business that resulted in a product rather than a service.

Goat cheese making (and later cows' milk as well) was begun at Westfield Farm by the Kilmoyers in the early 1980s. In the mid-1990s, they decided to retire from the life of cheesemakers and head south for the Florida sun. Since the Kilmoyers' retirement coincided with the Stetsons' dream, the four joined forces for one month when the Kilmoyers taught everything they knew about cheesemaking and the Stetsons were willing students at the makeshift cheesemaking boot camp.

After the intensive training, Bob and Letty Kilmoyer took off for Florida with cellular phone in hand, just in case the Stetsons had any further questions. They did, and many conversations were exchanged on the highways between Massachusetts and Florida in the ensuing weeks.

That was in 1996. Since then the Stetsons have carried on the Westfield Farm tradition, including the superb cheeses that got their start there. Their signature cheeses are the Hubbardston Blue, made with cows' milk, and the Westfield Blue Log, made with goats' milk. Both of these cheeses are snow-white on the inside while the outside consists of a soft blue mold layer. This is achieved by adding the *Penicillium roqueforti* mold to the milk or to the curds, depending on the cheese that is being made, which creates just enough of the blue mold to form on the surface, where the cheese can breathe. Since neither of the cheeses is perforated to allow oxygen and the consequent blue mold to form, neither has blue veins inside. Instead, the outer blue mold lends just a hint of blue cheese taste to the otherwise mild but flavorful soft cheese.

Another unique feature of the Westfield Blue Log, in particular, is that the flavor compounds with each taste. That distinction eliminates the possibility of bored taste buds, and creates a unique symbiosis in the mouth between the tart goats' milk flavor and the mustiness of the blue mold. It lends loads of flavor to cooked dishes, especially because the flavor of blue cheese gets stronger when it is heated. It becomes noble when spread on thin toasted slices of walnut-studded baguette and topped with a dried fig, or heavenly when it becomes the crowning glory on an old classic, the hamburger. These unique qualities earned this cheese a blue ribbon at the 1999 American Cheese Society annual conference.

(continued on page 194)

WHAT THEY MAKE
Goats' milk cheeses
Capri: chocolate, herb,
   herb & garlic, pepper,
   plain, smoked
Classic Blue Log
White Buck

Cows' milk cheeses
Capri/Camembert
Hubbardston Blue

HOW TO REACH THEM
Hubbardston, Massachusetts
978-928-5110
978-928-5745 (fax)
website: www.chevre.com

The Stetsons have acclimated to country living and especially to cheesemaking, and they are making about twelve cheeses—so far. They continue to explore new ideas, so it is hard to tell what they might be churning out next. In the meantime, their goat cheese with chocolate bits might win the prize for most unusual, while their newest experiment—a Stilton-like cheese—gives cheese devotees something to anxiously anticipate.

Spinach Sauté with Blue Goat Cheese and Caramelized Onions

Because of the way Westfield Farm makes its goats' milk Blue Logs, the cheese has a mild blue cheese flavor, even though it is technically not a blue cheese. In this dish, that slightly tart "blue" quality provides a surprising counterpoint to the sweet currants and caramelized onions, while the creaminess of the cheese contrasts nicely with the slightly crunchy peppers and pine nuts. If you cannot find blue goat cheese, use any type of mild and creamy blue cheese. Try to avoid crumbly blue cheeses; they will create a different texture and flavor.

1 tablespoon olive oil
1 large red onion, thinly sliced
2 cloves garlic, finely chopped
1 red bell pepper, roasted, skinned, and cut into ½-inch pieces
2 pounds fresh spinach, stems removed, leaves rinsed well and drained but not dried
⅓ cup dried currants, plumped in hot water for 20 minutes and drained
3 tablespoons pine nuts, toasted
Salt and freshly ground pepper
4 ounces Westfield Farm Blue Log, cut into teaspoon-size chunks (or use a creamy mild blue cheese)

In a large nonstick sauté pan, heat the oil over medium-high heat. Add the onions and sauté until they begin to soften, about 10 minutes. Reduce the heat to medium-low, add the garlic, and cook for about 5 minutes, or until both the onions and the garlic are softened but not browned. Add the red pepper and continue cooking until the onions are caramelized (browned on the edges and slightly gooey) and the red pepper is heated through, 12 to 15 minutes. (You may need to add a little water to the pan if the onions are browning too fast.)

Return the heat to medium-high and add the spinach. Cook until the spinach wilts, about 5 minutes; then add the currants and pine nuts. Season with salt and pepper to taste. Remove from the heat and add 3 ounces of the cheese. Stir the ingredients until the cheese begins to melt. Transfer the mixture to a serving plate, and top with the remaining cheese. Serve at once.

Serves 4

SAGPOND VINEYARDS

YOU'VE HEARD OF WINE AND CHEESE PAIRING, but you may never have heard of a winemaker and a cheesemaker being the same person. Until now. Roman Roth, winemaker at Wolffer Estate–Sagpond Vineyards on Long Island, wears both hats. His cheese: Sagpond Farmstead Emmentaler.

Roth fell into cheesemaking by virtue of the four cows that lived down the road from him (the only remaining dairy cows on Long Island). He hated to see their milk going to waste, but the owner couldn't find anyplace to sell the milk. So, have milk, make cheese, right? Except that Roth, who grew up in the Black Forest region of Germany, had only *eaten* good cheese. He had never made it.

Fortuitously, Roth happened to attend a dinner party where he was seated near a cheesemaker from Ohio. He soon tapped that cheesemaker's expertise, hiring him as a consultant, and two months later he became a full-fledged cheesemaker himself. In 1998 Roth's first twenty-pound wheels of Emmentaler were born.

Roth's reason for making Emmentaler stems from his childhood, when he would spend his summers in Switzerland. He relished observing how the Swiss made their Emmentaler and Swiss cheeses in the summertime so that they would be ready for the long, harsh winters. When he decided to make cheese, Roth reversed this method, since the high season on Long Island is the summer. Consequently he begins making his cheese in the winter so it will be ready in the summer. Since his Emmentaler is aged up to six months, this system has worked perfectly in its short life.

The output of cheese is fairly small, though impressive. Roth has only one twenty-seven-gallon kettle in which to make the cheese, and every step of the cheesemaking is done by hand, including the stirring. Nonetheless, that kettle manages to churn out three twenty-pound wheels a week, which is a figure that will likely increase.

The bulk of the cheese is sold at the winery, although it is also found in a few upscale Manhattan restaurants and cheese shops. Roth thinks that he will expand his operation one day, but for now he is taking it one day at a time, since cheesemaking is still very new for him. In fact, Roth seems slightly bemused by his success as a cheesemaker. Maybe that's understandable, as his degree and experience are in winemaking. But everyone knows that wine and cheese are a natural fit. Roth just happens to give that concept a whole new meaning.

Wölffer

The Hamptons, Long Island

Farmstead Cheese

Produced at Wölffer Estate

WHAT THEY MAKE
Sagpond Farmstead Emmentaler

HOW TO REACH THEM
Sagaponack, New York
631-537-5106
631-537-5107 (fax)
websites: www.wolffer.com
www.sagpondvineyards.com

Emmentaler and Savoy Cabbage-Stuffed Potatoes

Twice-baked potatoes must have been invented by someone with very little time yet a wonderful palate. They require little fuss, can be made in advance, and deliver magnificent flavor that goes well beyond the work that goes into them. Kids, in particular, seem to like them, but then kids usually like potatoes and they like melted cheese, so putting the two together isn't much of a stretch.

These twice-baked potatoes part ways with other similar recipes because of their two main ingredients: Emmentaler and Savoy cabbage. Savoy cabbage is smaller than conventional cabbage, it has a wrinkly texture, and it is milder than the common green variety. Once it has been cooked for a little while, it becomes slightly soft though still crunchy, while the flavor mellows into something only slightly reminiscent of its brassica, or mustard family, roots.

Emmentaler is a mountain cheese similar to Gruyère or Swiss cheese. It, too, can be on the mellow side (if it isn't aged very long), and together with the creamy potatoes and crisp cabbage, becomes the crowning glory in a wholly satisfying dish.

---

5 russet potatoes (about 3¾ pounds total),
    scrubbed clean
¼ cup (½ stick) unsalted butter
2 small heads Savoy cabbage (about 1 pound
    total), cored and thinly sliced
¼ cup (½ stick) salted butter, softened and
    cut into small pieces
8 ounces Emmentaler cheese, such as
Sagpond Farmstead, coarsely grated (about 2
    cups; or use Gruyère, Swiss, or Fontina)
¼ cup heavy cream, half-and-half, or milk
Salt and freshly ground pepper

Preheat the oven to 400°F.

With the tines of a fork, poke a few holes in each potato. Place them in a baking pan and bake for 1 hour. Remove from the oven and set aside until cool enough to handle, about 10 minutes.

While the potatoes are baking, prepare the cabbage: In a large sauté pan, melt the unsalted butter over medium-low heat. Add the cabbage, stir to coat with the butter, and cover. Cook, stirring occasionally, until cabbage is wilted but still has some crunch, about 15 minutes. If the cabbage begins to brown, add a little water or chicken stock to the pan, stir, and cover once again. Set aside.

Cut the potatoes in half lenthwise. Into a mixing bowl, gently scoop out the potato flesh, leaving a ¼-inch-thick shell. Add the salted butter, 1 cup of the cheese, and the cream. Mix on medium-high speed or beat vigorously with a wooden spoon until the ingredients are blended and are smooth and creamy. Add salt and pepper to taste. If the mixture isn't silky smooth, add a little more cream, 1 tablespoon at a time.

Divide the potato mixture among 8 of the potato skins. (Save the remaining 2 skins for another use, or smear them with a little butter and salt for a tasty snack.) Gently spoon about ¼ cup of the cabbage over the top of each potato. Distribute the remaining 1 cup cheese over the potatoes. (At this point, you can cover the potatoes with foil and refrigerate them for as long as 24 hours. Bring to room temperature before baking.) Bake for 15 minutes or until heated through. Turn the oven to broil and finish the potatoes under the broiler, until the cheese is bubbling, 2 to 3 minutes. Serve hot.

Serves 4 to 8

ORB WEAVER FARM

THEY DON'T MAKE A LOT OF CHEESE, but the cheese that Marjorie Susman and Marian Pollack do make is swept up as fast as you can say "Orb Weaver." On their small farm in New Haven, Vermont, the two women, using the milk from their six Jersey cows, create just two types of cheese. Their Vermont Farmhouse Cheese is a Colby-like creamy cheese that has the distinctive golden color of a cheese made from Jersey milk. Their other cheese is longer-aged, with a natural rind, and over time becomes a hard grating-type cheese. As a result, it can be used in just about any dish where a grating cheese is called for.

Cheesemaking is just one of Susman's and Pollack's many farm-based ventures. During the months between May and November when they aren't making cheese ("We want to give our cows and ourselves a break," says Susman), they are tending to their extensive organic garden, which sports a variety of vegetables and fruits that nearby residents can purchase at their local farmstand. Local restaurants also partake in the bounty.

Both women are longtime practitioners of sustainable agriculture, having bought their farm in 1982 and turned it into an organic operation. At one time the farm hosted a herd of thirty cattle and cheesemaking was at a more intense level, but Susman and Pollack chose to return to the simpler life they had originally sought when moving to the Champlain Valley.

Perhaps the name of the farm best symbolizes its two owners. An orb weaver is a garden spider that spins a beautiful symmetrical web. For Susman and Pollack, that web symbolizes the rhythms of farming and the importance of nurturing the soil to help it grow back richer and healthier with each passing year.

WHAT THEY MAKE
Vermont Cave-Aged Cheeses
Vermont Farmhouse Cheese

HOW TO REACH THEM
Lime Kiln Road, New Haven, Vermont
802-877-3755

Fennel, Apple, and Celery Root Gratin

This satiny gratin brings to life the essence of winter. It is warm, rich, and gratifying. The surprise ingredient is the apple. Sandwiched between the fennel and the celery root, it separates the savory flavors and injects its own sweetness. Bathed in cream and covered with melted cheese, this gratin could not be more satisfying. It is also simple to make. Try it with your next Thanksgiving turkey, or alongside a pork roast.

2 large celery roots (about 1 pound each)
2 fennel bulbs (about ½ pound each)
2 Granny Smith or other tart, firm apples
   (about 1 pound total), peeled and cored
Salt and freshly ground pepper
8 ounces Colby-style cheese, such as Orb
   Weaver, coarsely grated (about 2 cups; or
   use aged, but not sharp, cheddar)
About 1½ cups heavy cream

Preheat the oven to 375°F. Butter a 2-quart gratin dish or other ovenproof casserole.

Cut off the entire rough exterior of the celery roots, making sure that all brown parts are removed. You will be removing about ¼ to ½ inch of the exterior of each. Next, cut each celery root in half lengthwise. Turn one half cut side down, and cut into ¼-inch-wide pieces. Repeat with the remaining celery root. Set aside.

Cut off the fronds and the dark green parts of each fennel bulb, leaving just the bulb. Cut each bulb in half lenthwise. Cut each half lengthwise into ¼-inch-thick slices.

In a vegetable steamer, combine the celery root and fennel and steam for 5 minutes. Remove from the steamer and set aside to cool slightly.

Cut the apples into ¼-inch-thick rings.

Place one third of the celery root on the bottom of the prepared dish. Sprinkle with salt and pepper to taste. Overlap with one third of the apple slices, and sprinkle with a little more salt but no pepper. Put one third of the fennel over the apples, and once again sprinkle with salt and pepper. Repeat with the remaining celery root, apple, and fennel. Pour cream around the sides of the dish until the cream reaches about halfway up the dish. Sprinkle the top of the gratin with the cheese. Cover and bake for 35 minutes, or until the vegetables and apple feel tender when pierced with a fork or skewer. Turn the oven to broil, remove the cover, and broil until the gratin is golden brown and bubbling, about 3 minutes.

Let cool 15 minutes to allow the cream to firm up slightly and serve.

Serves 6 to 8

BUTLER FARMS

IT SEEMS UNLIKELY THAT A SOCIAL WORKER and a systems analyst in New York would become sheep dairy farmers and cheesemakers in Wisconsin. But Janet and Bill Butler did just that, opting for a simpler life that would provide a good place to raise their son as well as some sheep.

Their foray into cheesemaking actually began in New York State, where a neighbor, American cheese-making pioneer Joan Snyder, then owner of Hollow Road Farms, wanted to buy sheep's milk to make cheese. The Butlers owned a few sheep and therefore had the milk, and Snyder had the cheesemaking skills. This union resulted in some hands-on experience for Janet Butler, who learned how to make yogurt and cheese at Hollow Road.

After the Butlers moved to Wisconsin, they began to make sheep's milk yogurt, selling it at farmers' markets. In 1997 Janet took the Wisconsin-mandated courses and tests and became a certified cheesemaker.

Today they make a stellar sheep's milk feta, which is a rare domestic cheese (cows' and goats' milk fetas are more commonly made in the United States), as well as a fresh sheep's milk cheese, ricotta, two flavored cheeses, and three types of yogurt. The feta has a somewhat stronger, gamier flavor than many domestic fetas, and it is also less salty. It is arguably one of the best fetas made anywhere, with its buttery rich and pronounced flavors. It is naturally the perfect ingredient in a fresh salad or the ultimate in a Mediterranean vegetable dish, such as the one on the next page. Because of the conservative amount of salt, the feta also makes a surprisingly good snacking cheese, although a little goes a long way.

Like sheep's milk feta, sheep's milk ricotta is a rare find in this country. It has an unparalleled rich milk quality and should be savored in its purest form. Try a dollop on some fresh summer tomatoes with a scattering of chopped basil leaves and a drizzle of olive oil. This is what farm-fresh food is all about.

Although the Butlers' lifestyle improved by moving to Wisconsin, especially since they moved closer to relatives, the struggles of sheep cheese making remain. Janet has resumed her career in social work while still maintaining her role as cheesemaker, and every weekend (except in the winter) she and Bill share farmers' market duties in Madison and occasionally in Chicago. To the outside world, their commitment is worthwhile because they are trying to make cheeses that have not been made in the United States before. It is a valiant effort, especially with their feta, since feta is one of the cheapest cheese imports and one of the most expensive to make domestically. It is an effort that should be rewarded, if for no other reason than its exceptional quality.

BUTLER FARMS

sheep milk

FETA CHEESE

Ingredients: Cultured Pasteurized Sheep's Milk, Salt, Rennet.

NET WT.   OZ.

made at our farmstead creamery
WHITEHALL, WISCONSIN 54773
DAIRY PLANT #551087

WHAT THEY MAKE
Aged beer-washed cheese
Feta
Fresh brebis
Ricotta
Yogurt: plain and flavored

HOW TO REACH THEM
Whitehall, Wisconsin
715-983-2285
715-983-2230 (fax)
website:
members.xoom.com/butlerfarms/html

Lemony Artichokes with Feta and Oregano

This side dish makes a wonderful spring or fall accompaniment, since artichokes are kind enough to give us a long season. It is also quite easy to make. The most time-consuming part is trimming the artichokes, though it is actually very simple. Because of the relatively large amount of garlic called for in this recipe, a small portion goes a long way. If you're not a garlic fan, don't despair. Just don't use any, or use less. With or without garlic, this dish is packed with flavor. Serve it with oven-roasted or grilled fish, along with some roasted potatoes.

1 quart cold water
¼ cup plus 1 tablespoon lemon juice
8 baby artichokes (see Note)
4 teaspoons olive oil
2 teaspoons unsalted butter
4 cloves garlic, minced
About ¾ cup chicken stock or water
Salt and freshly ground pepper
2 teaspoons finely chopped fresh oregano
  leaves
2 ounces Butler Farms sheep's milk feta
  cheese, crumbled (about ⅓ cup; or use
  another cow, sheep, or goat milk feta)

In a large nonreactive bowl, combine the water and ¼ cup of the lemon juice.

Cut ½ inch off the top of one artichoke. Cut off the stem. Next, peel off and discard most of the outer leaves until you reach the tender, light green inner leaves. You will be removing more than half of the leaves. Cut the artichoke in half lengthwise, and then cut each half lengthwise again to make quarters. Put in the bowl of acidulated water. Repeat with the remaining artichokes. Set aside.

In a large sauté pan, heat the olive oil and butter over medium heat. Add the minced garlic and cook for 1 minute. Remove the artichokes from the acidulated water, shake off the excess water, and add them to the pan.

Sauté, stirring frequently, just until the edges of the artichokes begin to turn brown and become caramelized, about 6 to 8 minutes. Add ½ cup of the chicken stock and cover. Cook the artichokes, stirring occasionally, until they are tender but still firm, about 10 minutes. If the artichokes or garlic is sticking to the pan, add a tablespoon or two of stock or water. You want to keep the amount of liquid to a minimum, but you naturally don't want the artichokes or garlic to burn. (The garlic, however, will have turned a dark brown color.) Remove the cover and turn the heat to high. Add the remaining ¼ cup chicken stock and bring to a boil. Reduce the liquid to 1 tablespoon. Reduce the heat to medium, and add the 1 tablespoon lemon juice, salt and pepper to taste, and the oregano. Stir well. Place artichokes on a serving platter or individual plates. Top with the cheese and serve immediately.

Serves 4

Note: If baby artichokes are not available, you can use large globe artichokes instead. Cut 1 inch off the tops. Peel off all the leaves except for the very thin inner leaves. (Since the tips of the leaves are sharp, you may want to use scissors to cut them off before peeling.) Once they have been trimmed, cut them in half and scrape out the fuzzy choke inside. Then cut them into eighths. Proceed as described.

Simple Stuffed Zucchini

This colorful side dish got me through many dinners when I was in college—and later, when I was trying to impress friends with my kitchen prowess, such as it was. I don't know if it worked, but I do know that this simple dish took its place in my section of "regulars" among the categories of "experimental," "difficult," "creative," and other recipe folders. You can assemble these four hours in advance, refrigerate them, and then bring them to room temperature before baking.

VEGETABLES AND SIDE DISHES

8 zucchini (about 2 pounds total), washed
  and cut in half lengthwise
2 tablespoons olive oil
1 large yellow onion, finely chopped
3 small cloves garlic, minced
4 large tomatoes (about 3 pounds total), cut
  in half crosswise, seeded, and diced
Salt and freshly ground pepper, to taste
8 ounces medium-aged cheddar cheese,
  coarsely grated (about 2 cups; or use
  medium-aged Provolone)

Preheat the oven to 350°F.

Scoop out the flesh of the zucchini, being careful not to break the skins. The small side of a melon baller works well for this. Cut the flesh into small pieces and set aside.

In a large sauté pan, heat the olive oil over medium heat. Add the onions and sauté for 5 minutes. Add the garlic and cook until the onions are soft, 10 minutes more. Add the tomatoes and reserved zucchini flesh. Cook until the zucchini softens and the tomatoes have released their juices, about 10 minutes. Add salt and pepper, and remove from the heat. Let cool slightly.

Place the zucchini shells in a baking pan. Fill them with the stuffing. Top each with about ¼ cup of the grated cheese. Cover with foil and bake until the zucchini shells are soft, 35 minutes. Remove the foil and bake for 5 more minutes, or until the cheese begins to brown. Serve immediately.

Serves 4

OPPOSITE: Quarky Chocolate Cake (see page 216).

Goat Cheese Cake with Peaches and Blueberries

To some, fresh goat cheese and fresh cream cheese taste pretty similar despite the fact they're entirely different. I happen to think that fresh goat cheese has a wonderful tangy quality that cream cheese doesn't have, although I love cream cheese too. That tangy quality from the goat cheese translates beautifully to desserts because it helps keep the "sweet factor" in control while taking the "rich factor" to new heights. The cake is a perfect example of that balance. This recipe is inspired by the talented executive pastry chef Emily Luchetti, at Farallon Restaurant in San Francisco.

¾ **pound fresh goat cheese, such as Haystack Mountain Boulder Chèvre, at room temperature**
¾ **cup plus 2 tablespoons sugar**
1½ **teaspoons fresh lemon juice**
1 **teaspoon minced lemon zest (from 1 small lemon)**
1 **teaspoon vanilla extract**
6 **large eggs, separated**
3 **tablespoons all-purpose flour**
3 **large peaches, peeled, pitted, and cut into ¼-inch-thick slices**
½ **cup blueberries**
Confectioners' sugar
Whipped cream or crème fraîche (optional)

Preheat the oven to 350°F. Butter a 9-inch round cake pan and dust it with 1 tablespoon of the sugar.

In a medium bowl, combine the cheese with the ¾ cup sugar, lemon juice, lemon zest, and vanilla. Beat at medium speed until smooth. Beat in the egg yolks, one at a time, incorporating each one completely before adding the next. Turn the mixer to low and add the flour.

In another bowl, using clean beaters, beat the egg whites until firm. Beat one third of the egg whites into the cheese mixture. Gently fold in the rest of the egg whites. Spoon the batter into the prepared pan and bake until a toothpick inserted in the center comes out clean and the cake is a deep golden brown, 35 to 40 minutes. Do not underbake or you'll have an eggy mess. Cool for 15 minutes on a cooling rack. Remove the cake from the pan and cool completely.

In a bowl, mix the peaches and blueberries together with the remaining 1 tablespoon sugar. (You may need less or more sugar, depending on the sweetness of the fruit.) Set aside.

When ready to serve, invert the cake onto a serving plate. Dust with confectioners' sugar, and spoon the fruit on top of the cake, leaving a 1-inch border all the way around. Cut and serve, garnishing each piece with a little whipped cream, if desired.

Serves 8 to 10

HAYSTACK MOUNTAIN GOAT DAIRY

IN THE SHADOW OF THE ROCKY MOUNTAINS, in Niwot, Colorado, 120 goats frolic in the high country while serious cheesemaking goes on beside them. Located near Boulder, Niwot seems an unlikely locale for a cheesemaking operation, but for owner Jim Schott it seemed natural to return to the area where he once was a student and worked in a cow dairy. That, along with some earlier training as a chef, the desire to acquire some land, and the idea Jim's wife, Arlene, had of opening a children's bookstore, brought the couple from Madison, Wisconsin, to Colorado. Cheesemaking was not initially on the "to-do" list for either of them.

Schott's long association with farming, stemming back to his childhood, is probably what eventually led him to goats. After moving to Colorado, he visited a goat dairy east of Boulder and saw that unlike cows, the goats were "human-size," and they were smart. He decided that they would be manageable, and six acres and five goats later, he had a farm. That was in the late 1980s. After that, he became a quick study in raising and tending to goats. The next natural step was cheesemaking.

Sadly, Arlene Schott passed away just after the goat dairy was completed. But Jim and his daughter and business partner, Gretchen, carried on and have built an operation that now puts out several soft as well as aged cheeses that are sold to restaurants and stores throughout Colorado, as well as in neighboring states and by mail order.

Haystack Mountain's farmstead fresh chèvre is a study in creaminess, while their olive oil–bathed chèvre is a little firmer but rich and tangy due to the fruity oil and herbs. One of the more interesting cheeses is one Schott calls "Grateful Chèvre," a humorous name to describe a dry grating cheese (hence the "grate"ful moniker) that is rindless but has the piquant characteristics of Parmesan and the distinctive flavor of goats' milk.

Humor, in fact, is not lacking in Schott's operation. Take his elaborate system for naming the goats and keeping track of the generations within the herd: Each year he comes up with a new theme, such as the periodic table of elements, or herbs and spices, for that generation of goats. He then gives every new kid from that generation a name that falls within that theme. That kid's name will also begin with the first letter of its mother's name. Schott was a professor for much of his professional life, so a system like this makes perfect sense. If only school had been that much fun.

That background as a professor means that Schott is naturally a perennial student as well. He is constantly learning new things about cheesemaking and is consequently experimenting with new cheeses. For this reason, as well as the fundamental quality of their cheeses, Haystack Mountain Goat Dairy will certainly be one to keep track of in this new century.

WHAT THEY MAKE
Boulder Chèvre: plain and flavored
Chèvre en Marinade
Chèvre Spread
Feta
Grateful Chèvre

HOW TO REACH THEM
Niwot, Colorado
303-581-9948
303-516-1041 (fax)
website: www.haystackgoatcheese.com

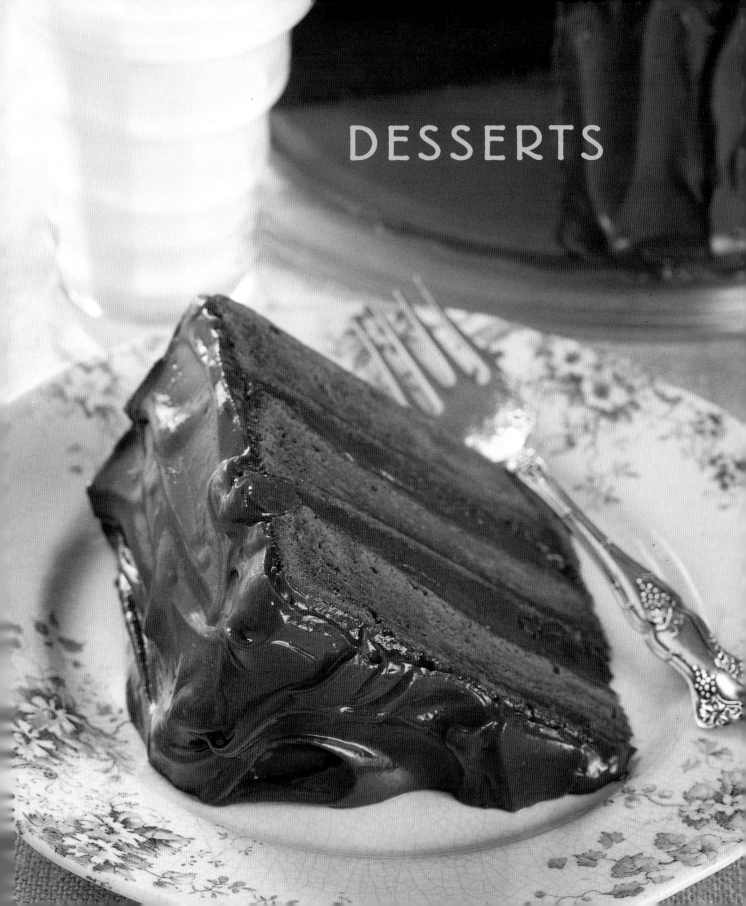

DESSERTS

Cranberry-Ricotta Tarts in a Toasted Almond Crust

When I first made these tarts, I was excited not only by how they tasted, but also by how they looked. They're festive little packages with a golden cheesy top that summons even the most reluctant dessert eater. As for the taste, the sweet ricotta filling and the tart cranberries create a pleasantly mild counterpoint to the rich, buttery almond crust. The cookie-like crust, in fact, is good for a variety of fillings, including a traditional cheesecake or a pastry cream topped with fresh fruit. You will need six four-inch tart pans, or one ten-inch tart pan, with removable bottoms, for this recipe.

FOR THE CRUST

2 cups almonds, lightly toasted
½ cup packed dark brown sugar
¼ cup (½ stick) unsalted butter, melted

FOR THE CRANBERRIES

½ cup apple brandy, such as Calvados
  (or use water)
⅔ cup dried cranberries

FOR THE FILLING

2 cups fresh whole milk ricotta, drained if
  necessary (see Note)
¾ cup sugar
2 eggs
½ teaspoon vanilla extract
2 tablespoons all-purpose flour

To make the crust: Preheat the oven to 325°F.

In a food processor, combine the almonds and brown sugar and grind until the almonds are finely chopped. Add the melted butter and pulse on and off, just until the butter is incorporated into the mixture. Place six 4-inch tart pans with removable bottoms on a baking sheet. (Or you can use one 9-inch pan with removable bottom.) Divide the almond mixture evenly among the tart pans, pressing the crust firmly against the sides and bottoms. Bake for 7 minutes. Remove and let cool.

To prepare the cranberries: In a small sauté pan, slowly heat the brandy, and pour it over the cranberries in a heatproof bowl. (Caution: Do not heat alcohol over a high heat or it will ignite. If this happens, simply let it burn away, making sure that there is nothing flammable near the stove. It will burn away in a matter of seconds.) Let the cranberries sit for 20 minutes and then drain.

To make the filling: In a medium-size bowl, combine all the filling ingredients and stir vigorously until the mixture is very creamy.

To assemble: Place the tart shells on a baking sheet. Sprinkle the cranberries into the shells. Carefully pour the cheese mixture into the tart shells, just until it reaches the top of the crust. Bake the tarts for 45 minutes, or until the cheese is golden brown. Let them cool completely before serving. As the tarts cool, the filling will fall and shrivel slightly. Nonetheless, they will still look irresistible. Remove tarts from pans just before serving.

Serves 6

Note: Sometimes fresh ricotta has a large amount of liquid, which can interfere with the baking process and create a runny tart. If your ricotta seems watery, place it in a colander lined with a double layer of cheesecloth, and let it drain for about an hour. If you do not have cheesecloth, use a thin paper towel or a coffee filter.

DESSERTS

EGG FARM DAIRY

TO USE WORDS LIKE "ECCENTRIC," "intelligent," and "energetic" to describe Jonathan White, owner of Egg Farm Dairy in Peekskill, New York, is as much an understatement about him as it is about his cheeses. "Setting the Dairy Industry Back 100 Years" is the Egg Farm Dairy credo, underscoring White's great hope of getting people refocused on the quality of their food rather than on quantity and mass production. This translates to a cheesemaking operation where small amounts of cheese are made, as are butter, chocolate butter, clabbered cream (crème fraîche), and mascarpone.

Another "setback" in the cheesemaking process at Egg Farm Dairy (also known as EFD) is White's venture into "wild ripening." This type of ripening has been practiced in the past, but not to any extent in this country. It means that Egg Farm Dairy cheese as well as cheese made by other cheesemaking operations is placed in an aging room where certain bacteria have been introduced. Those bacteria then go to work ripening the cheeses. It's a dicey proposition since this type of ripening is hard to control, and it is one that concerns some of White's fellow cheesemakers. But with his science background and insatiable curiosity, White has managed to harness the proper bacteria to age his cheeses successfully without cross contamination.

The result: cheeses with unusual names, like Amawalk and Taconic, and often with unusual shapes as well. Cheeses sold under the EFD label are made with cows', goats', as well as sheep's milk.

White is practically evangelical about cheese and cheesemaking, even though he's been at it only since 1994. Because of his unconventional methods and keen marketing skills, he has developed a high profile in a short amount of time. As a result, he has brought attention—albeit sometimes of a dubious kind—to his brand of cheesemaking. Nonetheless, it is White's type of risk taking, as well as his willingness to pursue cheesemaking in a new—and old—way that have been crucial to the success of American cheesemaking in general. Besides, fans of Egg Farm Dairy

---

WHAT THEY MAKE
Cows' milk products
Amawalk
Amram
Chocolate butter
Clabbered cream
Cultured butter
Hollis (smearcase)
Hudson
Mascarpone
Mohansic
Mozzarella
Muscoot
Peekskill Pyramid
Quarg (quark)

Ricotta
Taconic
Wild Ripened Cheddar

Goats' milk cheeses
Amelia
Egg Farm Dairy Goat Cheddar

Sheep's milk cheeses
Delphina
Old Croton

HOW TO REACH THEM
Peekskill, New York
1-800-CREAMERY
914-734-7343
914-734-9287 (fax)
website: www.creamery.com

cheeses are grateful that White is as unorthodox as he is—there's always an exciting new cheese emerging from his plant.

Egg Farm Dairy's wild-ripened cheeses run the gamut from mild to strong, and can be served alone or used for cooking. One of their most popular cheeses, Muscoot, is a soft-ripened cheese that is mild yet pronounced and can be served plain, melted on a piece of thinly sliced toast, or with a glass of red wine.

The Peekskill Pyramid is a celebration of creaminess and earthiness, all in one bite. At the peak of ripeness, this pyramid-shaped cheese is almost souplike in the center, and the rind takes on different colors as it develops its harmless molds. Sometimes it actually looks like a science experiment, but these molds lend flavor too. One bite of the oozing interior makes you wish you had a straw.

One of White's many passions is cooking, and he, along with his wife, Nina, and one of EFD's early supporters, New York restaurateur Charlie Palmer, has developed a booklet of recipes tailored to their cheeses and fresh milk products.

If you're interested in trying your hand at making your own mozzarella, Egg Farm Dairy sells frozen curds. All you have to do is heat up some water, stretch the curds, and watch mozzarella form before your very eyes. Try it in the summertime when bright red tomatoes are available, and "freshness" will take on a whole new meaning.

Fresh Goat Cheese, Pears, and Candied Walnuts with Lavender Honey

Sometimes the simplest desserts are the most satisfying. I first had a version of this at a bustling bistro in the Napa Valley, and while those around me were eating their crêpes suzette and crèmes brûlées, I was happily enjoying the wonderful flavors of tangy cheese and herbaceous honey. Not only that, I realized that this was a dessert—or an appetizer—that I could throw together at the last minute. You can vary the fruit and the type of honey, depending on your taste as well as what's in season.

12 small rounds fresh goat cheese (about 1 ounce each)

⅓ cup lavender honey (or use regular honey)

½ cup candied walnuts (see pages 102-103)

3 fresh pears, preferably Bosc, cored and cut into ⅛-inch-thick slices

Place 2 goat cheese rounds on each plate. Pour 1 tablespoon of the honey over each round. Scatter 5 or 6 nuts over and around the cheese, and arrange several pear slices on each plate.

Serves 6

Toasted Polenta Cake with Mascarpone and Cherry Compote

This cake is based on an old family recipe belonging to John Ash, the wonderfully talented culinary director of Fetzer Vineyards in Hopland, California. His grandmother was also talented, and her recipe for this cake proves it.

The use of coarse polenta rather than the finer cornmeal creates a very grainy, crumbly texture that provides a natural counterpoint to the creamy mascarpone. John's grandmother used vegetable oil in her cake, but I have taken the liberty of using olive oil instead. I like the lightness that it brings. Be sure to use a lighter-styled olive oil rather than the heavier extra-virgin.

Whether you choose to toast the cake or not, be sure to cut small portions since the cake is very rich. Once toasted it becomes crunchy on the outside while remaining soft on the inside. It is then an ideal surface for the marscarpone cheese and the compote. The cake is also very pretty, taking on a golden shimmer after it has been baked. Although rich, it is not terribly sweet, making it as good at breakfast or with tea as after dinner.

The compote can be made with just about any fresh fruit you like. If the fruit is quite ripe, then don't make a compote—use it as is. In the wintertime, pears are a good bet, either fresh or as a compote. A dried fruit compote is also nice, but it will require a longer cooking time and a little more liquid and sugar.

FOR THE CAKE
1 cup polenta
½ cup all-purpose flour
1½ teaspoons baking powder
¼ teaspoon salt
½ cup sugar
2 large eggs
1 large egg white
2 tablespoons unsalted butter, softened, cut into small pieces
¼ cup olive oil (not extra-virgin)
½ cup sour cream or plain yogurt (low-fat if desired)

FOR THE COMPOTE
5 ounces fresh cherries (about 1 cup), pitted
About 1 tablespoon sugar (depending on the sweetness of the cherries)
⅓ cup orange juice

8 ounces mascarpone
1 tablespoon sugar

To make the cake: Preheat the oven to 350°F. Butter an 8-inch cake pan. Line the bottom of the pan with a piece of parchment. Butter the parchment and then lightly flour the entire pan. Set aside.

In a medium bowl, sift together the polenta, flour, baking powder, and salt. Set aside.

In a large mixing bowl, mix the sugar, eggs, and egg white on medium-high speed until smooth. Add the butter and mix for 1 minute. (The mixture will not be completely smooth.) Add the olive oil and sour cream, and continue mixing for 2 more minutes.

Turn the mixer to low speed and add the reserved dry ingredients. Mix just until they are moistened. Pour the batter into the prepared pan and bake for 30 to 35 minutes, or until a tester inserted into the center comes out clean and the cake is a nice golden color. (Be careful not to overbake; the cake can quickly turn from moist to dry.) Let cool on a wire rack for 15 minutes. Remove the cake from the pan and let it cool completely on a wire rack.

To make the compote: In a medium-size saucepan, mix the cherries and sugar together.

Place over medium-high heat and cook just until the sugar has melted. Reduce the heat to medium and add the orange juice. Simmer for about 5 minutes, or until the cherries are soft to the touch. Remove from the heat and allow to cool.

To assemble: Preheat the broiler.

In a small bowl, stir together the mascarpone and the sugar.

Cut the cake into thin slices (a little goes a long way). Set the slices on a broilerproof baking sheet and broil until the edges turn dark brown. The middle of the slices will not brown. Turn and repeat on the other side, watching carefully so they don't burn. Remove them from the broiler and place the slices on individual serving plates. Top with a generous spoonful of compote, and then with a dollop of the mascarpone. Serve immediately.

Serves 8 to 10

Ricotta-Brioche Bread Pudding

I think I have read more do's and don'ts about making bread pudding than about any other type of dessert (except pie crusts). But what I have discovered is that while some people think white bread is the only bread to use in bread pudding, I like the richness yet relative lightness of brioche. It's sweeter than white bread and because of that plays a welcome host to the slightly tangy ricotta cheese. The orange zest bridges the sweet with the tangy and creates a new flavor all its own. This batter rises high above the pan, creating a golden cloud, but fortunately it has yet to actually run over the edge whenever I've made it. Feel free to serve this with a caramel sauce, a traditional hard sauce (butter, sugar, and bourbon), or whipped cream, although I prefer it just as it is. Another variation is to add dried prunes that have been soaked in sherry.

1¼ pounds brioche (or use any type of egg
  bread), crusts removed, cut into 1-inch
  slices, then into 1-inch cubes (about 9 cups)
5 extra-large eggs
1⅛ cups sugar
2 cups ricotta cheese, drained in cheesecloth
  if watery
2 teaspoons pure vanilla extract
2 cups heavy cream or half-and-half
2 cups whole or 2% milk
5 tablespoons unsalted butter, melted
1 tablespoon finely chopped orange zest

Place an oven rack into the second-lowest slot and preheat the oven to 325°F. Butter the bottom and sides of a 9 x 13-inch baking pan (preferably glass). Set aside.

In a large mixing bowl, whisk 4 of the eggs. Add 1 cup of the sugar and mix well. Add 1⅓ cups of the ricotta. Mix well. Add the vanilla, cream, milk, 4 tablespoons of the melted butter, and the orange zest and beat until smooth. Stir 7 cups of the bread cubes into the egg mixture. Let sit for 20 minutes, stirring occasionally.

Meanwhile, in a small bowl, beat together the remaining 1 egg, remaining ⅛ cup sugar, and ⅓ cup of the ricotta cheese.

Pour the bread mixture into the prepared pan. Scatter the remaining bread cubes over the mixture. Distribute the remaining ricotta mixture over the top in large spoonfuls. (It will not cover it all.) Dot with the remaining ⅓ cup ricotta cheese, and drizzle with the remaining 1 tablespoon melted butter. Bake until the corners of the bread cubes are toasted and the pudding is very puffy, 50 to 60 minutes. The pudding should jiggle slightly (like Jell-O) in the middle, but it should not be runny.

Let rest on a cooling rack for at least 15 minutes or up to 6 hours. Warm the pudding before serving or serve at room temperature.

Serves 12

Variation
⅓ cup dried prunes or figs, or a combination, cut into pieces, about the size of raisins
3 tablespoons cream sherry

Soak the prunes in the sherry for 20 minutes. Add the fruit and sherry to the pudding mixture at the same time you add the orange zest.

Cinnamon-Coated Panela

Panela is a fresh Mexican cheese that can usually be identified by the basket-weave decoration on the outside. This ornate exterior is formed when the cheese is placed in a basket to drain the excess whey. The cheese is pressed with weights, and that weight causes the basket weave to be "carved" into the cheese.

Unlike most other fresh cheeses, panela does not really melt when heated. Paradoxically, that very quality makes it a good cooking cheese when the cheese itself is the focus. You wouldn't want to put it on a pizza, since it would remain too firm. But in this dish, the cheese is put directly into the pan, and even though it gets very hot it keeps its shape. Since panela is a mild cheese, it can be used in both sweet and savory preparations. Try it with sautéed peppers and Mexican sausages, or as a dessert as described here. It makes a novel dish and is not too filling.

2 tablespoons sugar
½ teaspoon ground cinnamon
½ pound panela, cut into six ¼-inch-thick slices
1 tablespoon unsalted butter
2 small peaches, peeled and cut into ½-inch pieces

Mix the sugar and cinnamon together on a plate. Dip the cheese slices in the sugar-cinnamon mixture, coating them on both sides and on the edges. Reserve any extra sugar-cinnamon mixture.

Have a small serving platter or six individual plates ready.

Heat a medium-size nonstick sauté pan over medium-high heat. Add the cheese and cook until it begins to form small bubbles around the edges and is brown on the underside, 2 minutes. Turn, and cook the other side for about 2 minutes. The cheese should be quite brown on both sides. Put the cheese on the platter or plates.

In the same pan, melt the butter over high heat, and add the peaches. Stir gently for about 2 minutes, making sure both sides of the peaches are slightly brown. Sprinkle with the reserved sugar-cinnamon mixture, and distribute over the panela slices. Serve immediately.

Serves 6

COWGIRL CREAMERY

WITH A NAME LIKE COWGIRL CREAMERY, it is pretty much a given that the people behind it have a sense of humor. While that is true, owners Sue Conley and Peggy Smith are dead serious about their operation, which is located in a traditional dairy area in northern California. Committed to the environment, to local food producers, and to area dairies, Conley and Smith have created a unique operation showcasing the bounty that exists within the breathtakingly beautiful Tomales Bay and Point Reyes National Seashore area in western Marin County. So committed are they to the region that they are trying to create a special Western Marin County appellation, or regional designation, that will denote the environmentally friendly practices utilized by local growers and food producers as well as the general high quality of Western Marin agricultural products.

The operation, which was started in 1994, has two components: The first is Tomales Bay Foods, which encompasses a small cheese distributorship, a store carrying regionally made jams, chutneys and mustards, and locally grown produce, and a carry-out operation that serves up dishes made with local products. Smith, who was a chef at the renowned Chez Panisse in Berkeley for seventeen years, runs the kitchen and the store. Also housed in the store is a cheese counter where American artisanal cheeses are sold along with English cheeses from Neal's Yard Dairy in London. The cheese counter is managed by Kate Arding, a British recruit from Neal's Yard Dairy, who is thoroughly committed to American cheese.

The second component, Cowgirl Creamery, is the cheese arm of the operation and is strictly Conley's domain. Utilizing organic milk from the nearby Straus Family Creamery (see page 84), Sue makes five fresh, organic cheeses that are throwbacks to the pre-mass production days. Surely more people would eat cottage cheese if they tried Cowgirl Creamery's; it has a tangy flavor and a creamy consistency due to the cultured cream Sue adds to the curds. She also makes a nonfat quark, crème fraîche, fromage blanc, and molded rounds of fromage blanc that are coated with tarragon, thyme, and parsley. In addition, she now makes several flavors of ice cream utilizing organic products. The Meyer lemon vanilla bean ice cream alone is worth a trip to California.

(continued on page 216)

WHAT THEY MAKE
Clabbered cottage cheese
Crème fraîche
Ellen's Nonfat Quark
Fromage blanc
Olema Valley Round

HOW TO REACH THEM
Point Reyes Station, California
415-663-9335
415-663-8153
415-663-5418 (fax)
website: www.cowgirlcreamery.com

Part of Conley's vision was to make food production more understandable to more people. Since Tomales Bay Foods and Cowgirl Creamery (housed together in a renovated barn) are positioned in the heart of a nature-lover's mecca and tourist destination, she decided that if people could actually watch cheese being made, they might have a better understanding of the connection between what they eat and where it comes from. With that in mind, she built the cheesemaking room behind glass so that visitors could peek in on the process and see how milk becomes cheese. That, combined with the use of organic milk and a decided lack of machinery, makes Cowgirl Creamery not only a producer of excellent fresh cheeses but also a symbol for the hardworking people, quality ingredients, and artistic efforts that go into making specialty cheeses throughout America.

Quarky Chocolate Cake

Sour cream cakes are a dime a dozen, but using German-style quark (a low- or nonfat fresh cheese that tastes like a combination of sour cream, yogurt, and cream cheese) takes this ordinary chocolate cake into the realm of the memorable. It's fudgy, yet slightly easier on your conscience. If you can't find quark, which is available in some supermarkets, you can make this cake with sour cream. Since this is a three-layer cake, plan to serve a lot of people or to have a lot of leftovers. This cake is best eaten the day it's made, though it will hold, covered, for twenty-four to forty-eight hours at room temperature. Do not refrigerate.

FOR THE FROSTING

1¼ cups heavy cream

1⅔ cups sugar

6½ ounces good-quality unsweetened chocolate, such as Scharffenberger or Callebaut, finely chopped

¾ cup (1½ sticks) unsalted butter, slightly softened, cut into tablespoons

1½ teaspoons pure vanilla extract

FOR THE CAKE

½ cup boiling water

½ cup unsweetened cocoa powder (not Dutch process), plus extra for dusting the pans

4 ounces high-quality unsweetened chocolate, such as Scharffenberger or Callebaut, coarsely chopped

1¾ cups cake flour

6 tablespoons all-purpose flour

½ teaspoon baking powder

¼ teaspoon salt

1¼ cups (2½ sticks) unsalted butter, softened

2½ cups sugar

1 whole egg

5 large eggs, separated

1 tablespoon pure vanilla extract

1 cup quark, such as Ellen's Nonfat, stirred until smooth

DESSERTS

To make the frosting: In a medium-size saucepan, heat the cream and sugar. Stir until the sugar has dissolved. Add the chocolate and stir until it is thoroughly melted. Remove from the heat, cover, and let cool for about 10 minutes.

Using an electric mixer, mix the butter on medium-high speed until it is smooth and creamy. Turn the mixer to medium-low and add half of the chocolate mixture along with the vanilla. Mix well. Add the remaining chocolate mixture and mix until smooth and creamy. Set aside until it hardens slightly, to become a spreadable consistency, 1 to 2 hours. (Or, you can refrigerate the frosting for about 30 minutes, or until it becomes thickened and spreadable. Bring it to room temperature before frosting.)

To make the cake: Preheat the oven to 350°F. Generously grease three 9-inch round cake pans. Cut a piece of waxed paper to fit the bottom of each pan and place inside the pans. Grease the waxed paper, and dust the pans with cocoa powder until well coated. Set aside.

In a small heatproof bowl, pour the boiling water over the ½ cup cocoa. Stir until the mixture is very smooth, and set aside to cool.

Melt the chocolate in a double-boiler or in a stainless-steel bowl set over a pan of hot, but not boiling, water. Stir occasionally until smooth. Remove from the heat.

Into a medium-size bowl, sift together both flours, the baking powder, and salt. Set aside.

In the bowl of a stand mixer, beat the butter until smooth and creamy, about 5 minutes. Add 2¼ cups of the sugar and beat until well blended, about 5 minutes. Beat in the whole egg and egg yolks, one at a time. Beat in the cooled cocoa mixture until very smooth, scraping down the sides as you go. Turn the mixer to medium-low and add the melted chocolate, beating until well incorporated. Add the vanilla. Turn the mixer to low and add half the dry ingredients. Then add the quark, mix well, and add the rest of the dry ingredients. Beat until smooth and creamy, 2 to 3 minutes.

In a copper or stainless-steel bowl, and using clean beaters, beat the egg whites at high speed. When frothy, add the remaining ¼ cup sugar and continue beating until the egg whites form stiff peaks, 5 to 6 minutes.

Using a large rubber spatula, fold about 1 cup of the chocolate mixture into the egg whites. Then gently fold that mixture back into the chocolate mixture, just until the egg whites are well incorporated. Do not overmix.

Distribute the batter evenly among the pans, and bake in the center of the oven for 20 to 25 minutes. Do not overbake. Cakes are done when the tops are just beginning to crack and a toothpick inserted into the center comes out with a few crumbs clinging to it. Let cool on a rack for about 15 minutes. Remove the cakes from the pans and let cool completely on a wire rack.

To assemble: Place the first layer on a serving plate and frost the top only. Place the second layer on top of the first and frost the top. Repeat with the top layer. Spread the remaining frosting along the sides until the cake is completely covered with frosting. Cut and enjoy!

Serves 12 to 15

BRIER RUN FARM

GREG AND VERENA SAVA started Brier Run Farm in a tent. Having lived in upstate New York, they decided to make the move to the rolling hills of West Virginia, and to a place that looked a little more like Verena's homeland, Switzerland. They fell in love with some land, bought it, and then decided that they ought to build a house. In the meantime, they bought their goats and called their tent home.

An overabundance of goat milk led them to cheesemaking in the mid-1970s, but it wasn't until the mid-1980s that they began to make cheese in earnest. They built a cheesemaking facility and milk barn by themselves, and in 1986 the prestigious West Virginia resort, The Greenbrier, started buying their cheese.

After nearly two decades of milking goats and making cheese, the Savas are beginning to cut back. To most people, though, their definition of "cutting back" seems almost laughable. Instead of 140 goats, they are paring their herd to 60. Their six employees are now gone, leaving the entire process to the two of them. "We love, love, love what we are doing," says Verena Sava, "so we decided to cut back to a level where we could enjoy it more."

For cheese aficionados in and around West Virginia—and New York, Boston, and Chicago—the Brier Run Farm cheese will still be available. And Verena hints that maybe she'll even begin to make an aged cheese when the milk is abundant.

All of the Brier Run Farm's cheeses are hand-ladled, which means that the curds are scooped up by hand and poured into small molds outfitted with tiny holes, which allows the whey to drain. This method results in a cheese that is a little more loosely structured. Brier Run may be the country's only certified organic facility making soft cheese, and their chèvre is flavorful, tart, yet sweet. Verena Sava's quark is authentic and wonderfully tangy, though its goats' milk origin differentiates it from the usual cows' milk quark.

The Savas also make fromage blanc, blue mold and white mold cheeses (they use a Camembert mold), and something they call "Farmhouse Special," which Verena Sava describes as a fresh Romano cheese without the age.

Although the Savas are trying to recapture a life outside of their goat farm operation, they cannot reverse what they have already established: a very high standard for goats' milk cheeses and an indisputable devotion to the land and to its future. For these and other reasons, they have justly earned the status of cheesemaking icons in America.

BRIER RUN CHÈVRE
BRIER RUN FARM · BIRCH RIVER, WV 26610
INGREDIENTS
Pasteurized goat's milk, culture, salt, rennet

WHAT THEY MAKE
Farmhouse Special
Fresh chèvre
Flavored chèvre
Fromage blanc
Goats' milk fudge
Quark

HOW TO REACH THEM
Birch River, West Virginia
304-649-2975

Creamy Fromage Blanc with Summer Fruit

The mixture of fromage blanc and crème fraîche is inherently creamy, but it is not sweet. That is one of its virtues. Adding a little sugar and combining it with ripe fruit is all it takes to create an elegant dessert that's not too rich. The mixture is also excellent on pancakes and waffles as well as bananas, pears, and berries.

This dessert can be served in two ways: One is to put the fruit in a bowl and top it with the cheese mixture. The other is to layer it in parfait glasses. Either way, it's an easy dish to put together at the last minute if the fruit and the cheese mixture are prepared in advance. The latter can be prepared up to forty-eight hours ahead and refrigerated.

½ **pound nectarines, pitted and sliced**
  ¼ **inch thick**
½ **pound peaches, peeled, pitted, and sliced**
  ¼ **inch thick**
About ¼ **cup sugar (depending on the**
  sweetness of the fruit)
About ½ **teaspoon fresh lemon juice**
½ **cup fromage blanc, such as Brier Run**
½ **cup crème fraîche**
2 teaspoons sugar
16 fresh mint leaves

In a medium-size bowl, mix together the fruit, sugar, and lemon juice. Taste, and add more sugar and/or lemon juice as needed. Let sit for about 20 minutes.

In another bowl, mix the fromage blanc, crème fraîche, and sugar together until smooth.

Spoon the fruit into serving bowls, and place about ¼ cup of the fromage blanc mixture on top of each serving. Top each with 4 mint leaves, and serve.

Serves 4

Mascarpone Brownies

Decadent, delicious, devilish. These brownies are that and more, thanks to their extremely fudgy consistency and the creaminess of the mascarpone. The brewed coffee gives them a rich flavor that, combined with the mascarpone, is reminiscent of the popular Italian dessert tiramisù.

The hardest part about making these brownies comes after they leave the oven: to taste their best, they really need to sit for at least two hours before they're cut. With the smell of warm chocolate permeating the house, this is a challenge! But it is definitely worth the wait.

FOR THE BATTER
⅔ cup all-purpose flour
¼ teaspoon salt
½ teaspoon baking powder
2 ounces unsweetened chocolate
2 ounces bittersweet chocolate
2 ounces semisweet chocolate
2 tablespoons strong brewed coffee
½ cup (1 stick) unsalted butter
1 cup sugar
2 teaspoons vanilla extract
3 extra-large eggs

FOR THE FILLING
8 ounces mascarpone cheese, softened (or
   use cream cheese)
¼ cup sugar
¼ teaspoon vanilla extract
1 egg yolk

Preheat the oven to 325°F. Generously butter and flour an 8-inch square baking pan.

To make the batter: In a small bowl, sift together the flour, salt, and baking powder. Set aside.

In a large double-boiler or in a heatproof bowl set over a pan of simmering water, combine the chocolates, coffee, and butter. Stir occasionally until the mixture is melted and smooth. Remove from the stove and whisk in the sugar and vanilla. Whisk in the eggs, one at a time, being sure each

is fully incorporated before adding the next. When smooth, whisk in the reserved dry ingredients.

To make the filling: In a small bowl, beat the mascarpone with the sugar, vanilla, and egg yolk.

To assemble: Pour half the brownie batter into the prepared pan. Dot the batter with large spoonfuls of half the filling. Repeat with the remaining batter and filling. Next, create swirls in the batter: Starting in one corner of the pan, insert the tip of a regular table knife about halfway into the batter. Gently bring the knife forward and back, as if to make an "S" shape. Do this four times to make four "lines" through the batter. Do it four more times in the opposite direction. The mascarpone should be swirled but not completely mixed with the chocolate, since you do not want to lose the marble effect.

Bake for 50 minutes or until center is still slightly jiggly and a toothpick inserted in the center comes out *almost* clean. A few crumbs should still be sticking to the toothpick because the brownies will continue to cook after they have been removed from the oven.

Let rest on a cooling rack for 2 to 3 hours. Cut and serve.

Any leftovers should be stored for up to 2 days in the refrigerator. Otherwise, wrap and freeze for up to 3 months.

Makes 16 brownies

OPPOSITE: Macaroni and Cheese (see page 234).

DESSERTS

CHEESE CLASSICS

SONOMA CHEESE FACTORY

LIKE ITS NEIGHBOR THE VELLA CHEESE COMPANY, the Sonoma Cheese Factory has been producing Jack cheese since the 1930s. In fact, Tom Vella and Sonoma Cheese Factory founder Celso Viviani were partners in cheesemaking until Vella went off to start his own plant after World War II (see pages 68-69). Viviani continued making mostly cottage cheese and cream and sold them to his one buyer: Kraft Cheese Company. Gradually Celso and his son, Peter, started making Jack cheese and its aged counterpart, dry Jack, and it is for those cheeses that they are now famous.

Sonoma County is California's "other wine country," just west of the famous Napa Valley. In the past few years it has become a tourist magnet because it is rustic and quaint, yet it has some of the best wine, bread, and cheese in the world. The town of Sonoma is distinguished by its large square with a park as its center; around the perimeter is a series of shops and restaurants. Among those shops is the Sonoma Cheese Factory, where visitors can watch cheese being made and sample any one of the over fifteen different types of cheese.

The company's current president is David Viviani, though he still shares his duties with his father, Peter. The cheesemaking is done almost identically to the way it began: little mechanization and hand-formed. This includes the traditional method for Jack cheese, in which the curds are scooped up into muslin cloth, tied, pressed, and eventually packaged.

The Sonoma Cheese Factory cheeses are all made with pasteurized milk. With the exception of the dry Jack, which is called "Parma Jack," the Sonoma Jack cheeses are high-moisture, flavorful cheeses, distin-

guished by the numerous flavors the Factory makes. ("Factory" is a bit of a misnomer since all of the production is still done at the original site, which is startlingly small.) Among those are Vidalia onion, pesto, habañero, garlic, salsa, Mediterranean, and hot pepper (slightly milder than the habañero). They also make quite decent reduced-fat versions of some of these cheeses.

All of these Jack cheeses are excellent representations of the genre: slightly tangy, firm yet moist, with fresh milk flavors coming through. The habañero Jack might be an exception because that pepper is one of the hottest in the world. When it mixes with the cheese it becomes the dominant flavor. For that reason, it is wonderful to cook with because the spiciness will definitely come through.

WHAT THEY MAKE
Cows' milk cheeses
Cheddar: white and orange
Chile-Cheddar
Havarti
Parma Jack
Pepato
Reduced-fat Sonoma Jack: traditional, garlic, hot pepper, pesto

Sonoma Jack: traditional, garlic, habañero, hot pepper, Mediterannean, pesto, salsa, smoked, Vidalia onion
Teleme

Goats' milk cheese
Billy Jack

HOW TO REACH THEM
Sonoma, California
707-996-1000
800-535-2855 (mail order)
707-935-3535 (fax)
website: www.sonomacheese.com

The Vivianis also play a part in the world of California-made Teleme cheese. Along with the Peluso family (see pages 80-81), they learned how to make this unusually elegant cheese. Now they are resuming that tradition by making Teleme once again.

The newest addition to the Sonoma line is Billy Jack, David Viviani's clever name for their goats' milk Jack cheese. They just began to make this cheese in June 1999, so it will be interesting to see how it evolves.

Sonoma Jack cheese is an integral part of California cheese history. The cheese itself is no different than Monterey Jack, but the Vivianis wanted to name their cheese after the town in which it was made. (Monterey is about 150 miles southwest of Sonoma.) With the continued emphasis on Jack cheeses, the Viviani family, like the Vella family, is carrying on a cheesemaking tradition in Sonoma that began at the turn of the century and, interestingly, has grown but not changed in nearly a hundred years.

Pepper Cheese Crisps

Certain hors d'oeuvres, especially those with cheese, have stood the test of time. Cheese crisps or twists are one of those, although there are many versions of them. My grandmother's were made with flour, butter, cheese, a little bit of salt, and sometimes caraway seeds. This has some of those same ingredients, except that the flour and butter are in the form of puff pastry. It is important to use a buttery puff pastry rather than one made with vegetable shortening. The flavor from the shortening just doesn't compare with real butter. You can find puff pastry dough at some of the better bakeries, gourmet stores, and some supermarkets. It is well worth seeking out.

These taste especially good when hot, but they are fine at room temperature as well.

½ **pound frozen puff pastry dough, defrosted**
3 **ounces pepper Jack cheese, such as Sonoma**
    Cheese Factory's Habañero, grated (or use
    plain Jack cheese, grated and mixed with
    ½ **teaspoon red pepper flakes)**
Dash of salt
1 **to 2 tablespoons milk**

Preheat the oven to 400°F.

Roll the puff pastry dough into a rectangle measuring 10 by 13 inches. Cut it in half lengthwise. Sprinkle the cheese and salt over one piece of the puff pastry, leaving a ½-inch border. Brush the edges of the pastry with the milk. Place the other piece of puff pastry over the first, matching the edges. Roll gently with a rolling pin, just until the edges are sealed. If necessary, pinch the edges closed with your fingers. Cut crosswise into ½-inch strips. Twist each strip several times, and place them on a baking sheet.

Bake for 12 minutes, or until the strips are a deep golden brown. Let cool 5 minutes and serve.

Makes about 26 twists

WASHINGTON STATE UNIVERSITY CREAMERY

IT SEEMS NATURAL THAT A UNIVERSITY in the Midwest or in California (the nation's largest dairy state) would specialize in dairy sciences, but a university with that focus in the northwestern part of the country is a little more unusual. However, Washington State University in Pullman, Washington, has been milking cows and making cheese for the better part of the 20th century, and Cougar Gold cheese is the result.

As testimony to its quality and longevity, Cougar Gold's champion and de facto spokesman up through the 1970s was singer Rudy Vallee. No one really knows why, except for the obvious: He liked the cheese.

Cougar Gold is a farmstead cheese; the milk used to make it comes from the WSU campus cows. The milk is then pasteurized, made into cheese (in a similar fashion to cheddar cheese, except that a second culture is added, lending its characteristic flavor), pressed, and left to drain for about twenty-four hours. After that, the cheese is placed in its surprising home: a thirty-ounce can. It is then aged for one year.

The idea of a cheese actually ripening in a can seems counterintuitive. But dairy manager Mark Bates explains that while bacterial-ripened cheese, such as a Camembert, needs air to develop, the Cougar Gold has certain enzymes that need no air to ripen the cheese. Bates should know. He has been teaching cheesemaking and dairy management to students as well as to cheesemakers from around the country for over twenty-five years. And one bite of Cougar Gold confirms its quality. The slight nuttiness is reminiscent of a Gouda, but the drier texture and fruitiness are more like a medium-aged cheddar.

Cougar Gold flies off the aging shelves at a rate of about 30,000 cans a year. Although it isn't sold at the retail level, it's accessible to anyone who has a phone and the desire to bring a little Cougar Gold into their own home. However, the cheese is often not shipped in the summertime, when the heat might diminish its quality.

The WSU creamery makes other "canned" cheese, including two types of cheddar—one-year-old and "smoky"—and a line of cheeses called Viking. Similar to Monterey Jack, the Viking cheese is aged for four months and is made in a variety of flavors as well as in a reduced-fat version.

Cougar Gold, however, is probably the most interesting cheese because of its combination of flavors brought about by the unique cheesemaking method. It is also a perfect melting cheese, which is why it is featured in the following grilled cheese recipe. It can be used in soups, soufflés, and vegetable dishes, or eaten plain. In fact, it is the perfect picnic cheese. All you have to do is open the can.

WHAT THEY MAKE
Cougar Gold
Cheddar: plain and smoked
Viking: plain, flavored, reduced-fat

HOW TO REACH THEM
Pullman, Washington
1-800-457-5442
website: www.wsu.edu/creamery

"New" Old-Fashioned Grilled Cheese Sandwich

Few cheese dishes come close to the comfort level offered by a grilled cheese sandwich. The buttery bread and the oozing cheese spill out ease and warmth. While grilled cheese sandwiches are hardly challenging to make, the right proportion of ingredients is key to the perfect sandwich. Ultra-thin-sliced hearty bread, butter, and the perfect amount of grated cheese is all it takes. This creates a crispy exterior for the soft melted cheese.

Although grilled cheese sandwiches are traditionally made with cheddar or (heaven forbid!) processed American cheese, almost any type of good melting cheese works perfectly. Use what you like. To make a more up-to-date version, try placing a few basil leaves in the center. It's a wonderful fresh surprise.

½ pound Cougar Gold cheese, coarsely
   grated (or use cheddar or Gouda)
4 large ⅛-inch-thick slices country, *pain
   levain*, or other hearty bread, cut in half
12 fresh basil leaves (optional)
3 tablespoons butter

Sprinkle the grated cheese over 4 slices of the bread. Top with the basil leaves, if using. Cover with the remaining 4 bread slices.

In a large sauté pan, melt the butter over medium-high heat. Place the sandwiches in the pan and cover. Cook until the sandwich is golden brown on the underside, about 3 minutes. Turn with a spatula and cook the other side until golden brown and the cheese has melted, about 2 more minutes. Serve immediately.

Serves 4

NORTHLAND SHEEP DAIRY

HUMILITY, FIRST AND FOREMOST, is the quality that sings out when Jane North tells her story. Never mind that she was one of America's first sheep cheese makers (some say she *was* the first); never mind that she was making sheep's milk cheese in the Pyrenees with other cheesemakers and hers were the ones bought by the local French people at the farmers' market; and never mind that she's been making some of the most sought-after, exclusive cheeses in this country for fifteen years. If you don't ask her about this, Jane North won't tell you.

Living in the middle of New York State, close to Ithaca and Syracuse, Jane and her husband, Karl, milk a flock of fifty sheep. They keep the flock small so they can manage it on their own. From that milk, she makes three cheeses: Bergère Bleue, Folie Bergère, and Tomme Bergère.

Her Bergère Bleue is a Roquefort-style cheese that has more creaminess than its French counterpart and not all of the salt, since North prefers blue cheese that way. She says that a visit to the Roquefort caves took much of the mystery out of cheesemaking for her, clearing the (psychological) way to making her own cheese.

All of North's cheeses are made with raw milk, and both her sheep cheese and her lambing operation are certified organic by the Northeast Organic Farming Association. Indeed, the philosophy that drives the Norths is that of sustainable agriculture. Jane says that they are simply "stewards of the land," and that it is their responsibility—and everyone's—to see that the land and its natural resources endure.

The Norths' cheesemaking journey began thirty years ago while they were taking care of a friend's farm. The farm included a few goats, and part of the house-sitting duties included milking them. Jane saw that as an opportunity to learn to make cheese.

In the 1970s she and Karl decided to move the family to the French Pyrenees, to a "small village clinging to the side of a mountain," says North, to immerse the children in French culture and language. This experience served to further North's interest in cheesemaking. She began with goats and then moved on to sheep. Her friends and fellow cheesemakers encouraged her to bring her cheese to the local farmers' market, where it became a treasured item.

The North family returned to New York, and in 1985 they got their first sheep. They sold their first cheese in 1988 at the Ithaca farmers' market, where it received the same enthusiastic response as it had in France. This prompted the Norths to continue making cheese, which fit in with their dream of creating a farm that was self-sustaining.

Unfortunately for cheeselovers who do not live in the midsection of New York State, getting Northland Sheep Dairy cheese is difficult, although they will do mail order. Jane North makes only the three cheeses, totaling about 1,500 pounds a year. By comparison, a very small cheesemaker might make around 30,000 pounds a year. Still, it is worth tracking down.

WHAT THEY MAKE
Bergère Bleue
Folie Bergère
Tomme Bergère

HOW TO REACH THEM
Marathon, New York
607-849-3328

Traditional Cobb Salad

What would an American cheese book be without one of America's most famous salads? For those who don't know, this salad originated at the Brown Derby restaurant in Los Angeles sometime in the mid-1920s. The chef there, named Cobb, apparently decided to chop just about everything in sight and call it a salad. It was an instant hit, made famous by the restaurant's celebrity clientele. Over the years, a Cobb salad has come to symbolize anything that is chopped in small pieces and called a salad. But this recipe is about as close to the original as you can get. Interestingly, the ingredients in this traditional salad are as contemporary as any that might be used today. Because of all of the chopping involved, it is a good idea to prepare everything two to three hours in advance, keeping the ingredients in separate containers in the refrigerator (except for the bacon). Bring it all to room temperature, and put it together just before serving.

FOR THE DRESSING
¼ cup red wine vinegar
¼ teaspoon sugar
1½ teaspoons fresh lemon juice
½ teaspoon Worcestershire sauce
¾ teaspoon dry mustard
1 small clove garlic, minced
Salt and freshly ground pepper
¼ cup olive oil
½ cup vegetable oil

FOR THE SALAD
½ head butter lettuce (also called Bibb),
    cored and coarsely chopped
½ head romaine lettuce, cored and coarsely
    chopped
1 bunch frisée, cored and coarsely chopped
1 bunch watercress, leaves only
2 tomatoes, cored, seeded and cut into
    ¼-inch dice
1 whole boneless, skinless chicken breast,
    cooked, cut into ½-inch dice
1 avocado, pitted, peeled, and cut into
    ½-inch dice

⅓ cup crumbled blue cheese, such as
    Northland's Bergère Bleue
3 hard-cooked eggs, peeled and coarsely
    chopped
8 slices bacon, cooked, crumbled
2 tablespoons chopped fresh chives

To make the dressing: In a medium-size nonreactive bowl, mix together all the dressing ingredients. Set aside.

To assemble the salad: mix together all the lettuces and the watercress. Place in a large wide bowl or on a large serving platter. Arrange the tomatoes in a strip down the center. On one side of the tomatoes place the following in strips: chicken, avocado, and blue cheese. On the other side of the tomatoes place the eggs and bacon in strips. The lettuces should be completely covered with these strips. When ready to serve, bring the salad to the table and toss it with the dressing. Sprinkle with the chives.

Serves 6 to 8 as a first course, 2 to 4 as a main course

MAYTAG DAIRY FARMS

IF YOU'RE TRAVELING ON INTERSTATE 80 in the middle of Iowa, about thirty-five miles outside of Des Moines, you'll find yourself in the backyard of Maytag Dairy Farms, makers of America's most famous blue cheese. You won't see a huge herd of Holsteins anymore, though until 1992 they were an integral part of the operation. "Impossible to get people to take care of them," says president and CEO James Stevens.

The affable chief knows just about all there is to know about his company, as most CEOs do. But Stevens is a little unusual, in that he's been with Maytag "forever," he jokes. Forever, in this case, is more than forty-five years. In the context of the history of Maytag, such longevity and loyalty begin to make sense.

"Forever" began not long after Maytag got its start as a cheese factory in 1941. At that time, the two Maytag brothers, who were running the family's appliance business, decided they weren't terribly interested in carrying on their father's hobby of collecting Holsteins. They wanted either to get rid of the sizable herd or to find a way to derive income from it.

At the same time, Iowa State College (now Iowa State University) had recently completed research on making a Roquefort-style blue cheese with cows' milk. (True Roquefort is made with sheep's milk.) The Maytag brothers seized the opportunity to draw on the university's expertise and sent one of their people to Iowa State to learn how to make blue cheese. Caves were dug, a cheese plant was built, and in October 1941, the first Maytag blue cheese was born.

What is particularly impressive is that the cheese that was produced displayed a sophistication and depth that, at that time, was more common to European cheeses. While the cheese recipe has been refined along the way, notably by cheesemaker-cum-company-president Jim Stevens, it has always been a superior cheese.

Maytag Blue is made from raw milk and therefore must be aged for a minimum of sixty days. However, it is usually aged much longer than that. It is an impeccable specimen of blue cheese, with its pronounced saltiness, spiciness, and its musty, creamy, yet crumbly texture. The cheese does not appear to have huge amounts of blue spores, and yet one taste tells a different story. It is unmistakably a blue cheese in all its glory.

The same underground aging caves that were built back in 1941 are used to age the Maytag cheeses today. But demand has finally surpassed Maytag's current capacity, so construction is under way to build more caves and enlarge the cheesemaking facility.

The Maytag cheese operation, rife with tradition, is still owned and run by the Maytag

WHAT THEY MAKE
Blue Cheese Spread
Goat Blue (limited)
Goat Edam (limited)
Maytag Blue

HOW TO REACH THEM
Newton, Iowa
800-247-2458
515-792-1133
515-792-1567 (fax)

family. One of those family members is Fritz Maytag, who owns the San Francisco-based Anchor Steam beer operation. He is now branching out into winemaking as well, bottling wine under the York Creek label. It is a superior wine and, not coincidentally, a good cheese wine.

Maytag Dairy Farms has not limited its repertoire to cows' milk cheese. Among others, they now make goat cheese, although Stevens is quick to say that the goat cheese falls between a hobby and a serious product since they don't make a lot of it. But their goat blue cheese is definitely worth an inquiry.

When a business has been run so well for so long, the idea of change is always a little daunting. But for now, Stevens says that he has no plans to retire in the near future. "As long as the family likes what I'm doing and as long as I'm happy, I don't see any reason to leave," he says. That type of loyalty is reflected in the quality of the cheese: it is consistent, and it shows the hand of experience in its beautiful texture, depth of flavor, creamy consistency, and balance. It remains one of America's finest cheeses.

Iceberg Lettuce with Creamy Blue Cheese Dressing

❖

Although there are many ways to make old-fashioned recipes more contemporary, there are certain recipes that should just stay as they are. This is one of them. In today's world of designer greens and edible flowers, it would be easy to stray, and while that wouldn't be a terrible mistake, it would mean an unnecessary break from the past. Nostalgia notwithstanding, crunchy iceberg lettuce beneath a creamy dressing is a timeless combination worth treasuring. If you must stray toward the 21st century, then try hearts of romaine lettuce instead, or top it with strips of crispy bacon.

---

1 head iceberg lettuce
1 cup regular or low-fat mayonnaise
1 cup regular or low-fat sour cream
4 ounces blue cheese, such as Maytag Blue, crumbled, at room temperature
2 tablespoons fresh lemon juice
Dash of Tabasco sauce
Freshly ground pepper
2 tablespoons finely chopped fresh chives, plus extra for garnish

Cut the lettuce into 4 wedges, and place on individual plates.

In a medium-size bowl, whisk together the remaining ingredients, except the extra chives, until the dressing is creamy but still slightly lumpy from the blue cheese. Spoon a generous amount of dressing over each wedge of lettuce, garnish with the extra chives, and serve immediately. (The dressing can be made 24 hours in advance and refrigerated.)

Serves 4

Maytag Cheddar Soup

The folks at Maytag Dairy Farms, while famous for their blue cheese, have also made a white cheddar cheese on and off through the years. That cheese became the inspiration for a soup recipe. The following is an adaptation of that recipe, which has no doubt been made and served by countless Midwesterners during the long days of winter. Unlike many ultra-thick cheddar cheese soups, this one is light in texture—but don't be fooled, because it couldn't be richer. To make the best possible soup, use an aged but not super-sharp cheddar—it will impart the most flavor.

¼ cup (½ stick) unsalted butter

6 scallions, chopped

3 stalks celery, diced

2 carrots, diced

¼ cup all-purpose flour

5 cups good-quality unsalted chicken stock

1 large russet potato, peeled and diced

1 cup milk or half-and-half

½ pound cheddar, preferably white, coarsely grated

1 teaspoon Tabasco sauce

1 teaspoon Worcestershire sauce

Salt (depending on the saltiness of the cheese)

In a large pot, melt the butter over medium-low heat. Add the scallions, celery, and carrots and cook until limp, about 10 minutes. Sprinkle the flour over the vegetables, stir, and cook for 3 minutes. Add the chicken stock, 1 cup at a time, stirring constantly. Add the potatoes. Bring to a boil and then reduce the heat to a simmer. Cook until the potatoes are soft, 20 to 30 minutes. At this point, you can puree the soup in a blender or you can leave it chunky. A puree will result in a thicker soup, while the non-pureed version provides a variety of textures. Both taste good. Whisk in the milk, cheese, Tabasco, and Worcestershire. Taste, and add salt if needed. Serve immediately.

Serves 4 to 6

WINCHESTER CHEESE COMPANY

AFTER THE AGE OF SIXTY-FIVE, most people start thinking about retirement. Jules Wesselink, owner of Winchester Cheese Company, started making cheese. Born in Holland, Wesselink was familiar with Dutch cheeses, and he also came from a cheesemaking family. He was a dairyman, having owned herds of Holsteins in the Los Angeles area for the better part of forty years. When milk production became unprofitable, he decided to turn that milk into cheese. But first, he had to learn how.

Wesselink returned to Holland in 1995 and learned to make *boerenkaas* (also called "boere kaas"), or farmstead cheese. Among those was Gouda. He then came back to the United States and to his Winchester, California, dairy and began making Gouda there. His first cheese was sold in 1996.

Winchester lies about seventy miles north of San Diego, above a reservoir and beneath towering mountains. It is a perfect setting for a 500-cattle dairy. The cheesemaking facility, however, strays from its natural environment as it is located on four wheels. Rather than constructing a building, Wesselink discovered that a refrigerated trailer did the job just as well. It even has a nonoperational motor vehicle license.

Jules no longer makes the cheese, concentrating on the business end instead. Early on, he passed the cheesemaking duties to his daughter, Valerie Thomas, and her husband, David, who have mastered the art of making Gouda. Unlike the ubiquitous and unimpressive red wax Gouda, theirs is a raw milk cheese that is carefully aged over the course of months or even beyond a year. Their "super aged" Gouda is aged at least one year and takes on a slightly granular, nutty, salty, and butterscotch-like flavor that is unparalleled in this country. It is a cheese that blends nicely with a glass of port or perhaps with a Dutch ale. The "sharp" Gouda is aged between six months and one year and has the same qualities as its older counterpart but to a lesser degree. It is balanced, a little bit sweet, and makes for a great eating and cooking cheese. Jules says he likes his on mashed potatoes.

Winchester Cheese has been made for a short time and yet it is getting worldwide accolades. Wesselink sends his cheese to Holland every year to be judged and graded there because of their strict rules about boerenkaas. So far, his cheese has been honored with the highest grades. Only Wesselink and cheesemakers Valerie and David Thomas know how Winchester Gouda takes on the haunting characteristics that make it such an outstanding cheese.

WHAT THEY MAKE
Gouda: mild, medium, sharp, super-aged, cumin, jalapeño

HOW TO REACH THEM
Winchester, California
909-926-4239
909-926-3349 (fax)
website: www.winchestercheese.com

Three-Onion Soup Gratinée

Like all soups, this tastes better the next day. But if time does not permit, serving it the same day is perfectly acceptable, especially since it is topped with rich melted cheese. As you will see, this recipe uses three different types of onions: yellow, red, and Vidalia, Maui, or Walla Walla. The blend of these onions lends a lovely sweetness to the soup, but if you can't find them, use all yellow onions.

You will need broiler-proof bowls for this soup. If you do not have them, see the alternative cooking method at the end of the recipe.

¼ cup (½ stick) unsalted butter

2 Vidalia, Maui, or Walla Walla onions (about ½ pound total), cut into ¼-inch-thick slices

2 red onions (about ½ pound total), cut into ¼-inch-thick slices

2 yellow onions (about ½ pound total), cut into ¼-inch-thick slices

Freshly ground pepper

2 tablespoons all-purpose flour

1¾ cups good-quality unsalted beef stock

5½ cups good-quality unsalted chicken stock

1½ tablespoons fresh thyme leaves

Salt and pepper to taste

4 to 8 thin slices country-style bread, toasted

1½ cups coarsely grated Gouda cheese, such as Winchester Cheese (or use Gruyère or Emmentaler)

In a large stockpot, melt the butter over medium-low heat. Add all the onions along with ¼ teaspoon pepper, and sauté until the onions begin to turn golden brown or caramelize, about 25 minutes. Stir occasionally to be sure the onions do not stick to the pan. Once the onions are brown, add the flour and stir constantly until it disappears. Turn the heat to medium-high and add both stocks and the thyme. Bring to a boil. Reduce the heat to low, cover, and cook until the soup is slightly thickened and is a medium-brown color, at least 1 hour. Taste, and add salt and pepper as needed.

Preheat the broiler.

Ladle the soup into broiler-proof bowls. Place 1 slice of toast in each bowl and top with the cheese. Heat under the broiler until the cheese is brown and bubbling, 3 to 5 minutes. Serve immediately.

Serves 4 to 8

Note: If you do not have broiler-proof bowls, use this method: Preheat the oven to 400°F. Ladle the soup into a large deep, round casserole or soufflé dish. Place the toast slices on top of the soup. Cover with the cheese and bake until the cheese is brown and bubbling, about 15 minutes. Serve in individual soup bowls.

BRAVO FARMS

PATT AND BILL BOERSMA ARE CALIFORNIA PIONEERS. Their raw milk white cheddar is the first and only farmstead cheddar produced in the Golden State and is still one of just two California-made raw milk cheddars. Bill Boersma marvels at this distinction: "We have a hundred and fifty years of Valley [dairy] history, and it's hard to believe we're the first to make this cheese."

The Valley he is referring to is California's Central Valley, the 300-mile-long agricultural strip that runs down the center of the state. It is where cotton, grapes, nuts, and orchard fruits grow in abundance, and it is also where dairy farmers produce much of the state's milk.

Bill Boersma has been in the dairy business for over twenty-five years, but cheesemaking is a relatively new venture. It is also a talent. The Bravo Farms raw milk cheddar, which was first made in 1995, is an ivory-colored nutty and mildly fruity cheese that, because of its perfect balance, is reminiscent of some of the longer-aged English cheddars. It does not have the sharp or pungent characteristics of many American-made cheddars. Instead, it is more mellow but full-bodied and definitely full-flavored. The raw milk certainly adds to the depth of this cheese, but so too do the Boersmas' cheesemaking skills. Patt and Bill, along with one worker, make about 52,000 pounds of cheese a year.

Their skills are also apparent in their Edam cheese. This might be due to the 500-year-old recipe Bill Boersma uses to make it. (Edam was the first cheese to be exported from Holland, in the year 1250.) Unlike most Edams, the Bravo Farms Edam, which they call Queso de Bola, or ball cheese, because of its spherical shape, is made with whole milk. Other Edams are made with part skim milk. As a raw milk cheese, it is aged for no less than sixty days and sometimes more. The Central Valley town of Visalia, in which Bravo Farms is located, has a large Hispanic population, and Boersma says his Edam is particularly popular within that community.

Now the Boersmas have begun to make goats' milk cheese as well, using a neighbor's goats' milk. Its first time out, the raw milk aged goats' milk cheddar garnered a 98.5 score in a cheese competition held in Wisconsin. That was after they had been making the cheese for a little less than a year. It will unquestionably be an interesting cheese to watch, as will the goats' milk feta they are just now developing.

The Boersmas are exceptionally devoted to their craft, underscored by their decision to produce a raw milk cheddar when no other farmstead cheesemakers in their area ever had. Indeed, farmstead raw milk cheddars are rare throughout the United States, which makes this one a treasure and a symbol of many American cheesemakers' commitment to breaking new ground in high-quality handcrafted cheese.

WHAT THEY MAKE

Cows' milk cheeses
Flavored cheddars: chipotle, jalapeño, garlic
Raw milk cheddar
Queso de Bola (raw milk Edam)

Goats' milk cheeses
Feta
Goats' milk aged cheddar
Goats' milk mild cheddar

HOW TO REACH THEM
Visalia, California
559-734-1282
559-625-0490 (fax)
websites: www.bravofarm.com
www.whitecheddar.com
www.farmstead.com

Macaroni and Cheese

The ultimate in comfort food, traditional macaroni and cheese also brings out the comfort qualities of cheese itself. In fact, I don't think there's anything like hot, melted cheese to bring a calm pleasure to the act of eating. As you'll see, this version calls for three of the best American-made cheeses. There's a reason for using these particular types of cheeses, although you may choose whichever cheese producer you'd like.

The sharp white cheddar has a smooth, creamy quality when it melts, rather than becoming grainy; the Wisconsin-made Swiss-style Gruyère (the same type of cheese used for fondue) melts particularly well, and the aged Dry Jack (you can also use an American aged Asiago) lends just enough sharpness to wake up the tongue.

Be sure to rinse your pasta well after cooking it, because you don't want any residual starch that could make the dish taste floury, and also be sure to undercook the pasta since it will cook further in the oven. You don't want a gummy mess. You can assemble and refrigerate this dish up to six hours ahead of time, but bring it to room temperature before baking.

½ pound dried elbow macaroni, large size

4 tablespoons (½ stick) unsalted butter

½ cup fresh bread crumbs

3 cups whole or low-fat milk

¼ cup all-purpose flour

½ teaspoon kosher salt

¼ teaspoon freshly ground black pepper

⅛ teaspoon cayenne pepper

10 ounces sharp white cheddar cheese, such as Bravo Farms' cheddar, coarsely grated (about 2¼ cups)

4 to 5 ounces Swiss-style Gruyère cheese, such as Roth Käse, coarsely grated (about 1 cup)

2 ounces dry Jack, such as Vella Dry Jack, finely grated (about ¼ cup)

Preheat the oven to 375°F. Butter a 1½-quart soufflé dish or other straight-sided casserole. Set aside.

Bring a medium-size pot of water to a boil. Add the macaroni and cook 2 to 3 minutes *less* than the package directions suggest. You want the pasta to be underdone. Transfer the macaroni to a colander, drain, and rinse with cold water. Shake off as much excess water as possible and set aside.

In a large sauté pan, melt 1 tablespoon of the butter. Add the bread crumbs and stir until thoroughly coated. Put the crumbs on a small plate and set aside. Wipe out the pan with a paper towel and set aside.

In a small saucepan, heat the milk over medium heat until very hot but not scalded.

In the sauté pan you used for the bread crumbs, melt the remaining 3 tablespoons butter over medium heat. When the butter begins to bubble, add the flour and stir until cooked, about 1 minute. Slowly pour in the hot milk and whisk continuously until all of the milk is incorporated and the sauce has begun to thicken, about 5 minutes. Remove the pan from the heat and add the salt, black pepper, cayenne, 1½ cups of the cheddar, ¾ cup of the Gruyère, and all of the Dry Jack. Mix well until all the cheese has melted.

Add the cooled macaroni to the cheese sauce and pour the mixture into the prepared dish. Sprinkle with the remaining cheddar and Gruyère, and top with the bread crumbs.

Bake for about 30 minutes, or until the bread crumbs are golden brown and the casserole is bubbling (or until you can no longer resist the aroma of melting cheese permeating your home).

Let sit for 5 minutes, then serve.

Serves 4 to 6

Note: Although I happen to think traditional macaroni and cheese is best, this recipe certainly lends itself to variations. Here are a few ideas:

- For a Mexican flavor, substitute an equal amount of Jack cheese for the Gruyère. Sauté 1 coarsely chopped onion together with 2 finely diced jalapeño or serrano chiles in 1 tablespoon olive oil until cooked through but not brown. Add to the milk mixture.

- For a more sophisticated dish, sauté one thinly sliced fennel bulb and one thinly sliced leek in 1 tablespoon butter until limp but not brown, about 6 minutes. Add to the prepared sauce along with the cheeses.

- For an Italian slant, crumble and sauté one Italian sweet or spicy sausage in a nonstick pan. Add to the cheese sauce. After you've poured the macaroni and cheese mixture into the prepared dish, dot the top with spoonfuls of ricotta cheese, using about ¼ cup altogether. Top with the buttered bread crumbs and bake.

CARR VALLEY CHEESE

SOMETIMES CHEESEMAKERS SOUND AMAZINGLY relaxed, despite the fact they may have a flurry of activity going on around them. Sid Cook, of Carr Valley Cheese in La Valle, Wisconsin, is one of those. His demeanor is laid back, but his cheesemaking couldn't be more serious.

In looking back, Sid says he didn't have much of a choice about becoming a cheesemaker. Although he was interested in becoming a lawyer after college, he realized that cheesemaking was in his blood, having grown up next door to a cheese plant. "You opened the kitchen door and there was the plant," he remembers. Cheesemaking had been in his family for three generations before him, and it had mostly been done in Plain, Wisconsin, northwest of Madison.

Just like his fifteen-year-old son, who gets up twice a week at 2:45 A.M. to make cheese with his dad, Sid learned cheesemaking early on. He became a licensed cheesemaker at age sixteen. Although he took a hiatus to go to college, he's been making cheese ever since.

He now owns three retail stores and two cheese plants. One of those plants is dedicated to European-style cheeses, including a washed-rind cheese. He also makes a cheese that combines cow, goat, and sheep milk, called "ménage," a Parmesan-style cheese, Gouda, Edam, feta, and a smoked cheese.

But cheddar is his cash cow and his love. He has been making it since the beginning but has become known for it because of how long some of it is aged. He has kept some cheddars as long as eight years. While a cheese that old is unusual, a five- or six-year-old cheese can often be found biding its time in one of Cook's aging rooms.

In addition to cheddar cheese, Carr Valley is also known for something affectionately called "squeakers," or fresh cheddar cheese curds. In cheddar cheesemaking, after the curds have been stacked and drained, they are cut into tiny pieces and salted. Usually these tiny pieces are then scooped up into cheese molds to take shape and become cheese. But in the case of squeakers, the curds are scooped up and put into bags for sale that day. Those are called fresh curds. If they are sold the

---

WHAT THEY MAKE
La Valle Plant
Fresh curd "squeakers"
Cheddar: day-old, mild, medium, sharp (up to 6 years), flavored, Guernsey mixed curd, smoked, white (up to 5 years)
Colby
Havarti
Monterey Jack

Mauston Plant
Edam: regular and smoked
Feta
Fontina
Gouda: regular and smoked
Ménage (mixture of cow, sheep, and goat)
Monastery

HOW TO REACH THEM
La Valle, Wisconsin
Mauston, Wisconsin
800-462-7258
608-986-2906 (fax)

next day, they are called Day-Old. They are called squeakers because they are said to squeak when one bites down on them.

Cook says the origin of squeakers comes from the days when cheese factories lined the roads of Wisconsin. Travelers would stop and get fresh cheese and continue on their way. While that tradition is mostly a memory, some of the older people still remember what that fresh cheese tasted like. They still want it, but so do people of all ages who appreciate the fresh curd taste. Many cheesemakers in Wisconsin make squeakers, but it is yet another niche that Carr Valley seems to have carved out for itself.

Cook clearly takes pride in his cheeses, and he is anxious for others to learn about them, too. That's partly why he has the retail shops, but it is also why he encourages the public to come watch cheese being made. Naturally that helps sell the cheese, but it also gives people a stronger connection to the cheese and the process of making it. Since the main plant in La Valle is only about ninety miles from Madison, it is a nice day trip for city folk.

Although Carr Valley makes many different cheeses now, Cook says he may increase his production of sheep's milk cheeses. But while he keeps adding new cheeses to his repertoire, Cook maintains almost a reverence toward his cheddar. And we're all the luckier for it.

Welsh Rabbit (Rarebit)

⇢◆⇠

Like many so-called classics, the origin of Welsh Rabbit (Rarebit) has lots of lore associated with it. Some say its proper name is indeed Welsh Rabbit because it is supposedly what rabbit hunters ate when they came home from their hard work. Another explanation is that "Rabbit" was a humorous term used to describe a melted cheese dish with ale, served on crackers. Another version has it that a Welsh chef tried to pass the dish off as rabbit. It is not seen on many menus these days, but rabbit hunting or not, it is definitely a dish worth considering when the days are long and cold. For a Dutch version, try it with Gouda cheese and a Dutch beer.

2 tablespoons unsalted butter

3 tablespoons all-purpose flour

$\frac{1}{2}$ cup beer or ale

6 to 7 ounces orange cheddar cheese, coarsely grated

2 teaspoons Worcestershire sauce

$\frac{1}{2}$ teaspoon dry mustard

Dash of cayenne pepper

4 to 6 slices hearty bread, toasted

8 slices bacon, cooked (optional)

8 slices tomato (optional)

In a medium-size saucepan, melt the butter over medium heat. Add the flour and stir vigorously for 1 minute. Add the beer and stir just until the bubbles start to subside, about 30 seconds. Add the cheese, Worcestershire, mustard, and cayenne. Stir constantly until the cheese melts and the mixture is smooth and creamy.

Place the toast slices on individual plates and top with the cheese mixture. If you like, place bacon and/or tomato slices on top of the cheese. Serve immediately.

Serves 4 to 6

SHELBURNE FARMS

TO HEAR ROSS GAGNON TALK ABOUT HIS ROLE as a cheesemaker is like listening to a sculptor talk about his stone. "I am guiding the cheese. I'm not producing it or making it," he says humbly. This is because the milk from Shelburne Farms' own superior Brown Swiss cows travels from the cows to the bulk tank and to the cheesemaking barn. From there, a starter, rennet, and salt are added as the milk becomes cheese, and finally cheese is created. Of course it is not that simple, but Gagnon believes so strongly in the quality of his cows, the clean grasses and clover they eat, and the milk that they produce, that he almost takes a back seat to the end product, the cheese.

Gagnon and Shelburne Farms make only cheddar cheese. It is made from raw unhomogenized milk and is aged anywhere from six months to over two years. It is all made by hand. One taste of Shelburne Farms' cheddar reveals a cheese unlike any other cheddar made in this country: it is rich, mellow, earthy, and smooth. It is not acidic and it is not sharp; it is balanced. The same can be said for Gagnon.

Having been making cheese for only a little over two years, Gagnon has more than the know-how. He has the feel. He also had a good teacher in Shelburne's former cheesemaker, Mariano Gonzales, as well as in Scott Fletcher, cheesemaker at Grafton Village Cheese Company. (See more about Grafton on page 251.). "I don't take shortcuts. There is a traditional method and I adhere to that," Gagnon explains.

In fact, Shelburne Farms is steeped in tradition, even though cheese has been produced there only since 1981. The 1,400-acre working farm, which is also a national historic site, got its start in 1886. At that time, Dr. W. Seward Webb and his wife, Eliza (Lila) Vanderbilt Webb, were instantly enamored of the setting on beautiful Lake Champlain. They bought farmland there and increased their acreage by buying more land belonging to about thirty nearby farmers. From that they created a large country estate and working farm.

Over the years, after Webb's death, many of the buildings he had erected fell into disrepair. From about 1940 until the 1970s, the farm was owned by Webb/Vanderbilt family members, who worked diligently to preserve it as best they could.

Thanks to the Webb family, Shelburne Farms is now a non-profit center dedicated to educating children—who visit from different schools

WHAT THEY MAKE
Raw milk cheddar: clothbound, medium, sharp, extra
  sharp, smoked

HOW TO REACH THEM
Shelburne, Vermont
802-985-8686
802-985-8123 (fax)

every day of the school year—and adults on the subjects of natural resources and sustainable agriculture. Part of this translates to the cheese because the pasture grasses eaten by the cows have not been sprayed with pesticides or herbicides. Visitors are also taught about vegetable farming, animal milking, bread baking, forestry, and other related topics.

Visitors also come in the form of hotel guests, since the original residence at Shelburne Farms has been converted into a twenty-four-room inn. Guests are treated to bird walks, croquet, lake swimming, fishing, and a host of other outdoor activities that are provided by this environmentally conscious organization.

They are also invited to sample some memorable cheese. Cheesemaker Gagnon has recently taken his art further by making a very small amount of clothbound aged cheddar in the English tradition. It is a cheese to behold, with its semi-hard texture and deep, rounded flavor. The clothbound cheddar's exceptional merits were duly noted by the American Cheese Society in 1999 when they honored it, along with another Shelburne cheddar, with a blue ribbon. Shelburne Farms makes a relatively small amount of cheese, about 100,000 pounds annually, but it is a cheese that is positively worth seeking out for a taste of how cheddar is meant to be.

The incomparable Brown Swiss herd at Shelburne Farms.

Jesse's Shepherd's Pie

Shepherd's pie may or may not be a dish that traditionally features cheese. It just depends which recipes—and which historical accounts—you read. But since most hearty dishes are enhanced by the addition of cheese, shepherd's pie naturally follows suit. What does make this version different is the use of celery root and highly spiced lamb sausage.

I must say that I was skeptical when I first saw this recipe, but since it came from someone who knows more about cheese than most cheese experts do, and who is a graduate of the Culinary Institute of America, I knew I had to try it. Now, every time I see Jesse Schwartzburg, cheesemonger and chef extraordinaire, I thank him not only for sharing his wonderful recipe but also for opening my eyes to yet another possibility to showcase American artisanal cheese.

---

1 pound spicy lamb sausage (about 4 sausages), casings removed, meat crumbled (or use regular lamb sausage or ground lamb)

1 large red onion (about ½ pound), cut in half lengthwise and then into ¼-inch slices

1 medium celery root (about ¾ pound), peeled, all brown spots removed, and cut into ¼-inch dice

¼ cup dried currants, soaked in hot water for 15 minutes and drained (optional)

6 Yukon Gold potatoes, peeled and quartered

6 tablespoons (¾ stick) butter, softened

½ cup milk or cream

Salt and freshly ground pepper, to taste

½ pound aged white cheddar cheese, such as Shelburne Farms', cut into ¼-inch dice

Preheat the oven to 400°F. Butter a 3-quart casserole and set it aside.

In a large sauté pan over medium heat, cook the lamb, sautéing until it just begins to turn brown, about 5 minutes. Add the onions, celery root, and currants, if using, and cook, stirring occasionally, until the vegetables are very soft and translucent but not brown, about 20 minutes. Set aside.

Meanwhile, in a large pot, cover the potatoes with water. Bring to a boil and cook until they are tender, about 15 minutes. Drain, and return the potatoes to the pot. Mash with a wooden spoon. Add the butter and milk, and mix vigorously until the potatoes are smooth. Add salt and pepper. Stir in the cheese.

Place the lamb mixture in the bottom of the casserole. Spread the potato mixture over the lamb. Bake for 20 minutes. Turn the oven to broil, and broil until the potatoes begin to turn brown, 2 to 3 minutes. Serve immediately.

Serves 6 to 8

ROTH KÄSE USA

IF GREAT CHEESE WERE ALWAYS AS DIFFICULT to make as Roth Käse USA's Gruyère, chances are we wouldn't have nearly as much first-rate cheese in this country as we do. Fortunately, the people who make this Gruyère have persisted, and in the process they have given us one of our finest alpine cheeses.

Roth Käse is located in Monroe, Wisconsin, in an area called "Swiss County" because of the large Swiss population that originally settled there. Not coincidentally, it is a place where a lot of cheese is made.

Roth Käse USA also has Swiss roots. It was started by its current chief executive officer, Fermo Jaeckle, and his cousin, Felix Roth. But the U.S. cheesemaking enterprise really began for the Roth family in the early 1900s. The family had been making cheese in Switzerland since before 1850, and by the 1900s they

determined that there was a market for Swiss cheeses in the U.S. They sent a family member named Otto Roth to America to develop a business selling their Swiss cheeses. He formed Otto Roth & Company, laying the foundation for cheese-making by the Roth family in the United States.

In the late 1950s, Karl Jaeckle, Fermo's father, took over the business. But in 1975 he suddenly passed away. His sons Fermo and André, both in their twenties, took over the business, and their youth notwithstanding, made Otto Roth & Company this country's largest importer of European specialty cheeses in just one year.

Over time the company was sold to General Foods, which then sold it again. It eventually ended up back in Fermo Jaeckle's hands, but by this time André had gone on to other things, and cousin Felix stepped in. That is when they located the Monroe, Wisconsin, plant. They put $2.5 million in renovations into their $500,000 investment, but at least the plant had the underground curing facilities that are integral to their cheese now.

Like the company, the cheese has had no easy road. In Switzerland, Gruyère is made in copper vats and cured on wooden boards. In this country, those are both

(continued on page 242)

WHAT THEY MAKE

Baby Swiss
Butterkäse
Buttermilk Blue
Farmers
Fontina: Italian-style,
  Swedish-style
Gruyère

Havarti: plain and flavored
Homestead
Muenster
Raclette
Rofumo (smoked Fontina)
St. Bernard's Smoked
  Butterkäse

HOW TO REACH THEM

Monroe, Wisconsin
800-257-3355
608-328-3355
608-329-7677 (fax)

unacceptable practices according to the U.S. Department of Agriculture. It took a flight to Switzerland by a Wisconsin inspector to visit the Roth Käse cheese factory and witness their procedures first-hand before they could receive approval to operate this way in Wisconsin. That gave Roth Käse state approval, but the plant will never receive USDA approval because of a rule that says that milk cannot come in contact with corrosive material. Copper is considered corrosive. Of course Gruyère has been made that way for centuries in other countries. The lack of USDA approval simply means that Roth Käse USA cannot export to countries that require that cheese be made in a USDA-approved plant; they cannot bid on government projects; and they cannot sell their cream for butter.

The concern about the wooden boards is that they hold moisture, which could contain certain unwanted bacteria. For curing Gruyère, those boards are essential because of the way the desirable bacteria interact with the cheese. Nonetheless, the company was able to prove, at least so far, that their sterilization method is safe. (The use of the boards remains an issue and may or may not ultimately be accepted by the inspectors.)

The cleaning method for the boards is quite elaborate. After the cheese is cured and removed, a hot kiln located in the curing room is turned on. Water is then sprayed in the room, creating a steam bath and raising the temperature to 180°F. This stays on for six hours. After that, the boards are considered clean since it is unlikely that anything could live after that kind of treatment.

The cheesemaking process is fairly standard. The relatively large curds are separated from the whey and cut into squares. The curds are then scooped into hoops and pressed. The cheese is then brined and taken to the drying room, where it is turned and washed twenty-three times in four months. The result is a four- to fourteen-month-old nutty yet slightly fruity cheese whose melting qualities are legend and whose edible features are practically indescribable. The Gruyère is buttery, rustic, and even musty. It has a solid yet pliable texture, and it literally melts in your mouth, not to mention a pot, making the perfect fondue.

Roth Käse USA makes about half a million pounds of Gruyère annually, but the bulk of the cheese they produce is Havarti. They also make a Buttermilk Blue, a Fontina, a Baby Swiss, and several other cheeses. The factory is still overseen by Felix as well as his brother Ulrich, who live in Switzerland, but the cheesemaker, Bruce Workman, is every bit a Wisconsinite. He has even earned Wisconsin's prestigious Master Cheesemaker status for his Gruyère and Baby Swiss. This is a distinction created by the state that requires three years of education and proven competence in the particular cheeses for which the cheesemaker is seeking a Master Cheesemaker certificate. A cheesemaker may receive only one certificate for up to two cheeses at one time. In Workman's case, it has paid off. In 1999, the American Cheese Society honored his Gruyère with its most prestigious award: Best of Show.

It is a long way from the Swiss Alps to the plains of Wisconsin, and it's an even longer road from the accepted cheesemaking practices in Switzerland to the more rigid standards in the United States. Roth Käse's Gruyère is an exceptional cheese, and we can only hope it will continue to be made in the way it has always been made: by hand, in copper vats, and on wooden boards.

Classic Cheese Fondue

What more friendly food is there than one where everyone sits around a table digging into a communal pot? Food definitely becomes the focus when everyone is dipping their bread in a vessel full of melted cheese, using a disproportionately long fork. Conversation over the drops of melted cheese that land between the pot and the plate, along with memories of a perfect evening, become the essence of fondue.

Cheese fondue has a rich history that comes from the mountains of Switzerland, where cheeses like Gruyère, Emmentaler, and Appenzeller sit in large wheels begging to be melted. Add to that the native kirsch, or cherry brandy, and fondue is as natural as snow on the Matterhorn.

In this country, fondue has made a comeback from its faddish phase in the 1970s. Fondue pots are once again on bridal registry lists and on the shelves of chic cookware stores, and cookbooks have been devoted entirely to fondue. But having a fondue pot is not essential. Instead, simply use a good insulated enamel pot to make the fondue. Then set the pot on a trivet in the middle of the table. The heat from the pot will keep the cheese in good condition for quite a while. If the cheese becomes hard, simply melt it again over low heat on the stove. You can also add a bit of warmed wine to the cheese to thin it out. Be sure to have long-handled forks (or skewers) on hand, since it will otherwise be too difficult to reach into the pot without the risk of burning a finger or a hand.

Finally, feel free to experiment with any of your favorite cheeses. Just be sure that the ones you choose have good melting qualities and that all rinds are removed.

---

1 pound Gruyère cheese, coarsely grated

1 pound Emmentaler or Swiss cheese, coarsely grated

1½ tablespoons cornstarch

1 clove garlic, slightly crushed

1 cup good-quality, slightly fruity white wine, such as a Riesling or Chenin Blanc

1 teaspoon fresh lemon juice

¼ teaspoon cayenne pepper

¼ cup kirsch (cherry brandy)

1½ pounds hearty country-style or sourdough bread, with crust, cut into 1-inch cubes

Warm a fondue pot by filling it with hot water. Pour out the water and wipe it dry.

In a medium-size bowl, toss together the cheeses and the cornstarch. Set aside.

Rub the inside of a medium-size saucepan with the garlic clove. Add the wine, lemon juice, and cayenne, and heat slowly over medium heat. Once it is hot but not boiling, slowly add the cheese, stirring with a wooden spoon until it is smooth. Add the kirsch and cook for about 3 minutes.

Pour the cheese into a fondue pot, or simply bring the cooking pot to the table and set it on a trivet.

Serve immediately, with the bread cubes.

Serves 6

BELGIOIOSO CHEESE

IN 1979 ERRICO AURICCHIO left his home in Italy to start making Italian cheese in the United States. His family had been making cheese, mostly Provolone, in Italy since the 1870s, and Errico was no exception.

Although he came to the U.S. to open a branch of Auricchio Cheese, by 1994 he had sold his interest in the Italian company and acquired the Denmark, Wisconsin, plant as his own. He christened the new plant's cheeses BelGioioso. Auricchio explains that *bel* means "beautiful" in Italian and *gioioso* signifies "joy and happiness." The company brochure sounds out the name as bel-joy-oso. The Italian company still maintains the name Auricchio.

The original small cheese factory has grown from one to four plants where fourteen different cheeses are made. Although BelGioioso is still probably best known for its Provolone—for good reason—they also make what might be this country's best creamy Gorgonzola. Errico Auricchio explains that unlike the long-aged Gorgonzola, BelGioioso's is deliberately made as a high-moisture cheese, making it creamy rather than crumbly. They achieve this by loosely packing large curds in molds by hand and keeping the cheese at a low temperature. Then air is allowed to circulate around the curds, and as fermentation takes place, the curds, because of their large size, retain a lot of moisture. More air is introduced from the outside when the cheese is pierced with long skewers in several places. This fosters the mold growth and creates the blueing that distinguishes Gorgonzola. The cheese is ready to eat within sixty days.

BelGioioso's Provolones—and there are many—are the company's raison d'être. They make mild to aged Provolones, rind and rindless, pasteurized and raw. Their shapes bear names like pear, bell, caciocavalli (the name of another Italian cheese distinguished by its shape), and Sicilian. The Sicilian might also be called "sandwich-style" since it is in the form of a brick and is meant to be sliced. Because of the varied shapes, many are hand-formed, tied with the rope that distinguishes Provolones here and in Italy, dipped in a plastic coating, and hung to age. They are made with whole cows' milk.

A taste of the aged Provolone erases all memories of the domestic Provolones many of us grew up with. It has body and depth; it is clean and buttery and yet somewhat sharp; and depending on its age, it is toothsome and textural. It lends itself to melting on a pizza, grating in a lasagna, or as a topping on a baked summer tomato drizzled with olive oil and a few herbed bread crumbs. The year-old Provolone can be grated over pasta or cut into chunks as part of an antipasto. It is also wholly satisfying by itself with a glass of red wine (and maybe a good book).

WHAT THEY MAKE

American Grana
Asiago
Auribella
Fontina
Gorgonzola
Kasseri

Mascarpone
Mozzarella
Parmesan
Pepato
Provolone: rindless,
   small-style, aged
Romano

HOW TO REACH THEM

Denmark, Wisconsin
920-863-2123 (no mail order)
920-863-8791 (fax)
website: www.belgioioso.com

Veal Parmesan

Although this dish may not be an American original, like a lot of Italian food it has been adopted into the American food repertoire as our own. Veal scallopine are best to use for this dish, but they can be exorbitantly expensive. A cheaper alternative, though not as desirable, is to purchase veal cutlets and pound them with a kitchen mallet to a paper-thin thickness. Another fine alternative is to use boneless, skinless chicken breasts.

FOR THE SAUCE

2 tablespoons olive oil

1 yellow onion, coarsely chopped

2 cloves garlic, sliced paper-thin

1 can (28 ounces) good-quality Italian whole peeled tomatoes, coarsely chopped, juices reserved

¼ cup slivered fresh basil leaves

Salt and freshly ground pepper

FOR THE VEAL

¾ pound veal scallopine (about 8 pieces; or 1 pound veal cutlets pounded ⅛ inch thick, or 2 boneless, skinless chicken breasts, about 2 pounds, pounded ⅛ inch thick)

2 cups fresh bread crumbs, toasted

2 tablespoons finely grated Parmesan or Asiago cheese

1 teaspoon kosher salt

Freshly ground pepper

1 egg, beaten

¼ cup (½ stick) unsalted butter

2 tablespoons vegetable oil

4 ounces young Provolone cheese, cut into 8 slices (or use mozzerella or Oaxaca)

To make the sauce: In a large sauté pan, heat the oil over medium heat. Add the onions and cook for 5 minutes. Add the garlic and cook for about 10 minutes, or until the onions begin to soften. Add the tomatoes and ½ cup of the reserved juices. Reduce the heat to medium-low, cover, and cook for about 20 minutes to let it thicken. Check occasionally to make sure the sauce isn't cooking away. If it is, add a little more tomato juice and/or water. Add the basil, season with salt and pepper to taste, and keep warm.

Meanwhile, preheat the oven to 375°F.

To prepare the veal: Cut the veal into pieces about 2 inches wide and 3 to 4 inches long. (If you bought scallopine, they should already be about the right size.)

Mix together the bread crumbs, cheese, salt, and pepper to taste. Pour onto a flat plate. Put the beaten egg in a shallow bowl. Dip the veal into the egg and then coat with the bread-crumb mixture. Repeat with all the slices.

Line a large plate or platter with paper towels.

In large sauté pan, heat the butter and oil together until the butter begins to bubble. Sauté 3 or 4 veal slices, or however many fit comfortably in the pan, until crisp and brown on the bottom, 3 to 4 minutes. Turn and cook 2 to 3 more minutes, or until the other side is crisp and brown. Remove to the plate to drain. Repeat with the remaining veal.

To assemble: Place the veal in a single layer in a 7 × 11-inch gratin dish or other baking dish. Put 1 or 2 slices of Provolone on each piece of veal. Smother with the sauce, and cover the dish with foil. Bake until the cheese has melted and is beginning to bubble, 20 to 25 minutes. Remove the foil and cook for 5 more minutes. Serve immediately.

Serves 4

BOGGY MEADOW FARM

A NAME LIKE "FANNY MASON" may sound fictional, but this Boggy Meadow Farm cheese harks back to the early days of this small operation in Walpole, New Hampshire. The farm has been in owner Powell Cabot's family for nearly 200 years, and the cheese is named after one of his most famous family members. As a very wealthy woman and a patron of the Boston Symphony Orchestra, Fanny Mason often invited entire orchestras to come and perform for the grand parties she held at her farm and summer home. Mason enjoyed having a working farm just a hundred or so miles from her Boston home, since it meant that she could have butter and fresh vegetables sent to her whenever the season allowed. The main house, in which she lived during the summers, was built in 1839.

Fanny Mason was born in the 1860s and lived into the middle part of the 20th century. She had no children of her own, and when she died, the property was turned over to a family member. It was then that Boggy Meadow Farm became a working dairy operation.

Powell Cabot took over the property in 1992, and in 1994 he decided to make cheese out of some of the milk from the farm's Holsteins. He hired a cheesemaker along with a cheesemaking consultant, whose recipe is now used to make two of their cheeses, Baby Swiss and Smoked Baby Swiss. Boggy Meadow Farm has recently developed a high-moisture Jack cheese as well.

Baby Swiss is a cheese that resembles the well-known Swiss cheese. It parts company with its better-known cousin, though, in many ways. First, it is called Baby Swiss because it has smaller holes relative to the large, deep holes in Swiss cheese. Also, the curds for regular Swiss cheese are cooked at a temperature of 120°F or higher. For Baby Swiss, the curds are cooked for a short time at a lower temperature, about 102°F. Additionally, Baby Swiss is made in small wheels, unlike the huge Swiss cheese wheels.

While the taste of Baby Swiss is unmistakably that of Swiss cheese, with its sharp overtones, it is pleasantly mellow at the same time because of its fruity notes. It is that balance that makes the Fanny Mason Baby Swiss particularly good for cooking. It won't overwhelm a dish, but it will let you know it's there. It also melts beautifully.

The Smoked Baby Swiss is made by the same process, its smoky flavor coming from maple chips in the smokers at Grafton Village Cheese Company in Vermont, about thirty minutes away (see page 251).

Although this farmstead cheese operation is relatively small, making about 50,000 pounds a year, it is the only small thing about Boggy Meadow Farm, which spans 900 acres and borders three miles of the Connecticut River. A farm like this deserves to be seen—and, in fact, can be. It is open to the public.

WHAT THEY MAKE
Fanny Mason Baby Swiss
Fanny Mason Smoked Baby Swiss
Jack Cheese

HOW TO REACH THEM
Walpole, New Hampshire
603-756-3300
603-756-9645 (fax)

Baby Swiss Cheese Soufflé

Baby Swiss is a cousin of Swiss cheese, but it does not have the big holes and is made in much smaller wheels. It has some of the flavor characteristics of Swiss cheese, but with less of a bite. Consequently, it is mellower and slightly sweeter. It is a perfect soufflé ingredient. The star anise called for in this recipe heightens that sweetness and adds an exotic twist, but the soufflé is none the worse without it.

Generally, a soufflé can be made with almost any cheese and with almost any favorite herbs or flavorings. It is a neutral host for anything seasonal, such as summer peppers, and it is a perfect showcase for cheese alone. Either way, soufflés never fail to impress. If a fallen soufflé is a frightening prospect, don't worry: It's par for the course. The only prerequisites to a good soufflé are to use a rich and flavorful cheese, to bring the eggs to room temperature before using them, and to serve it as hot as possible. Room-temperature eggs will help increase the volume of the egg whites, resulting in a billowy soufflé.

1 tablespoon finely grated Asiago or
   Parmesan cheese
1¼ cups milk
1 star anise (optional)
3 tablespoons unsalted butter
3 tablespoons all-purpose flour
1 scant teaspoon kosher salt
¼ teaspoon cayenne pepper
Freshly ground black pepper, to taste
4 egg yolks, at room temperature
6 egg whites, at room temperature
½ pound Baby Swiss cheese, such as Fanny
   Mason, coarsely grated (or use Swiss
   cheese, Emmentaler, or Gruyère)

Preheat the oven to 375°F.

Butter a 1½-quart soufflé dish or casserole. Coat the dish with the Asiago. Set aside.

In a small saucepan, simmer the milk and star anise over medium-low heat, until it is hot but not boiling.

In a medium-size saucepan, melt the butter over medium-low heat. Whisk in the flour, stirring constantly so it doesn't burn. Slowly add the hot milk, whisking constantly until the mixture thickens, about 5 minutes. Add the salt, cayenne, and black pepper. Cook over very low heat for 15 minutes, stirring occasionally. Remove from the heat and discard the star anise. Beat in the egg yolks one at a time.

In a medium-size bowl, using clean beaters, beat the egg whites until soft peaks form. Fold the cheese and one quarter of the egg whites into the egg yolk mixture. Gently fold the remaining egg whites into the mixture, folding just until the whites are coated with the yolk mixture and are about the size of large grapes. Pour into the prepared dish and bake on the middle rack of the oven for 35 to 40 minutes, or until the soufflé has risen about 3 inches above the sides of the dish and the top of the soufflé is a deep brown color. Serve immediately.

Serves 4 to 6

SONTHEIM FINE CHEESES

IN A LARGE MEADOW IN SOUTHWEST COLORADO, about thirty Brown Swiss cows lazily spend their day wandering. Their singular duty is to provide one of the best types of cows' milk that exists. That milk is then transformed into some of the finest cheeses produced in this country. Indeed, Sontheim Fine Cheeses live up to their name.

The Tilsit cheese, in particular, is remarkable. It is a round, golden, raw milk washed-rind marvel that is relatively mild but entirely flavorful in its youth (around three months) and bursts with flavor as it ages. To some, the aged version is simply strong, as ripe German Tilsit traditionally is. But to those who like assertive cheese, this is robust with truffly, rustic, savory, and earthy tones that explode in the mouth. It is firm but not hard, reminiscent of the texture of an aged Gouda. It is a cheese that is not made elsewhere in this country.

Bruno Sontheim, patriarch of the family, is the cheesemaker, having learned his craft in his homeland of Bavaria. He has chosen to stay close to his German roots in his cheesemaking, which is proving to be an education for American consumers, who may never have tried these types of cheeses. In addition to the Tilsit and Soft Tilsit, Sontheim also makes a hard, dry, washed-rind cheese called *bergkaese*. Traditionally bergkaese is eaten with bread, butter, and a salad of greens, onions, some radishes, and vinegar and oil. But Bruno's wife, Sylvia, who manages their household of four children and works ninety hours a week outside the home to support the fledgling cheesemaking business, says she enjoys bergkaese another Bavarian way: homemade spaetzle (a German noodle) layered with the cheese and topped with onions that have been caramelized in butter. The dish is then cooked until the cheese is melted and the flavors have melded.

The Sontheims received early accolades for their cheese, having garnered awards from the American Cheese Society for their Tilsit soon after they began making cheese in the U.S. in 1997. Like many cheesemakers, they have not had an easy time gaining recognition beyond a few specialized cheese sellers who grasp that this cheese is special. This is partly due to their remote location, and it is also because marketing cheese is a Herculean task for which, paradoxically, they have little time. For now, their cheeses are sold at the better retail shops around the country, through mail order, and at Colorado farmers' markets, where they always sell out.

The Sontheim cheeses have a certain air about them that is a departure from other cheeses made in America. Perhaps that comes from the traditional names and recipes for the cheeses, or perhaps it's because these people are relatively recent immigrants, much like the Europeans who started the cheesemaking traditions in American. Whatever the case, the Sontheim cheese is stunning, and it is a treasure waiting to be found.

WHAT THEY MAKE
Bergkaese
Edamer
Soft Tilsit
Tilsit

HOW TO REACH THEM
Powderhorn, Colorado
970-641-6671
website: members.xoom.com/sontheim

Grilled Two-Cheese Burgers

What would a book about American cheese be without a recipe for a cheeseburger? And since American cheesemakers are making such sensational cheeses, why not showcase not one but two of them in an old-time favorite food? These burgers are simple to make, but they enter the gourmet realm with the herbed goat cheese that comes spilling out after the first bite. The burgers can be made into patties and refrigerated for up to four hours before cooking. They are especially good with a dollop of the tomato jam on page 180. It is sweet and jammy and by far outdoes any ordinary ketchup.

1⅔ pounds ground beef, preferably 15% fat
1½ tablespoons Worcestershire sauce
Salt and freshly ground pepper
4 ounces herbed goat cheese, such as Laura Chenel or Doeling Dairy (see Note)

6 ounces medium-aged Tilsit, such as Sontheim, cut in thin slices, (or use medium-aged Provolone or Gouda)
6 hamburger buns or English muffins, toasted

Prepare an outdoor grill or preheat the broiler.

In a large bowl, mix together the meat, Worcestershire sauce, and salt and pepper to taste. Divide the meat into 12 equal balls and flatten 1 ball to form a thin patty. Take about 1 tablespoon of the goat cheese and place it in the center of the patty. Make a second patty. Put the two patties together to form a "sandwich" around the goat cheese, and pinch the edges together. Repeat with the remaining meat and goat cheese.

Place the meat on the grill or under the broiler, and cook for 4 minutes. Turn, and top each burger with a slice of Tilsit cheese. Cook about 4 minutes more, or until the meat feels firm but not hard to the touch for medium-rare, or almost hard for well-done hamburgers. (Well-done hamburgers should have a total cooking time of about 10 minutes.)

Serves 6

Note: If you can't find herbed goat cheese, make your own. Simply buy fresh goat cheese and roll it in a mixture of dried herbs.

Banana Cheesecake

Few cheese-related desserts are as classic as cheesecake. This cake is baked slowly and then left to bake a little further in the turned-off oven, a method that yields a creamy texture and a cake that doesn't crack, as cheesecakes often do. For non-banana-eaters, this recipe works fine without the fruit. Simply boost the sugar in the batter to a full cup.

You may use low-fat cream cheese or a combination of regular and low-fat, but do not use nonfat.

FOR THE CRUST

1¾ cups graham cracker crumbs

½ cup sugar

6 tablespoons (¾ stick) unsalted butter, melted

FOR THE CAKE

1½ pounds cream cheese, at room temperature

5 tablespoons crème fraîche (or use sour cream)

⅔ cup sugar

4 large eggs

3 very ripe bananas, pureed in a blender or food processor to make 1 cup

1 teaspoon vanilla extract

FOR THE TOPPING

1 cup sour cream

2 tablespoons sugar

1 teaspoon pure vanilla extract

½ firm but ripe banana, sliced into ¼-inch-thick rounds

2 teaspoons sugar

1 teaspoon fresh lemon juice

Preheat the oven to 325°F.

To make the crust: In a small bowl, mix together the crust ingredients. Carefully press the mixture onto the bottom and sides of a 9-inch springform pan. Bake for 10 minutes. Remove from the oven and set aside.

To make the cake: In a large mixing bowl using an electric mixer or a wooden spoon, mix the cream cheese for 5 minutes or until smooth. Add the crème fraîche and mix for about 1 minute. Add the sugar and beat until the granules have disappeared, about 2 minutes. Add the eggs, one at a time, beating well after each addition. Add the banana puree and vanilla, and mix until the ingredients are blended well, about 3 minutes. The batter will be very liquidy.

Pour the batter into the crust and place the cake in the center of the oven. Bake for 50 minutes. Do not open the oven at the end of the 50 minutes. Turn the oven off and leave the cake for 20 minutes. Remove it from the oven and place it on a cooling rack. Let cool completely.

To make the topping: In a small bowl, mix together the topping ingredients. When the cake is completely cool, spread the sour cream topping over the top of the cake.

Gently mix together the banana, sugar, and lemon juice. Arrange the banana slices in a ring around the edge of the cake, spacing them 1 inch apart. Refrigerate the cake for at least 2 hours or overnight. The flavors will develop further as the cake rests.

Serves 10 to 12

CHEESE CLASSICS

GRAFTON VILLAGE CHEESE COMPANY

GRAFTON VILLAGE CHEESE COMPANY is an operation whose grand reputation belies its relatively small size. Part of that has to do with cheesemaker Scott Fletcher, and most of it has to do with his cheese. Cheddar is all he makes. With the luxury of concentrating on one type of cheese, the talent to make outstanding cheeses, and a quaint, beautiful area in Vermont in which to make it, Scott Fletcher can transform milk like few others.

Grafton Village Cheese has been around since the 1890s, but a fire in 1912 abruptly ended cheesemaking until the 1960s, when the nonprofit Windham Foundation restored it. Devoted to the restoration of old buildings, the Foundation also owns and has refurbished almost half of the other buildings in the historic town of Grafton in south central Vermont.

Cheesemaker Fletcher has been there since the '60s also. He was, in fact, one of the company's first employees. Having just graduated from high school, he was taught cheesemaking on the job. Eventually he became the cheesemaker-in-charge.

Recently Fletcher has turned Grafton cheese into gold. His "newest" cheese is three-year-old Grafton Gold, which is sharp, rich, and surprisingly moist for its age. Although other Grafton cheeses had been aged as long as two years, none had been aged as long as the Grafton Gold. It brings new meaning to a grilled cheese sandwich, but it is also a standout on a cheese board. A dried date or two is a perfect companion.

Grafton Village cheddar is made from the milk of Jersey cows, and like most Vermont cheddars, it is the color of the milk. No orange dye is added. In the case of Grafton, the cheese has a yellowish tinge because of the creamy color of Jersey milk. The milk is not pasteurized, though it is heated in the course of making the cheese. From there, traditional cheddar methods are followed, with Fletcher constantly monitoring the cheesemaking. What results are blocks and wheels of cheddar that are aged anywhere from one year to three.

In the course of making cheese for Grafton, Fletcher also helps out other cheesemakers. For example, he lends the company smoker to Boggy Meadow Farm in nearby New Hampshire (see page 246). Fletcher also lent his expertise to the cheesemaker at Shelburne Farms, who had never made cheese before landing the job (see pages 238-239).

Judging by the full and intense flavors that define the Grafton cheddars—and their 1999 blue ribbon from the American Cheese Society for smoked cheddar—Fletcher is a worthy role model. Although he's been making cheese for thirty-three years, he hasn't lost his edge or, by all accounts, his enthusiasm. The proof is in the cheese.

WHAT THEY MAKE
Cheddar: Classic Reserve, Grafton Gold, Premium
Flavored cheddars: garlic, sage, smoked

HOW TO REACH THEM
Grafton, Vermont
800-472-3866
802-843-2221
802-843-2210 (fax)
website: www.graftonvillagecheese.com

Apple-Cheddar Pie

If there's any doubt that apple pie is the ultimate symbol of Americana, adding cheddar cheese will convince even the most cynical. After all, what's more American than apples and cheese? But this pie is more than just a symbol. It tastes great. The slight tanginess of the cheese serves to showcase the wonderful sweetness of the apples, while at the same time bringing an added richness and depth to the standard apple pie. Serve the pie with vanilla ice cream or sweetened whipped cream for an added treat.

Although this pie isn't hard to make, it does require a little patience. It is probably easiest to prepare the piecrust dough a day ahead (or as much as a week ahead if you freeze it), and then assemble and bake the dish on the day you plan to serve it. It will keep for a day or two, but it's really best when eaten on the day it is baked.

FOR THE CRUST

2½ cups all-purpose flour

1 tablespoon sugar

½ teaspoon salt

½ cup grated medium-aged cheddar cheese, such as Grafton Premium

10 tablespoons (1¼ sticks) very cold unsalted butter, cut into ½-inch cubes

2 tablespoons very cold shortening, cut into ½-inch pieces

3 tablespoons sour cream or plain yogurt

2 teaspoons fresh lemon juice or cider vinegar

¼ cup very cold water (or less, as needed)

FOR THE FILLING

4 to 5 sweet-tart apples, such as Gala, Fuji, Braeburn, Jonathan, or Pippin, peeled, cored, and sliced into ½-inch pieces, then cut in half crosswise

2 tablespoons fresh lemon juice

2 tablespoons all-purpose flour

½ teaspoon ground cinnamon

About ¼ cup packed brown sugar (depending on the sweetness of the apples)

About ½ cup white sugar (depending on the sweetness of the apples)

To make the crust: In a large bowl, mix together the flour, sugar, salt, and cheese. Freeze, covered, for 30 minutes.

Remove the flour mixture from the freezer. Using a pastry blender or two knives, cut in the butter and shortening until they are well coated with the flour mixture and are the size of small gumballs. (Or use a food processor, pulsing until the butter and shortening are the size of small gumballs, about 8 pulses.)

Mix in the sour cream and lemon juice, just until incorporated (about 5 pulses on the food processor). Slowly add the cold water until moist clumps begin to form. You don't want the mixture to become gummy by adding too much water, but you need enough so that the mixture isn't crumbly when you go to roll it out. (If using a food processor, mix in the water but do not overprocess. It should take only about 30 seconds to incorporate the water.)

Once the dough holds together fairly well (erring on the dry side will ultimately create a flakier crust), it's ready to be refrigerated. Divide the dough in half (handling it as little as possible because your warm hands will break down the fat in the dough, leading to a tough crust). Put each half in plastic wrap and form into a 4- to 5-inch disk. Refrigerate for at least 1 hour or preferably overnight.

Have a 9-inch pie plate ready.

Begin with two large sheets of parchment. Set one on the counter and lightly flour the paper. Place one piecrust disk on top of the paper (leave the other crust in the refrigerator). Lightly flour the other piece of parchment and set it on top of the piecrust. Begin rolling the dough, turning the parchment a quarter-turn after each roll. Continue until the crust measures 11 to 12 inches in diameter. Remove the top piece of parchment. Then, making sure your rolling pin is well floured, gently roll the piecrust around your rolling pin. Carefully unroll the crust over your pie plate, being sure to center it over the plate. If it isn't centered, just put it into the refrigerator for 15 minutes. After it's cold, you'll be able to gently slip your hand under the crust to center it. Press crust down gently into the pie plate and against the sides. Return the crust to the refrigerator while you roll out the second crust.

Follow the same procedure for the second crust, rolling it out to the same 11- to 12-inch diameter.

Refrigerate it, still sandwiched between parchment, while you make the filling.

Preheat the oven to 400°F.

To make the filling: In a large bowl, toss the apples with the lemon juice. Mix together the flour, cinnamon, and sugars, and add to the apple mixture, making sure that the apples are well coated. Let sit for 15 minutes, until juices begin to form. Do not let it sit any longer.

To assemble: Remove the first piecrust from the refrigerator and fill it with the apple mixture. Gently wrap the second crust around the floured rolling pin and slowly unroll it over the apples, being careful to center it. Trim the edges of both crusts to ½ inch larger than the rim of the pie plate, and join the top and bottom crusts together by pinching them. Tuck the edge of the crust just under the edge of the pie plate. Crimp the edge with your thumb and forefinger or simply leave it as is. Make three or four slashes in the crust to allow steam to escape. (If you have leftover crust, you can make decorations, such as leaf shapes. Place them around the pie.)

Bake on the lowest rack of the oven for 30 minutes. Then move the pie to the next rack up and reduce the oven temperature to 350°F. Bake for another 30 to 35 minutes, or until the piecrust is golden brown, the juices are bubbling, and a skewer inserted in the pie indicates that the apples are very soft. If the apples do not seem done but the piecrust is getting too brown, simply drape a large piece of foil over the pie.

Remove the pie from the oven and let it cool on a wire rack for at least 1 hour. This allows the filling to set. If you want to eat the pie warm, return it to the oven for about 15 minutes, or until heated through.

Makes 1 double-crust 9-inch pie
Serves 6 to 8

GLOSSARY

Acidic: Describes a slightly sour and sometimes biting flavor in cheese.

Acidification: When the milk is becoming acidic due to the introduction of starter culture bacteria.

Acidity: The level of acid in raw milk. It also refers to the level of acid in the milk after starter culture bacteria have been added. The cheesemaker must know the acidity level before proceeding to the next phase.

Affineur: The "cheese finisher," or person whose specialty and responsibility is to age cheese.

Aged: Describes a cheese that has been left to mature, and in the process to lose moisture and develop flavor. The term can refer to a cheese that is as young as three weeks, as in the case of a crottin, but usually it refers to cheeses that are allowed to mature for a minimum of two months.

Aging: The process cheese undergoes as it evolves from its liquid to its solid state. The longer cheese ages, the less moisture it will have and usually the more flavor it will develop.

Ammoniated: The condition of overripeness, usually of soft-ripened cheese, where the aroma and taste are similar to ammonia. An undesirable quality.

Annatto: A seed from which color is extracted to create the orange hue found in some cheddar and Colby cheeses.

Aroma: The odor or smell that emanates from a cheese. It can be mild to overpowering, though the aroma does not always translate directly to the flavor.

Asadero: A mild, fresh Mexican-style cheese, either processed or natural, that is often molded into a log and sliced.

Asiago: A pressed-curd salted cheese that is sold as a fresh cheese as well as an aged, or *grana-style*, cheese. It has a sweet, mild flavor when young and a piquant flavor when aged.

Baby Swiss: A smaller, milder version of Swiss cheese. The holes, or eyes, in the cheese are smaller than those found in the large wheels of Swiss cheese, and the wheels are usually only five pounds or less. Baby Swiss is also higher in moisture than Swiss.

Bacteria: The microorganisms that circulate just about everywhere, including cheese aging rooms, which contribute to the cheese's final flavor. Bacteria also occur naturally in the cheese, fostering the aging and flavor of the cheese.

Bacterial cultures: Used as starters in cheesemaking, to bring the milk to the proper acid level. They also contribute to the flavors and textures found in cheese.

Bacterial-ripened cheese: See *Surface-ripened cheese.*

Bakers' cheese: Also known as pot cheese, bakers' cheese is a nonfat, dry, soft-curd cheese used in baking. It is also the favored ingredient for cheese blintzes.

Balanced: Describes the concentrations of milk and acid in a cheese. If it is balanced, the milk flavors and acid level in the cheese are correctly proportional.

Barnyardy (sometimes called **barny**): Describes a flavor and aroma in some cheese that is reminiscent of the smells that emanate from a barn or barnyard. Usually it is similar to a strong, musty, and even sometimes dirtlike flavor or aroma, and despite that description, can be a favorable quality in many cases. Some aged goat cheeses and some sheep's milk cheeses might be described as barnyardy.

Beer Kaese (also **Beer Käse**): Also known as beer cheese, beer kaese is a surface-ripened cheese that is usually quite strong in both flavor and aroma. Some believe it was invented to accompany beer, giving it its name. It is made primarily in Wisconsin.

Bitter: Refers to an unfavorable component in cheese that is often detected after the cheese has been swallowed. It leaves a lingering off-taste in the mouth. This bitter flavor can be likened to the taste of caffeine.

Blind: Refers to a Swiss cheese that has little or no holes, or eye formation. The traditional Swiss cheese flavor might also be missing from a blind cheese.

Bloomy rind: The white, flowery, and desirable down-like surface of a soft-ripened cheese such as Camembert or Brie, the result of a bacterial spray, usually *Penicillium candidum*.

Blue-surface cheese: A cheese that has blue mold characteristics on the outside, usually due to the addition of both internal and external molds, but is not pierced to allow blue veins to form.

Blue-veined cheese: A cheese in which a mold (usually *Penicillium roqueforti*) is added to the curds. Once the cheese is pressed and formed, it is skewered to create veins, allowing air to penetrate the cheese and foster mold growth. The mold that is formed in those veins and throughout the cheese is blue or blue-green, resulting in the name for the cheese. Blue cheese can be made from cows', goats', or sheep's milk.

Body: The texture of the cheese.

Brick cheese: A surface-ripened cheese that is mild when young, but when aged becomes very pungent. It is made in the form of a brick, although it is said it got its name because of the bricklike shape of the weights that were originally used to press the cheese.

Brie: A round, creamy, soft-ripened cheese with a bloomy rind. American-made Brie is usually made in four- to six-ounce sizes.

Brine: A solution, usually salt and water, in which certain cheeses are soaked for anywhere from a few hours to several months. It is a means of salting the cheese as well as creating a protective exterior for longer aging. Gouda, Emmentaler, Gruyère, and dry Jack are cheeses that are brined before they are aged. Feta cheese is often stored and sold in brine and can be kept that way for over a year, while mozzarella is often briefly soaked in brine before it is packaged.

Brushed rind: A process where the rind of a natural-rind cheese is brushed to keep mold from forming and to keep the interior of the cheese moist.

Butterfat: The fat portion of milk. This varies according to animal, with sheep's milk having the highest proportion of butterfat.

Butter Kaese (or Butterkäse) : A mild, semi-soft cheese that in some cases is spreadable and in other cases more firm. It is up to the individual cheesemaker how it is made. It is made in a loaf shape for easy slicing. It is usually found in the Midwest.

Butterscotch: The caramel-like flavor that develops in some aged cheeses. It is most often found in a well-aged Gouda.

Buttery: Can apply to both texture and flavor. In the case of texture, it is the quality of butter: creamy yet with body. A ripe California Teleme or a ripe Camembert might be described as buttery in texture. When used to describe the flavor, buttery pertains to the creamlike, rich flavor in the cheese. Again, a ripe Camembert could be described as buttery.

Camembert: Originated in Normandy, France, Camembert is a creamy, bloomy-rind, soft-ripened cheese. The desirable outer mold is usually created by the spraying of the *Penicillium candidum* or *P. camemberti* mold. Sometimes, though, it is not sprayed and instead mold forms naturally as the result of particular molds that have been added to the curds. Unlike in France, where the wheels are larger, American Camemberts are usually made in four- to six-ounce wheels. Traditionally this is a cheese made with cows' milk, but many American cheesemakers are making Camemberts from goats' and sheep's milk as well.

Casein: The protein in milk that coagulates to form curds. This coagulation is brought about by the introduction of cultures to the milk. These cultures raise the acid level, causing the casein proteins to clump together or coagulate. Rennet is then introduced, which causes the protein bonding or coagulation to intensify, leading to curd formation.

Caves: Aging rooms that are usually built underground. These cavelike venues allow for greater control over temperature, light, and humidity.

Cellar: Similar to a cave, a cellar is a room used for aging or ripening cheese. It, too, is usually underground, but it may be part of a home, barn, or cheese plant, similar to a basement.

Chalky: Refers to the texture of a cheese, often a goat cheese, where the consistency is dry, crumbly, and leaves an undesirable coating on the tongue.

Cheddar: A natural cream-colored or dyed orange cheese that is usually classified by its age and is the result of a process of cheesemaking called cheddaring. The classifications are mild (usually two to four months old), medium (four to eight months old), sharp (nine to twelve months old), and extra-sharp (anything over one year up to as much as four years old).

Cheddaring: The process by which cheddar cheese is made. The curds are formed into long sheets and stacked to promote the draining of the whey. They are usually restacked several times to allow for maximum whey drainage. They are then milled, or cut into tiny pieces, and pressed into molds.

Cheese board or **Cheese course:** A grouping of cheeses that is served either before, after, or instead of a meal.

Cheesecloth: Thin cotton cloth material used to drain cheese curds and/or line cheese molds.

Chèvre: The French word for goat, chèvre refers to a fresh cheese made with pasteurized goats' milk. It comes in many shapes, including logs and rounds, or it can be sold in small tubs or in bulk at some cheese shops. It is a soft, spreadable cheese that is equally good on its own or as an ingredient in salads or cooked dishes, both sweet and savory.

Chontaleño: A semi-hard Central American–style cows' milk cheese, similar in texture and taste to the salty, crumbly cheese known as cotija.

Citrusy: A flavor characteristic that is similar to the tart, sometimes sour, and sometimes herbal qualities found in citrus fruits. It might be specific, such as orange-like or lemony. It often pertains to high-acid cheeses, such as a young goat cheese.

Clean: A flavor characteristic in a cheese that shows a bright, pronounced flavor with no aftertaste.

Cloth-wrapped or **bandaged:** Describes a cheese, usually cheddar, that is "bandaged" or wrapped in cloth and then aged.

Coagulation: The state in cheesemaking when the casein, or milk protein, clumps together to form curds.

Coffee-flavored: A flavor characteristic, often of a well-aged Gouda, that is similar to the flavor of coffee.

Colby: A cheese thought to have been invented near the town of Colby, Wisconsin. It is similar to cheddar but differs in the cheesemaking process. The curds are washed with cool rather than hot water and they are not stacked and drained. Colby is a higher-moisture cheese that is generally mild. Some Colby is aged, in particular the Colby-like cheese called Crowley.

Cooked curds: A process in cheesemaking where the curds are heated, sometimes to very high tempera-tures, to help expel the whey. Examples of cooked-curd cheeses include Emmentaler and Gruyère.

Cotija: A hard, aged, white, crumbly Mexican cheese. Similar to feta, it is often sprinkled on dishes such as black beans or enchiladas or can even be used as a salt substitute in salads and potatoes. It is a very dry cheese that does not melt when heated. Cotija is also sometimes called queso añejo.

Cottage cheese: A fresh washed-curd cheese to which cream, milk, or nonfat milk is added to create a creamy consistency. The curds vary in size from small to large. It may be eaten plain or with fruit.

Crescenza: A fresh, runny cows' milk cheese that looks melted even when it hasn't been heated because of its creamy consistency. It is used in a variety of savory dishes because it melts so well, but it also pairs nicely with dried or fresh fruit. The flavor is similar to a mild Jack cheese.

Crumbly: Describes a cheese that literally crumbles when cut. Older blue cheeses may be crumbly, as are some fetas, cotija, queso blanco, and enchilado.

Cracked: When a cheese has visible fissures running through it. Sometimes this is the natural result of aging, but sometimes it signifies that the cheese has dried out and is likely past its eating prime.

Creamy: A favorable textural consistency and/or flavor of certain cheeses. It indicates a smooth and often runny consistency. It usually refers to the ripe forms of Brie, Camembert, California Teleme, and crescenza, among others. It can also refer to certain fresh cheeses, such as some cottage cheese, mascarpone, and crème fraîche. Creamy is also used to describe a flavor denoting rich or buttery characteristics.

Crème fraîche: Cultured milk or cream, or a combination of both. The result is a thick fresh cheese similar in consistency to sour cream. The flavor is buttery and a little tangy, and is good on fruit tarts or pies instead of whipped cream. It is also a good ingredient in cooked dishes, both sweet and savory.

Crottin: A cylindrical cheese with a brownish, yellowish rind, made from goats' milk. Crottins are generally mild and are sold anywhere from ten days to three weeks old. If kept well, they can become hard grating cheeses in about eight weeks.

Crowley: A unique cheese invented in the mid-1800s.

It is made by America's oldest continuously operating cheese factory, the Crowley Cheese Company in Vermont. It is a natural-colored cheese similar in texture and flavor to Colby.

Curds: The solid or coagulated portions of the milk. Curds are the result of the casein or milk proteins clumping together after they are exposed to starter bacteria. The starter(s) raise the acid level of the milk, causing the casein molecules to bond together. The curds undergo further solidifying once rennet is introduced, and eventually the curds become cheese.

Curing: Synonymous with *aging* or *ripening*. Refers to the period when a cheese is left in a cave, or curing or aging room, to mature and lose some of its moisture.

Cutting the curd: After the rennet has been introduced and the curds have begun to form, the curds are then cut with various-shaped metal wires to help expel the whey.

Delicate: Describes the light, gentle aroma and/or flavor that comes from cheeses that are usually younger. The aroma from a young Jack, Teleme, or Fontina might be considered delicate.

Dry Jack: Jack cheese that has been aged at least one year to become a hard grating cheese.

Dry matter: The portion of the cheese that is comprised of solids. Most cheese has at least 25 percent of its weight in dry matter or solids. The non-dry matter is the liquid portion of a cheese. For example, a young Jack cheese will consist of about 50 percent dry matter, while the other 50 percent is moisture. This is also the portion of the cheese that is measured for total fat content.

Earthy: A generally positive term to describe a depth of flavor that has characteristics of the earth, or soil, the area where the cheese is made and/or the feed of the animal. It often speaks to a slight mustiness in the cheese.

Edam: A mild cows' milk cheese in the family of Dutch cheeses that is usually shaped into an elongated sphere and waxed. It can be eaten as a table cheese. Its slight saltiness lends flavor to cooked dishes as well.

Emmentaler: Often called Swiss cheese in the U.S., Emmentaler is named after a river valley in Switzerland, where the cheese originated. It is usually made in large wheels weighing as much as 200 pounds and is distinguished by its large eye formation and hazelnut flavor.

Enchilado: A soft, crumbly Mexican cheese distinguished by its red coating, which is made from either chile powder or paprika. Enchilado añejo is a harder, longer-aged version of enchilado.

Explosive: A term used to describe a quality in cheese that simply lights up the flavor sensors. It does not necessarily equate to "strong," and instead refers to a cheese that, when tasted, literally explodes in the mouth with flavor.

Eyes: These are the holes formed in cheese as a result of the introduction of certain bacteria. In the case of Swiss cheese, eyes are encouraged, usually by the introduction of the *Propionicacter shermanii* bacterium. This bacterium produces carbon dioxide, which creates bubbles that eventually burst, leaving the grape-size eyes, or holes, behind. Other cheeses, such as Havarti, have smaller eyes because the bacteria used in those are not as aggressive.

Farmer cheese: A fresh cheese that is similar to cottage cheese, though it is less creamy, the curds are often smaller, and its taste is more sour.

Farmlike: The flavor characteristic that might also be described as grassy or hay-flavored. It is often a fresh, milky, or earthy flavor as compared to barnyardy, which can be stronger and more gamy.

Farmstead: A cheese that is made exclusively from milk that comes from the cheesemaker's own animals.

Feed-flavored: When the characteristics of the feed eaten by the animals are discernible in the taste of the cheese.

Fermentation: The process by which milk transforms into cheese and other milk products such as sour cream and yogurt. Technically, fermentation is the process leading to the breakdown of carbohydrates. In the case of milk, *Lactococci* or *Lactobacilli* bacteria are introduced to the milk, which causes the breakdown of lactose into lactic acid. This conversion sets up the proper acid levels and textural consistency for the milk to be made into cheese.

Feta: A fresh cheese that originated in Greece, where it was traditionally made with goats' milk or sheep's milk. In the U.S. it is made with either sheep's, goats', or cows' milk, or sometimes a mixture of two milks. Feta is usually kept in a saltwater brine and can be preserved for well over a year. It is a rindless cheese that, despite the brine, is dry and crumbly.

Firm: Refers to the body of the cheese when it is strong and smooth rather than weak or soft.

Flat: Indicates that the flavor of the cheese is neutral, with no particular standout characteristics; lacking flavor.

Floral: The fragrant quality in cheese that can pertain to both aroma and flavor. A floral flavor is a sweet though not sugary taste, such as in a fresh sheep's milk ricotta. It can also refer to a cheese that might have a floral component added to it.

Fontina: Originated in Italy, Fontina is a semi-hard, mild to strong-flavored cows' milk cheese. It is distinguished by its tiny eyes and is a brushed-rind cheese. In the U.S., however, Fontina is not always a brushed-rind cheese, and at least one producer is making Fontina from goats' milk.

Fresh cheese: Cheese that has not been aged or ripened. Cottage cheese, pot cheese, and mozzarella are a few examples of fresh cheese.

Fresh milk: A flavor and/or aroma characteristic that is reminiscent of the pre-fermented milk. A just-made mozzarella, especially one made with the milk from a water buffalo, has this milk or lactic flavor.

Fromage blanc: A fresh (unripened) cultured cheese that can be made from cows', goats', or sheep's milk. Its consistency falls somewhere between ricotta and sour cream, and its taste lies somewhere between those two products as well. Tangier than ricotta but not as sour as sour cream, it can be used as a spread, and is also very good for cooking since it melts nicely and adds creaminess and body. It can be used in pastas, risotti, and pizzas or in fruit and baked desserts.

Fruity: A flavor and/or aroma characteristic that is reminiscent of fresh fruit. The flavor or aroma can be that of a specific fruit, such as an apple-like flavor in a Gruyère, or more general, as in fruity, or with notes of sweetness. The aroma of a cheese might also have the natural sweetness that is associated with fruit.

Furry: Can be used favorably to describe the light downlike bacteria that surrounds a bloomy-rind cheese such as a Camembert, or it can be a disparaging term to describe unwanted mold growth on other cheeses.

Gamy: Can be a favorable or unfavorable characteristic, depending on the individual and on the cheese. Gamy refers to the flavor and/or aroma in a cheese that has strong animal-like characteristics. If a goat cheese tastes gamy, it usually means that it has a strong, earthy flavor that the taster might be associating with the smell or taste of a goat. A young cheese generally should not have a gamy flavor or aroma.

Garlicky: Pertains to a garlic flavor occasionally detected in cheese. It usually comes from the feed or grasses that the animal has eaten. It is generally not a favorable characteristic.

Gorgonzola: An Italian blue-veined cheese that has been adopted by a few American cheesemakers. Gorgonzola is a cows' milk cheese made from pasteurized milk. It has two distinct styles, based on the length of aging. A young Gorgonzola may be called Gorgonzola dolce. It is creamy (sometimes so creamy it is best eaten with a spoon), with greenish-blue veins and a relatively mild but spicy "blue" flavor. Longer-aged Gorgonzola is firmer, spicier, and stronger-flavored.

Gouda: Of Dutch origin, Goudas were originally wax-wrapped mild cows' milk cheeses. While those are still made in great quantities, many American cheesemakers are now making Goudas in the Dutch *boerenkaas*, or farmstead, fashion. These are handcrafted raw milk, cooked-curd, brined Goudas that are aged for as long as two years. Longer-aged Goudas are golden in color and have a nutty, caramel, and sometimes coffee flavor. They can also be earthy, somewhat strong, and salty. Gouda is a good melting cheese, and because of that is good in many cooked dishes. Some Goudas are now made with goats' milk.

Grana style: A cheese that is made by cooking, pressing, and salting the curds. The pressed curds are then washed and turned constantly during the aging process to become a dry, granular ("grana") cheese. Asiago is a type of grana cheese.

Grassy: Refers to a flavor, and sometimes an aroma, in a cheese that is reminiscent of grass. It usually relates to a certain acidic element that might even be perceived as sour by some. Fresh goat cheeses often have a grassy element, which is usually considered favorable. The grassy flavor and aroma can also pertain to the flavors and/or aromas that are the result of the grasses eaten by the animals.

Graviera (also known as **Kefalograviera**): A sheep's milk cheese found primarily in Greece, its country of origin, but made by Skunk Hollow Farm in Vermont as well. There it is called Graviera. In Greece it earns the prefix *kefalo*, which means "head." It refers to the size of the cheese, which is larger than a person's head. Graviera is made with raw milk and aged anywhere from about eight to fourteen months. It has very small eyes and a natural rind. It is a full-flavored cheese that is sweet yet nutty. It melts very well and is also a lovely table cheese.

Gruyère: A so-called mountain or Alpine cheese because of its origins in the Swiss and French Alps. (French Gruyère is called Comté). Gruyère is a cooked-curd brined cheese that is aged from three months to one year. It has legendary melting qualities and is the usual ingredient in cheese fondue. It can range in flavor from mild to medium-strong and has nutty, earthy, and floral qualities. The most authentic Gruyère in the U.S. is made by Roth Käse in Wisconsin, which has a sister plant in Switzerland.

Gummy: Of or pertaining to a gumlike or chewy quality in the texture of cheese, often due to excessive moisture or condensation. An unfavorable characteristic.

Hard: Term used to describe cheeses that have been aged for a long period, and/or salted, and/or pressed, causing them to lose their moisture and become hard. Grating cheeses are hard cheeses.

Havarti: A generally mild cows' milk cheese made throughout the United States, but especially in Wisconsin. It has very small eyes and is a very good melting cheese. Havarti is often made with flavorings such as caraway seed, dill, or garlic.

Heat-treated milk: Falling somewhere between raw milk and pasteurized milk, this milk is quickly heated at a lower temperature. This might mean that the milk is heated at 130°F for two to sixteen seconds. The goal is to kill off any of the potentially unhealthful organisms that might exist in raw milk yet retain certain flavor and other characteristics that also exist in raw milk.

Herbaceous: A term that can apply to the flavor and/or the aroma of a cheese, referring to an herbal quality in the cheese. This quality can be the result of herbs added to the cheese, or herbs used in the curing process, but usually it is the result of the way the cheese is made, the area in which it is made, and the type of feed or grasses eaten by the animals whose milk was used for the cheese. It is often found in aged sheep's milk and goats' milk cheeses.

Holes: The same as eyes, holes are the distinguishing characteristic of Swiss or Emmentaler cheese. They are the result of carbon dioxide bubbles that form in the body of the cheese. This carbon dioxide occurs in response to specific bacteria that are deliberately introduced into the cheese. Other cheeses, such as Havarti and Fontina, have much smaller holes because of the less aggressive bacteria present in these cheeses.

Homogenization: A process which breaks down and incorporates the fat globules found naturally in milk. This prevents the cream from separating and rising to the top. It also helps in cheesemaking because less of the fat is lost in the whey, which means the yield will be higher. Some cheesemakers deliberately avoid homogenization, however, because they believe the larger fat globules are beneficial to the consistency and flavor of their cheese.

Ivory: The light cream color in many cows' milk and some sheep's milk cheeses, including some undyed cheddars, the inside or paste of Camembert and Brie, Jack cheese, crescenza, and California Teleme.

Jack cheese: See *Monterey Jack*.

Kasseri: Usually a Greek sheep's milk cheese, in the United States it is made by some producers with cows' milk. It is a very mild cheese that is best used in cooking.

Lactic: The strong presence of milk in flavor and/or aroma.

Lactic acid: The acid that is produced by the breakdown of lactose. That breakdown results from starter bacteria being added to the milk.

Lactose: A natural sugar present in milk.

Lactose intolerance: The inability of the body to break down lactose. Symptoms of lactose intolerance can include bloating, diarrhea, and nausea.

Liederkranz: Introduced in this country in the late 1800s, Liederkranz is a strong surface-ripened cheese that is made in a small oblong shape. It has a moist rind and a hefty aroma. It is not, however, made in any great quantities in America any longer.

Limburger: A very pungent semi-soft surface-ripened cheese made and enjoyed primarily in the Midwest, though it originated in Belgium. Often served with raw onion on dark rye or pumpernickel bread. To some the aroma and taste of Limburger is overpowering.

Longhorn: A style of cheddar or Colby cheese that is so named because of its cylindrical shape.

Mascarpone: A naturally sweet, spreadable cream made with only two ingredients: cream and citric or tartaric acid. These ingredients are combined and left to drain, allowing all of the non-cream components, including the sodium, to separate out. The cream that is left is buttery in taste and texture. It is very rich and is used as an ingredient in sweet dishes or as a topping for desserts. It also melts well and can sometimes be used in place of cream cheese, though it is creamier. Its best known use is in the Italian dessert tiramisù.

Metallic: Refers to a metal flavor detected in cheese. It is an unfavorable characteristic.

Mold: Spores that are added to the milk or the curds and/or the surface of a cheese to encourage mold growth as the cheese is formed. Surface molds are sometimes sprayed on the outside of the cheese, as in the case of Camembert. These types of molds are edible. Mold is also the undesirable growth that forms on the outside of old and/or poorly wrapped cheeses. This can often be cut away from the cheese, however, and the cheese can then be consumed.

Molding: The step in cheesemaking when the curds are poured or hand-ladled into molds, usually plastic, that are outfitted with tiny holes to allow for drainage of the whey. Molding also contributes to the final shape of the cheese. Sometimes the molds are muslin or nylon bags that are tied in a particular shape. These bags allow for drainage and also create the final shape of the cheese.

Monterey Jack: Originated in California in the mid-1800s, Jack cheese is a cows' milk cheese that can be sold as a young, high-moisture semi-soft cheese or aged to become a hard grating cheese. The young version melts very well and is often used in Mexican cooking. It has a fruity flavor and aroma, but it also has a bit of a tang. The aged version, called Dry Jack by California's Vella Cheese Company, becomes golden after two or three years and is nutty, still somewhat fruity, and moderately salty. High-moisture Jack cheese is often made with flavors, including hot peppers, pesto, onion, or garlic.

Mossholder: The name of a cheese and of the person, Otto Mossholder, who invented it in the early 1900s. It is a unique cheese, still made in Wisconsin by the Mossholder family. This is a raw milk cheese that has characteristics of brick, Swiss, and Colby cheeses. It is made in brick form, although it does not become as strong as brick cheese because it is not surface-ripened. Instead, it is salted and wrapped in plastic. It is aged anywhere from two months to two years and is made plain and in several flavors.

Mottled: Describes a spotty and uneven appearance on the outside of the cheese, or an unevenness of color, usually due to the combining of curds from two different vats.

Mouthfeel: The way a cheese feels in the mouth. It might be smooth, dense, granular, buttery, or any number of other possible consistencies.

Mozzarella: A mild fresh cheese, made from either cows' milk or, in Italy, the milk of water buffalos. Hot water is added to the curds and whey, causing them to separate. The hot curds are stretched or kneaded for a short period and formed into their final shape, usually a ball. Because of this process, mozzarella is called a *pasta filata*, or stretched-curd cheese. Fresh mozzarella is sold in brine or water, and is often cut in slices and served in a salad with sliced fresh tomato, basil, and olive oil. In its drier form, mozzarella is packaged in plastic and used primarily as a grating cheese for pizzas and other cooked dishes. For this reason, it is often referred to as a pizza cheese. It can be made with either whole milk or part skim milk.

Muenster: Traditionally a strong French washed-rind cheese. American Muenster is a very mild, slightly sweet cows' milk cheese, used mainly for melting in grilled cheese sandwiches or eaten plain alongside some fresh apples. It is an excellent "beginner's cheese" because of its mildness.

Mushroomy: Describes the flavor and/or aroma in a cheese that is reminiscent of mushrooms.

Musty: Often due to mold growth, a musty flavor or aroma that can be likened to dirt. It is earthy to the point of dankness, and such flavor often lingers well after the cheese has been consumed. It is not a favorable characteristic.

Mutton-like: Describes the aroma or flavor in a cheese that is similar to the taste or smell of sheep or lamb; a strong, gamy flavor or aroma.

Natural rind: A rind that develops naturally due to bacteria in the cheese, and/or introduced to the surface of the cheese, and/or found in the cheese aging room. Molds may also be added to the surface of the cheese to create the rind.

Nutty: A favorable flavor and sometimes aromatic characteristic often found in aged cheeses. As the word implies, nutty refers to the toasty and sometimes woody flavors that are found in nuts. Those same flavors can be found in certain cheeses, including Swiss, Gruyère, and Parmesan.

Oaxaca: A mild Mexican cows' milk cheese that is nearly identical in taste to mozzarella. It, too, is a stretched-curd cheese, or *pasta filata*, but instead of a ball, Oaxaca is formed into the shape of a braid.

Oniony: A flavor of onion that comes through in the cheese. This is usually due to the feed or grass that has been eaten by the animals. It is generally an unfavorable characteristic.

Open: Refers to the body or texture of a cheese that contains holes or openings.

Panela: A Mexican fresh cows' milk cheese that is molded in baskets and gently pressed to release some of its moisture. Panela is an excellent frying cheese because it softens but does not melt when cooked. It can even be sliced and grilled. It can be used in both sweet and savory dishes.

Parmesan: A grana-style cheese that, in the United States, is made with pasteurized or heat-treated milk. The curds are then cooked and the salt is either added to the curds, or the pressed cheese is placed in a saltwater brine. Domestic Parmesan is aged a minimum of ten months. In Italy, traditional Parmigiano-Reggiano is made from raw milk and is aged for a minimum of eighteen months.

Pasta filata: Literally "stretched curd," *pasta filata* cheeses are those that are hand- or machine-stretched while still warm and made into a variety of shapes. This stretching creates the stringlike characteristic common to all *pasta filata* cheeses. Examples of *pasta filata* cheeses are mozzarella, Oaxaca, Provolone, and the well-known string cheese.

Paste: The interior of a cheese. In French, the interior is called the *pâte*.

Pasteurization: The process by which milk is heated with the intent of killing any unwanted or unhealthful organisms. The standard formula for pasteurization is 160°F for fifteen seconds. This, however, varies according to the pasteurization equipment and sometimes the intended cheese. Fresh, unripened cheeses are heated at 145°F for thirty minutes.

Pasty: Describes an unfavorable sticky consistency in the body of the cheese.

Pencillium camemberti: A mold spore sometimes used in the production of Camembert cheese.

Penicillium candidum: A mold that is often used in certain soft-ripened cheeses to create flavor as well as the growth of a particular type of rind.

Peppery: Refers to a spicy flavor often found in some blue cheeses. Certain aged cheddars might also have peppery characteristics.

Perfumy: Term used for the perfume-like aroma that is emitted from certain cheeses. Aged Goudas and Gruyères often have this characteristic.

Piquant: A bright, tangy, and sometimes sharp flavor characteristic. It can be detected in certain young goat cheeses and also in some cheddars.

Plymouth Cheese: A unique cheese invented in 1890 by the father of President Calvin Coolidge. Its flavor lies somewhere between a Havarti and a cheddar, and it is aged anywhere from two months to four years. It is named for the town Plymouth Notch, which contains historic buildings, many of which the Coolidge family either built or occupied.

Pot cheese: A low-fat plain cottage cheese that has no added salt. It is also called dry curd cottage cheese. The name comes from the time when cheese was made from skim milk and heated in a pot on the stove.

Provolone: A stretched-curd, or *pasta filata*, cheese made with either raw or pasteurized milk. It can be aged for as long as two years, at which time it becomes hard and salty. The younger versions of Provolone are a common sandwich ingredient, but Provolone also melts well in cooked dishes.

Pungent: A strong and possibly acrid flavor or aroma found in some cheese. Many surface-ripened cheeses, such as brick and Limburger, might be described as pungent. To some this is a desirable characteristic, and to others it is not. Some cheeses might have a pungent quality because they are poorly made or are too old. In this case, the result is undesirable.

Quark (or **quarg**): A staple for most Germans, quark is a nonfat or low-fat fresh cheese whose consistency lies somewhere between yogurt and a creamy cottage cheese. It is, in fact, similar to bakers' cheese. Some producers make nonfat versions of quark, while others include butterfat in their recipes. It can be used in place of sour cream or yogurt in baking, and it can also be used as a tart topping on toast. It is also a tangy addition to a fresh fruit salad.

Queso añejo. See *Cotija.*

Queso blanco: A mild Mexican semi-hard cheese made from cows' milk. Used primarily in cooking.

Queso blanco fresco: A mild, fresh Mexican cheese that is very firm yet moist. It can be used in cooking, but it does not melt. It is similar in consistency to feta cheese and can be similarly crumbled. When used for frying, queso blanco fresco is called *queso para freir*, or "frying cheese."

Rancid: Refers to a soapy, bitter, and off flavor that is usually the result of poorly handled milk.

Raw milk: The milk that comes directly from the animal. It is milk that has not been pasteurized.

Red-hued: The color of the rind on some surface-ripened cheeses, such as brick and Limburger. Also, the undesirable color of an overripe soft-ripened cheese, such as a Camembert.

Rennet: An animal, vegetable, or microbial substance that contains the enzyme rennin, which is crucial to the coagulation of milk. Traditionally rennet came from the stomach lining of a calf, but it also comes from sheep and goats. Non-animal sources include the vegetable known as cardoon, and microbial rennet is the laboratory-made genetic equivalent of animal rennet.

Rennin: The enzyme that coagulates milk.

Rich: Used mostly to describe a full-flavored, high-butterfat cheese. It can also describe a cheese whose earthiness or saltiness is the predominating characteristic. A Parmesan cheese might be considered rich because it is high both in butterfat and in salt.

Ricotta: A slightly granular and mild fresh cheese most often made with cows' milk. It is made in several ways: entirely from the whey; with whole or part skim milk; and without the whey. It can be quite watery or it can be fairly dry, depending on the producer and packager. Although rare in this country, sheep's milk ricotta is particularly flavorful and worth trying.

Ricotta salata: The dry form of ricotta. Ricotta salata

is made, usually from whey, and then placed in a basket to drain. It is pressed to release further moisture from the cheese and left to dry for weeks or months. It is then used as a grating cheese.

Rind: The outside of a cheese, either natural or artificial. The rind protects the interior of the cheese and often imparts a flavor of its own to the cheese. Some cheeses have no rind at all because the cheesemaker has chosen to package the cheese before a rind has the chance to form. This packaging can be in the form of wax, plastic, or in the case of Cougar Gold, a can.

Rind rot: The visible soft spots, discoloration, or rotting of a cheese rind.

Ripe: A cheese that is ready to be eaten. Refers to any cheeses that are aged, regardless of the period of time they are aged. A ten-day-old cheese might be considered ripe.

Ripening: Synonymous with aging, ripening is the process of maturing a cheese.

Robust: Rich and full-bodied. The cheese might burst with a number of flavors, including but not limited to buttery, gamy, herbal, or floral flavors.

Romano: A granular-style cheese made almost exclusively from cows' milk in this country. It is quite salty and is used primarily as a grating cheese.

Rubbery: A term that pertains to an undesirable quality in the texture of a cheese. It suggests a certain stiffness and a lack of the textural qualities normally found in the particular cheese. Certain bulk-manufactured part-skim mozzarellas are inherently rubbery, as are many low-fat and nonfat cheeses. This is due to the relative lack of fat globules and the particular protein structure found in these types of cheeses.

Runny: The state of a ripe cheese when it oozes outside of its rind after being cut or is no longer keeping its original shape. Examples might include some soft-ripened cheeses, California Teleme, and crescenza.

Rustic: Earthy and/or herbal qualities present in the flavor and/or aroma of a cheese. Certain natural-rind aged sheep's milk cheeses might be considered rustic.

Saggy: A cheese that is drooping. In the case of soft-ripened cheese, this can be favorable since it means that the cheese is ripe. However, it can just as easily mean that the cheese is overripe. A quick whiff will usually tell whether it's ripe or ready to be discarded.

Salting: The step in cheesemaking when salt is added to the cheese. It varies according to the type of cheese. For example, salt is added to the curds during cheddar making while it is added in brine form to the outside of a Gouda after the cheese has been molded.

Savory: Loosely defined as the "fifth sense" after sweet, sour, bitter, and salty. Several cheeses are characterized as savory, including aged cheddar and Parmesan. See *Umami*.

Scamorza: A fresh, oval-shaped *pasta filata* cheese that is made in both plain and smoked styles. It is very similar to mozzarella, though slightly more tangy, and can be used interchangeably.

Semi-hard: Term used for a cheese that has about 50 percent moisture or less. Examples are Emmentaler, aged Gouda, and aged cheddars.

Semi-soft: A cheese that has between 50 and 75 percent moisture. Examples are high-moisture Monterey Jack cheese, Havarti, and American Muenster.

Sharp: A flavor in cheese that straddles the line between piquant and bitter. Many bulk-manufactured American cheddars are labeled "sharp." Usually refers to a step in the cheesemaking process where the enzymes are quickly heated to boost the acid level of the cheese. This translates to a sharper cheese. In specialty cheesemaking, the sharpness also comes about because of the acid content, but the full sharp flavor manifests itself slowly as a result of the aging process.

Silky: A term used to describe the texture of a cheese if that cheese is particularly smooth or runny.

Smoked: The flavor that is produced after a cheese has been subjected to a natural smoking process. Cedar chips, hickory chips, and other types of regional wood are most often used to make smoked cheese.

Smoky: Describes a flavor and/or aroma in a cheese that is reminiscent of smoke from a wood-burning fire. More loosely, it might simply mean an earthy component in the cheese.

Soft cheese: An unpressed, high-moisture cheese that is aged for a very short time. Crescenza is an example.

Soft-ripened cheese: A cheese that ripens from the rind inward due to the mold or bacteria added in the cheesemaking process and/or sprayed on the surface of the cheese. Evidence that a soft-ripened cheese has begun its ripening or softening is that the part of the cheese that lies just under the rind is becoming soft, sometimes to the point of being runny. Camembert and Brie are the best-known examples.

Solid: Term used when the texture of the cheese is firm and has no discernible openings. It also shows no weakness or "give" when pressed.

Sour: Refers to the condition when a cheese has an overpowering acidic component.

Sour milk: Refers to a generally unfavorable flavor in cheese that is reminiscent of sour milk, which would be sour and possibly musty.

Spicy: A characteristic in cheese that might be piquant, pungent, and/or aromatic. Blue cheese is often described as spicy because of its mold characteristics, while a cheese flavored with black pepper or chile peppers is also described as spicy.

Springlike: A flavor and/or aromatic characteristic in cheese that is fresh, herbaceous, perfumy, fruity, floral, or any combination of these.

Squeakers: Just-made cheddar cheese curds that are scooped up and packaged by the cheesemaker and sold on the day they are made. Squeakers were invented in Wisconsin, where they remain popular today. They are said to squeak when they are eaten, due to their freshness. Technically, if squeakers are sold the day after they are made, they are then called Day-Old.

Starter: The bacteria that is added to milk at the beginning of the cheesemaking process to raise the lactic acid level. This in turn creates "sour" milk, which then helps the milk to coagulate. The starter also lends flavor to the final cheese.

Stravecchio: Named for the Antigo Cheese Company's aged Parmesan. Meaning "very old," Stravecchio is aged for twenty months.

Sulfurous or **Sulfide flavor:** The flavor and/or aroma in a cheese that is reminiscent of rotten eggs. It is thought to come about when, for some reason, an enzyme found in certain bacteria breaks down two of the sulfur amino acids in cheese.

Supple: Refers to a texture that is pliable, smooth, and/or satiny.

Surface-ripened cheese: A cheese on which bacteria is

encouraged to grow on the surface, such as with brick cheese or beer kaese, to achieve distinct (usually strong) flavors. Also called **bacterial-ripened cheese**.

Sweet: Can refer to the flavor or aroma of a cheese. It usually signifies a lower-acid cheese and possibly one with a less pronounced sodium component.

Sweet Swiss: A cheese developed in Wisconsin by Randy Krahenbuhl, owner of Prima Käse. It is, as the name implies, a milder, less sharp version of Swiss cheese and its holes are smaller than those found in the traditional Swiss cheese.

Swiss cheese: The famous "cheese with the holes." It originated in Switzerland, though in that country it is referred to as Emmentaler, which is a slightly different cheese. In this country, as in Switzerland, it is a cooked- and stirred-curd cheese that is salted after it has been lightly pressed. The large eyes form as a result of carbon dioxide, which is created by the introduction of certain bacteria. Ohio is this country's largest producer of Swiss cheese.

Tangy: Used when describing goat cheese, due to its piquant flavor. It often suggests a higher-acid cheese.

Teleme: A cheese that is in the brine family of cheeses (of which feta is one), originating in Greece. In this country, it is a soft, sometimes runny cheese (depending on ripeness) that was created in the early 1900s in California, where it is still made today. Similar to Jack cheese, though with more pronounced fruitiness.

Tilsit: A semi-soft to semi-hard washed-rind cows' milk cheese that has roots in several European countries. In this country, Sontheim Fine Cheeses in Colorado makes it in a German style. The wheel-shaped cheese is mild when it is young, and when aged becomes strong and favorably earthy. It is a particularly good cooking cheese because of its melting properties and its full flavor.

Truffly: A flavor and/or aroma in cheese that is earthy, almost dirtlike, but favorably so. The characteristic pertains to the prized fungus known as a truffle.

Umami: A term used to describe the "fifth taste," after sweet, sour, salty, and bitter. It was identified by the Japanese and is now being studied in this country. *Umami* is loosely equated to the term *savory*. Many foods fall into the *umami* category that don't fall neatly into the other four taste categories, such as mushrooms, tomatoes, and some shellfish. Aged cheddar and Parmesan, among others, are said to have *umami*.

Vegetal: Describes a plantlike flavor or aroma in a cheese. It can include any type of plant or vegetable.

Veiny: Containing an abundance of veins. This is caused by the proliferation of bacteria in the cheese, brought about by the introduction of oxygen. This is how the veins in blue cheese are formed, where it is a favorable characteristic. It is an unfavorable characteristic in a cheese in which the veins are unintended.

Velvety: Pertains to the texture and/or mouthfeel of a cheese. Both the rind and the paste of a ripe soft-ripened cheese might be said to have velvety characteristics.

Washed-rind cheese: Cheese in which the rind is literally washed with a solution, usually of salt and water, to keep the cheese moist as well as to lend flavor. This moisture can translate to a stronger cheese, depending on the cheese. A washed-rind cheese can also be washed with liquids besides saltwater, such as cider, beer, or wine.

Wax or **paraffin:** The wax coating of a cheese. If the wax is applied well and is of good quality, it should adhere tightly to the cheese and show no signs of cracking.

Weedy: Refers to a flavor in a cheese that is overly vegetal and/or grassy and/or earthy.

Whey: The high-protein liquid portion of milk that forms after the milk protein, or casein, begins to coagulate and becomes curds.

Yeasty: A flavor and/or aroma in a cheese that is reminiscent of baking bread, a good Champagne, or brewed beer. A blue cheese might have a yeasty aroma, as might certain soft-ripened cheeses.

CHEESEMAKERS AROUND THE COUNTRY

(*denotes cheesemaker profiled in the book)

ALABAMA
Clear Creek Farm
Valley Head, Alabama
256-635-6123

Fromagerie Belle Chèvre
Elkmont, Alabama
256-423-2238 or 800-735-2238

Sweet Home Farm
(cows' milk cheese)
Elberta, Alabama
334-986-5663 (mail order at
Christmastime only)

ARKANSAS
Doeling Dairy Goat Farm*
Fayetteville, Arkansas
501-582-4571 or 888-524-4571
501-582-1213 (fax)
website: www.doelingdairy.com

CALIFORNIA
Andante Dairy
St. Helena, CA
707-963-2337
415-681-4110 (fax)

Ariza Cheese Company
(Mexican cheeses)
Paramount, California
562-630-4144 or 800-762-4736
562-630-4174 (fax)
website: www.mexicancheese.com

Belfiore Cheese Company
Berkeley, California
510-540-5500
510-540-5594 (fax)

Bellwether Farms*
Petaluma, California
707-763-0993 or 888-527-8606
(mail order)
707-763-2443 (fax)
website:
www.bellwethercheese.com

Bodega Goat Cheese
Bodega, California
707-876-3483 (phone and fax)

Bravo Farms*
Visalia, California
559-734-1282
559-625-0490 (fax)
website: www.bravofarm.com
    www.whitecheddar.com
    www.farmstead.com

Cacique Cheese Company
(Mexican and Caribbean
cheeses)
City of Industry, California
626-961-3399
626-961-4676 (fax)
website: www.caciqueusa.com

California Mozzarella Fresca
Benecia, California
707-746-6818
707-746-6829 (fax)

California Polytechnic University
Creamery
San Luis Obispo, California
805-756-1243
805-756-1228 (fax)

Cowgirl Creamery / Tomales Bay
Foods*
Point Reyes Station, California
415-663-9335 or 415-663-8153
415-663-5418 (fax)
website:
www.cowgirlcreamery.com

Cuatro Piedras (goats' milk
cheese)
Santa Barbara, California
805-682-4511

Cypress Grove Chèvre*
McKinleyville, California
707-839-3168
707-839-2322 (fax)
website:
www.cypressgrovechevre.com

Formaggi di Ferrante
(Italian cheeses)
Sacramento, California
916-332-6397
916-332-6398 (fax)

Goat's Leap Cheese (farmstead)
St. Helena, California
707-963-2337 (phone and fax)

Imperial Valley Cheese Company
Cheese (cows' milk cheese)
El Centro, California
760-337-1573

Italia Latticini
Wilmington, California
310-830-8321 or 310-549-1994
310-549-4510 (fax)
website:
www.italialatticini@thegrid.com

Karoun Dairies
(Mediterranean cheeses)
Los Angeles, California
323-666-6296 or 323-666-6222
323-666-1501 (fax)

Kendall Farms (crème fraîche)
Atascadero, California
805-466-7252

Laura Chenel Chèvre*
Sonoma, California
707-996-4477
707-996-1816 (fax)

Loleta Cheese Company
(cows' milk cheese)
Loleta, California
707-733-5470 or 800-995-0453
707-733-1872 (fax)

Marin French Cheese Company
Petaluma, California
707-762-6001
707-762-0430 (fax)
website:
www.sfnet.net/cheesefactory

Marquez Brothers International
(Mexican and Central American
cheeses)
San Jose, California
408-960-2700 or 800-858-1119
408-960-3213 (fax)
website:
www.marquezbrothers.com

Joe Matos Cheese Factory*
Santa Rosa, California
707-584-5283

Oakdale Cheese & Specialties
Oakdale, California
209-848-3139
209-848-1162(fax)

Parker Dairy & Cheese
Orland, California
530-865-5700 (phone and fax)

Pedrozo Dairy and Cheese Company (farmstead cows' milk cheese)
Orland, California
530-865-9548

Peluso Cheese Company*
Los Banos, California
209-826-3744
209-826-6782 (fax)

Redwood Hill Farm*
Sebastopol, California
707-823-8250
707-823-6976 (fax)
website: www.redwoodhill.com

Rumiano Cheese Company
Crescent City, California
707-465-1535
707-465-4141 (fax)

Sea Stars Goat Cheese
Pescadero, California
650-879-0480
650-879-9161 (fax)

Sequoia Specialty Cheese Company (cows' milk cheese)
Tipton, California
559-752-4106

Skyhill Napa Valley Farms
Napa, California
707-255-4800
707-252-9297 (fax)

Sonoma Cheese Factory*
Sonoma, California
707-996-1000 or 800-535-2855 (mail order)
707-935-3535 (fax)
website: www.sonomacheese.com

Spring Hill Jersey Cheese (farmstead)
Petaluma, California

707-762-3446
707-762-3455 (fax)

Straus Family Creamery*
Marshall, California
415-663-5464
415-663-5465 (fax)
website: www.strausmilk.com

Udderly Gold Dairy
Helendale, California
760-243-1166

Vella Cheese Company*
Sonoma, California
707-938-3232 or 800-848-0505
707-938-4307 (fax)
website: www.vellacheese.com

Winchester Cheese Company*
Winchester, California
909-926-4239
909-926-3349 (fax)
website:
www.winchestercheese.com

Yerba Santa Dairy*
Lakeport, California
707-263-8131

COLORADO
Bingham Hill Cheese Company
Fort Collins, CO
970-472-9650
970-472-9655 (fax)
website: www.binghamhill.com

Haystack Mountain Goat Dairy*
Niwot, Colorado
303-581-9984
303-516-1041 (fax)
website:
www.haystackgoatcheese.com

Sontheim Fine Cheeses*
Powderhorn, Colorado
970-641-6671 (phone and fax)
website:
members.xoom.com/sontheim

CONNECTICUT
Calabro Cheese
East Haven, Connecticut
203-469-1311 or 800-969-1311
203-469-6929 (fax)

FLORIDA
Turtle Creek Dairy (goat cheese)
Loxahatchee, Florida
407-798-4628

HAWAII
Hamakua Farms (goat cheese)
Hamakua, Hawaii
808-878-6226

Heather Threlfall (goat cheese)
Honokaa, Hawaii
808-885-6988

Ku`oko`a Farm*
Kurtistown, Hawaii
808-966-7792

IDAHO
Rollingstone Chèvre
Parma, Idaho
208-722-6460

INDIANA
Capriole Inc.*
Greenville, Indiana
812-923-9408 (phone and fax)

IOWA
Maytag Dairy Farms*
Newton, Iowa
515-792-1133 or 800-247-2458
515-792-1567 (fax)

MAINE
Nezinscot Farm (cows' and goats' milk cheese)
Turner, Maine
207-225-3231

State of Maine Cheese Company
Rockport, Maine
207-236-8895 or 800-762-8895
website: www.cheese-me.com

MARYLAND
Gemelli, Inc. (Italian-style cheeses)
Silver Spring, Maryland
301-384-0674 or 800-GEMELLI
(800-436-3554)
301-384-0674 (fax)
website: www.gemelliinc.com

MASSACHUSETTS
Great Hill Dairy*
Marion, Massachusetts
508-748-2208 or 888-748-2208
508-748-2282 (fax)
website: www.greathillblue.com

Smith's Country Cheese (farmstead; cows' milk cheese)
Winchendon, Massachusetts
978-939-5738

Westfield Farm*
Hubbardston, Massachusetts
978-928-5110
978-928-5745 (fax)
website: www.chevre.com

MINNESOTA
**Dancing Winds Farms
(goat cheese)**
Kenyon, Minnesota
507-789-6606

Happy Ours Farm (goat cheese)
Byron, Minnesota
507-365-8098
507-365-8921 (fax)

**Morning Meadows
(cow and goat cheese)**
Redwing, Minnesota
651-388-6393

MISSOURI
Stoney Acres Sheep Dairy
Falcon, Missouri
417-668-5560 (phone and fax)
website:
www.geocities.com/heartland/
    bluffs/2479/

NEVADA
**Oasis Farmstead Dairy
(goat cheese)**
Fallon, Nevada
702-867-4283
website:
www.oasisfarmsteaddairy.com

NEW HAMPSHIRE
Boggy Meadow Farm*
Walpole, New Hampshire
603-756-3300
603-756-9645 (fax)

NEW MEXICO
Sweetwoods Dairy (goat cheese)
Peña Blanca, New Mexico
505-465-2608
505-465-0904 (fax)

NEW YORK
Cappiello Dairy Products
Schenectady, New York
518-398-5325
518-374-4015 (fax)
website: www.cappiello.com

Coach Farm*
Pine Plains, New York
518-398-5325
518-398-5329 (fax)

Egg Farm Dairy*
Peekskill, New York
914-734-7343 or 800-CREAMERY
914-734-9287 (fax)
website: www.creamery.com

Goat Hill Farm (farmstead)
Manlius, New York
315-655-3014 (phone and fax)

**Hawthorne Valley Farm
(cows' milk cheese)**
Ghent, New York
518-672-4465
518-672-4887 (fax)

Lioni Latticini
Brooklyn, New York
718-259-8378 or 800-528-3252

**Little Rainbow Chèvre
(farmstead)**
Hillsdale, New York
518-325-GOAT (4628)

Northland Sheep Dairy*
Marathon, New York
607-849-3328

**Old Chatham Sheepherding
Company***
Old Chatham, New York
518-794-7733 or 888-SHEEP-60
518-794-7641 (fax)
website:
www.blacksheepcheese.com

Sagpond Vineyards*
Sagaponack, New York
516-537-5106
516-537-5107 (fax)
websites:
www.sagpondvineyards.com
www.wolffer.com

NORTH CAROLINA
Celebrity Dairy (goat cheese)
Siler, North Carolina
919-742-5176
919-742-1432 (fax)
website: www.celebritydairy.com

Goat Lady Dairy
Climax, North Carolina
336-824-2163

OHIO
Brewster Dairy
Brewster, Ohio
330-767-3492
330-767-0151 (fax)

Caprine Estates (goat cheese)
Bellbrook, Ohio
937-848-7406
937-848-7437 (fax)
website: www.caprineestates.com

Miceli Dairy Products
Cleveland, Ohio
216-791-6222
216-231-2504 (fax)

Minerva Cheese Factory
Minerva, Ohio
330-868-4196
330-868-SWIS (7947) (fax)

OREGON
**Bandon Cheese
(cows' milk cheese)**
Bandon, Oregon
541-347-2456
541-347-2012 (fax)

**Covered Wagon Farm
(goat cheese)**
Sherwood, Oregon
503-628-2447 (phone and fax)

Juniper Grove Farm*
Redmond, Oregon
541-923-8353 (phone and fax) or
888-FROMAGE (376-6243)
website:
www.junipergrovefarm.com

**Rogue Valley Creamery
(blue cheese)**
Central Point, Oregon
541-664-2233
541-664-0952

**Tillamook County Creamery
Association**
Tillamook, Oregon
503-842-4481 or 800-542-7290
(mail order only)
503-815-1309 (fax)
website:
www.tillamookcheese.com

PENNSYLVANIA
**LeRaysville Cheese Factory
(cows' milk cheese)**
LeRaysville, Pennsylvania
570-744-2554
570-744-2192 (fax)

**Menhennett Farm
(sheep's milk cheese)**
Cochranville, Pennsylvania
610-593-5726

Woodchoppertown Chèvre
Boyertown, Pennsylvania
610-689-5498

TEXAS
**Cheesemakers, Inc. & Yellow
Rose Goat Dairy
(Mexican and goat cheeses)**
Cleveland, Texas
281-593-1319
281-593-2898 (fax)

Mozzarella Company*
Dallas, Texas
214-741-4072 or 800-798-2954
214-741-4076 (fax)
website: www.mozzco.com

**Pure Luck Grade A Goat Dairy
(farmstead)**
Dripping Springs, Texas
512-858-7034
website: www.purelucktexas.com

**Texas Jersey Cheese Company
(farmstead)**
Schulenburg, Texas
800-382-2880
409-743-5019 (fax)

**White Egret Farm
(goats' milk cheeses)**
Austin, Texas
512-276-7505
512-276-7489 (fax)
www.whiteegretfarm.com

VERMONT
Blythedale Farm, Inc.*
Corinth, Vermont
802-439-6575

Boucher Family Farm
Highgate Center, Vermont
802-868-4193
802-868-7395 (fax)

**Cabot Creamery
(cows' milk cheeses and butter)**
Cabot, Vermont
802-563-2231
802-563-2604 (fax)
website: www.cabotcheese.com

Crowley Cheese*
Healdville, Vermont
802-259-2340 or 800-683-2606
802-259-2347 (fax)
website: www.vtcheese.com/
   crowleystory.htm

**Franklin County Cheese
Corporation**
Burlington, Vermont
802-860-0215
802-933-2300 (fax)

**Grafton Village Cheese
Company***
Grafton, Vermont
802-843-2221 or 800-472-3866
802-843-2210 (fax)
website:
www.graftonvillagecheese.com

K.C.'s Kritters
Brattleboro, Vermont
802-257-4595

Kingsey Cheese of Vermont
Hardwick, Vermont
802-472-5763

Lazy Lady Farm (goat cheese)
Westfield, Vermont
802-744-6365

Major Farm/Vermont Shepherd*
Putney, Vermont
802-387-4473
802-387-2041 (fax)
website:
www.vermontshepherd.com

Orb Weaver Farm*
New Haven, Vermont
802-877-3755

The Organic Cow
Tunbridge, Vermont
802-685-3123
802-685-4332 (fax)

Rivendell Meadows Farm
Irasburg, Vermont
802-755-6349

The Seward Farmily
E. Wallingford, Vermont
802-259-2311

Shelburne Farms*
Shelburne, Vermont
802-985-8686
802-985-8123 (fax)

Skunk Hollow Farm*
Greensboro, Vermont
802-533-2360
802-533-9916 (fax)
website:
www.skunkhollowfarm.com

Sugarbush Farm
Woodstock, Vermont
802-457-1757 or 800-281-1757
802-457-3269 (fax)
website: www.sugarbushfarm.com

**Three Shepherds of the Mad
River Valley***
Warren, Vermont
802-496-3998
802-496-4096 (fax)

Vermont Butter & Cheese*
Websterville, Vermont
802-479-9371 or 800-884-6287
802-479-3674 (fax)
website:
www.vtbutterandcheeseco.com

Willow Hill Farm*
Milton, Vermont
802-893-2963
802-893-1954 (fax)
website: www.sheepcheese.com

VIRGINIA
Briar-Patch Goat Cheese
Disputanta, Virginia
804-991-2121 (phone and fax)
website:
www.geocities.com/napavalley/
   cellar/2493/benttree.html

**Everona Dairy (farmstead;
sheep's milk cheese)***
Rapidan, Virginia
540-854-4159
540-854-6443 (fax)

**Meadow Creek Dairy
(farmstead; cows' milk cheese)**
Galax, Virginia
540-236-4955
website: www.ls.net/~mcd

Monastery Country Cheese
Crozet, Virginia
804-823-1452

Mountain Hobby Cheeses
Willis, Virginia
540-789-4277

WASHINGTON
Quillisascut Cheese Company*
Rice, Washington
509-738-2011

Sally Jackson Cheeses*
Oroville, Washington
(no mail order; see Resources)

Washington State University Creamery*
Pullman, Washington
509-335-7516 or 800-457-5442
website: www.wsu.edu/creamery

White Oak Farm (goat cheese)
Battle Ground, Washington
360-576-7688
website: www.white-oak.com

WEST VIRGINIA
Brier Run Farm*
Birch River, West Virginia
304-649-2975

WISCONSIN
The Antigo Cheese Company*
Antigo, Wisconsin
715-623-2301 or 800-356-5655
715-623-4501 (fax)
website: www.antigocheese.com

Bass Lake Cheese Factory*
Somerset, Wisconsin
715-247-5586 or 800-368-2437
715-549-6617 (fax)
website: www.blcheese.com

BelGioioso Cheese*
Denmark, Wisconsin
920-863-2123 (no mail order)
920-863-8791 (fax)
website: www.belgioioso.com

Butler Farms*
Whitehall, Wisconsin
715-983-2285
715-983-2230 (fax)
website: members.xoom.com/
   butlerfarms/

Carr Valley Cheese*
LaValle, Wisconsin
800-462-7258
608-986-2906 (fax)

Cedar Grove Cheese
Plain, Wisconsin
608-546-5284
608-546-2805 (fax)

Chalet Cheese Co-op
Monroe, Wisconsin
608-325-4343
608-325-4409 (fax)

**Fantome Farm
(farmstead; goats' milk cheese)**
Ridgeway, Wisconsin
608-924-1266

Henning Cheese
Kiel, Wisconsin
920-894-3032

Klondike Cheese
Monroe, Wisconsin
608-325-3021
608-325-3027 (fax)

LoveTree Farm*
Grantsburg, Wisconsin
715-488-2966
715-488-3957 (fax)

Meister Cheese Company
Muscoda, Wisconsin
608-739-3134
website: www.meistercheese.com

Montchèvre (Betin Inc.)
Belmont, Wisconsin
608-943-6419

Mossholder Cheese*
Appleton, Wisconsin
920-734-7575
920-734-7696 (fax)

Organic Valley
LaFarge, Wisconsin
608-625-2602
608-625-2600 (fax)
website: www.organicvalley.com

Park Cheese
Fond du Lac, Wisconsin
414-923-8484 or 800-752-7275
414-923-8485

Prima Käse*
Monticello, Wisconsin
608-938-4227
608-938-1227 (fax)

Roth Käse*
Monroe, Wisconsin
608-328-3355 or 800-257-3355
608-329-7679 (fax)

Specialty Cheese Company
Lowell, Wisconsin
414-927-3888 or 800-367-1711
414-927-3200 (fax)

Widmer Cheese Factory
Theresa, Wisconsin
920-488-2503
920-488-2130 (fax)
website:
www.widmerscheese.com

RESOURCES
INFORMATION AND ORGANIZATIONS

American Cheese Society
P.O. Box 303
Delavan, WI 53115
262-728-4458
262-728-1658 (fax)
website: www.cheesesociety.org

The American Cheese Society is a non-profit organization dedicated to helping American cheesemakers by educating the public, government, and cheesemakers on all facets of farmstead and specialty cheese. For cheesemakers, it is a valuable resource for networking as well as for information about cheesemaking, including marketing. For the public, the American Cheese Society is a resource for cheese aficionados, retailers, restaurateurs and chefs, and others, to learn more about American farmstead and specialty cheese. In addition, the ACS represents cheesemakers on governmental issues that affect them. For example, the government's interest in banning the use of raw milk in cheesemaking affects many cheesemakers, and the ACS is serving as their collective voice on the issue.

American Dairy Association
10255 West Higgins Road
Rosemont, IL 60018
847-803-2000
website: www.ilovecheese.com

California Milk Advisory Board
400 Oyster Point Blvd., Suite 214
South San Francisco, CA 94080
650-871-6459
650-583-7328 (fax)
website: www.realcaliforniacheese.com

Cheeses of New England (New England Dairy Promotion Board)
376 Chandler Street
Worcester, MA 01602
508-755-6882
508-792-6042 (fax)
website: www.newenglandcheese.com

International Dairy Foods Association
National Cheese Institute
1250 H Street NW, Suite 900
Washington, DC 20005
202-296-2909

New England Cheesemaking Supply
P.O. Box 85
Ashfield, MA 01330
413-628-3808
413-628-4061 (fax)
website: www.cheesemaking.com

Slow Food Movement
Via della Mendicitá Istruita, 14
12042 Bra (cuneo)
Italy
877-756-9336
website: www.slowfood.com

The Slow Food Movement is designed to celebrate regional foods and small producers, including cheesemakers. It is also set up to keep these foods and their producers vibrant and to promote the enjoyment of food and flavors. It was founded in Italy, but so-called conviviums, or regional groups, exist throughout the country. The Slow Food Movement encourages people to start their own conviviums if they do not exist in their area.

Vermont Cheese Council
116 State Street
Montpelier, VT 05620-2901
1-888-523-7484
website: www.vtcheese.com

Wisconsin Milk Marketing Board
8418 Excelsior Drive
Madison, WI 53717
608-836-8820 or 800-373-9662
608-836-5822 (fax)

Wisconsin Specialty Cheese Institute
P.O. Box 1264
Madison, WI 53701
800-697-8861
website: www.wisspecialcheese.org

SELECTED CHEESE RETAILERS ACROSS THE COUNTRY

CALIFORNIA

Andronico's Market
510-524-2696
Locations throughout northern
    California
Mail order: No

Artisan Cheese Shop
2413 California Street
San Francisco, CA 94115
415-929-8610
415-929-8619 (fax)
Mail order: Yes

Bristol Farms
1570 Rosecrans Boulevard
Manhattan Beach, CA 90266
310-643-5229
website: www.bristolfarms.com
Locations throughout southern
    California
Mail order: No

The Cheese Board Co-Op
1504 Shattuck Avenue
Berkeley, CA 94709
510-549-3183
Mail order: No

Dean & Deluca
607 South St. Helena Highway
St. Helena, CA 94574
707-967-9980
website: www.dean-deluca.com
Mail order: Yes
(See New York listings for more
    on Dean & Deluca)

Full of Life
333 West Bonita Avenue
Claremont, CA 91711
909-624-3420
Mail order: Yes

Oakville Grocery
7856 St. Helena
Oakville, CA 94562
800-736-6602
website: www.oakvillegrocery.com
Locations throughout northern
    California
Mail order: Yes

Pasta Shop
5655 College Avenue
Oakland, CA 94618
510-547-4005
1 other location in Berkeley,
    California
Mail order: Some; call for details

Tomales Bay Foods
80 Fourth Street, PO Box 594
Point Reyes Station, CA 94956
415-663-9335
415-663-5418 (fax)
website:
www.cowgirlcreamery.com
Mail order: Yes (farmstead and
    artisanal cheeses only)

Wally's
2107 Westwood Boulevard
Los Angeles, CA 90025
310-475-0606
website: www.wallywine.com
Mail order: No

The Wine House
2311 Cotner Avenue
Los Angeles, CA 90064
1-800-626-WINE (9463)
website: www.winehouse.com
Mail order: No

COLORADO

**Wild Oats Corporate
    Headquarters**
3375 Mitchell Lane
Boulder, CO 80301
303-440-5220 or 800-494-WILD
website: www.wildoats.com
Several locations around the
    country; also operates under
    the names Alfalfa's and Nature's
    Northwest
Mail order: No

CONNECTICUT

Say Cheese! la grande pantrie
924 Hopmeadow Street
Simsbury, CT 06070
860-658-6742 or 888-243-3373
website: www.saycheese-lgp.com
Mail order: Yes

FLORIDA

Epicure Market
1656 Alton Road
Miami Beach, FL 33139
305-672-1861 or 800-232-3218
Mail order: Yes

ILLINOIS

**Dominick's Finer Foods &
    Dominick's Fresh Stores**
708-492-5443
website: www.dominicks.com
Locations throughout Illinois;
    1 location in Indiana
Mail order: No

LOUISIANA

Spice, Inc.
1051 Annunciation Street
New Orleans, LA 70130
504-558-9992
website: www.spiceinc.com
Mail order: Yes

MARYLAND

Sutton Place Gourmet
6903 Rockledge Drive, #900
Bethesda, MD 20817
301-564-6006 or 800-346-7863
website: www.suttongourmet.com
Other locations include Balducci's
    in New York and Hayday
    Country Farm Markets in New
    York and Connecticut
Mail order: Yes

MASSACHUSETTS

Formaggio Kitchen, Inc.
244 Huron Avenue
Cambridge, MA 02138
617-354-4750 or 888-212-3224
617-547-5680 (fax)
Mail order: Yes

**Wasik's
The Cheese Shop**
61 Central Street
Wellesley, MA 02482
781-237-0916
Mail order: Yes

MICHIGAN
Zingerman's
422 Detroit Street
Ann Arbor, MI 48104
734-663-3354 or 888-636-8162
734-930-1942 (fax)
website: www.zingermans.com
Mail order: Yes

Holiday Market
1203 So. Main Street
Royal Oak, MI 48067
248-541-1414
Mail order: No

MINNESOTA
Byerly's and Lunds stores:

Byerly's
3777 Park Center Blvd.
St. Louis Park, MI 55416

Lunds Uptown
1450 West Lake Street
Minneapolis, MI 55408
612-825-2440

website: www.byerlys.com
Locations throughout Minnesota
Mail order: Limited; call for
 details

MISSOURI
The Cheese Place
7435 Forsyth Boulevard
St. Louis, MO 63105
314-727-8878
2 other locations in St. Louis
Mail order: Some; call for details

NEW JERSEY
Madison Shoppers
121 Main Street
Madison, NJ 07940
973-822-0200
website: www.shopperswine.com
1 other location in Madison
Mail order: No

NEW YORK
Balducci's
Mail order:
Shop From Home
95 Sherwood Ave.
Farmingdale, NY 11735
516-843-0383
800-BALDUCCI
www.balducci.com

Store:
424 Avenue of the Americas
New York, NY 10011
212-673-2600

Dean & Deluca
Mail order:
800-221-7714
2526 East 36th North Circle
Wichita, KS 67219
website: www.dean-deluca.com
Other locations throughout U.S.
Main store:
560 Broadway
New York, NY 10012
212-226-6800 or 800-999-0306

Fairway
2127 Broadway
New York, NY 10023
212-595-1794
1 other location in New York
Mail order: No

Ideal Cheese Shop
1205 Second Avenue
New York, NY 10021
212-688-7579 or 800-382-0109
212-223-1245 (fax)
website: www.idealcheese.com
Mail order: Yes

Murray's Cheese Shop
257 Bleeker Street
New York, NY 10014
212-243-5001 or 888-692-4339
Mail order: Yes

Zabar's
2245 Broadway
New York, NY 10024
212-787-2000 or 800-697-6301
212-580-4477 (fax)
Mail order: Yes

NORTH CAROLINA
Dean & Deluca
6903 Phillips Place Court
Charlotte, NC 28210
704-643-6868
website: www.dean-deluca.com
Mail order: Yes
(See New York listings for more
 on Dean & Deluca)

Fowler's
112 South Duke Street
Durham, NC 27701
919-683-2555 or 800-722-8403
website:
 www.fowlersfoodandwine.com
Mail order: Yes

OHIO
Dorothy Lane Market
6177 Far Hills Avenue
Dayton, OH 45459
937-434-1294
1 other location in Dayton
website:
 www.dorothylane.com/ordering
Mail order: Some; call for details

West Point Market
1711 West Market Street
Akron, OH 44313
330-864-2151
website:
 www.westpointmarket.com
Mail order: Yes

PENNSYLVANIA
DiBruno Brothers
930 S. Ninth Street
Philadelphia, PA 19147
215-922-2876 or 888-DBCHEESE
website: www.dibruno.com
Mail order: Yes

TENNESSEE
Corner Market
6051 Highway 100
Nashville, TN 37205
615-352-6772
website: www.cornermkt.com
Mail order: No

TEXAS
Central Market
4001 North Lamar Boulevard
Austin, TX 78756
512-206-1000 or 800-360-2552
1 other location in Austin and 1 in
 San Antonio
website: www.centralmarket.com
Mail order: Some; call for details

**Whole Foods Market (extensive
 cheese program)**
Corporate Headquarters
601 North Lamar Boulevard
Austin, TX 78703
512-477-4455 or 888-945-3637
Nearly 100 locations throughout
 the U.S.
Depending on location, also oper-
 ates under the names Fresh
 Fields, Bread and Circus,
 Nature's Heartland, Bread of
 Life, Merchant of Vino, and
 Wellspring Grocery
website: www.wholefoods.com
Mail order: Some; call for details

UTAH
Liberty Heights Fresh
1100 East and 1300 South
Salt Lake City, UT 84105
801-467-2434
Website:
www.libertyheightsfresh.com
Mail order: Yes

VERMONT
Cheese Outlet/Fresh Market
400 Pine Street
Burlington, VT 05401
802-863-3968 or 800-447-1205
website: www.cheeseoutlet.com
Mail order: Yes

Cheese Traders
1186 Williston Road
South Burlington, VT 05403
802-863-0143 or 800-540-4261
Mail order: Yes

VIRGINIA
The Cheese Shop
424 Prince George Street
Williamsburg, VA 23185
757-220-0298 or 800-468-4049
757-564-3927 (fax)
Mail order: Yes

WASHINGTON
Brie & Bordeaux
2227 N. 56th Street
Seattle, WA 98103

206-633-3538
206-633-1742 (fax)
Mail order: No

Larry's Markets
10008 Aurora Avenue North
Seattle, WA 98133
206-527-5333
206-244-9663 (fax)
5 other locations
Mail order: Some; call for details

DeLaurenti
1435 First Avenue
Seattle, WA 98101
206-622-0141
Mail order: Yes

BIBLIOGRAPHY

Apps, Jerry. *Cheese: The Making of a Wisconsin Tradition*. Amherst, Wisconsin: Amherst Press, 1998.

Bodyfelt, F. W., J. Tobias, and G. M. Trout. *The Sensory Evaluation of Dairy Products*. New York: Van Nostrand & Reinhold, 1988.

Brown, Bob. *The Complete Book of Cheese*. New York: Gramercy Publishing Company, 1955.

Cheese Grading, Packaging and Labeling, Chapter ATCP 81. Madison, Wisconsin: Wisconsin Department of Agriculture, Trade, and Consumer Protection. January, 1996.

Corriher, Shirley O. Cookwise: *The Hows and Whys of Successful Cooking*. New York: William Morrow & Company, 1997.

Duyff, Roberta Larson, MS, RD, CFCS. *The American Dietetic Association's Complete Food & Nutrition Guide*. Minneapolis: Chronimed Publishing, 1996.

Farmer, Fannie Merritt. *The Boston Cooking-School Cook Book*. 6th ed. Boston: Little, Brown and Company, 1937.

Haskell, Patricia, and Vivienne Marquis. *The Cheese Book: A Definitive Guide to the Cheeses of the World*. New York: Simon & Schuster, 1965.

Jenkins, Steven. *Cheese Primer*. New York: Workman Publishing Company, 1996.

Kosikowski, Frank V., and Vikram V. Mistry. *Cheese and Fermented Milk Foods. Volume I, Origins and Principles*. 3rd ed. Great Falls,Virginia: F. V. Kosikowski, L.L.C., 1999.

Madison, Deborah. *Vegetarian Cooking for Everyone*. New York: Broadway Books, 1997.

Masui, Kazuko, and Tomoko Yamada. *French Cheeses*. New York: DK Publishing, 1996.

McGee, Harold. *On Food and Cooking: The Science and Lore of the Kitchen*. New York: Fireside, Simon & Schuster, 1997.

Pearl, Anita May, Constance Cuttle, and Barbara B. Deskins. *Completely Cheese*. Middle Village, New York: Warner Books, 1978.

Stamm, Eunice R. *The History of Cheese Making in New York State*. New York: The Lewis Group Ltd., 1991.

METRIC CONVERSION CHART

WEIGHT EQUIVALENTS

The metric weights given in this chart are not exact equivalents, but have been rounded up or down slightly to make measuring easier.

Avoirdupois	Metric
¼ oz	7 g
½ oz	15 g
1 oz	30 g
2 oz	60 g
3 oz	90 g
4 oz	115 g
5 oz	150 g
6 oz	175 g
7 oz	200 g
8 oz (½ lb)	225 g
9 oz	250 g
10 oz	300 g
11 oz	325 g
12 oz	350 g
13 oz	375 g
14 oz	400 g
15 oz	425 g
16 oz (1 lb)	450 g
1½ lb	750 g
2 lb	900 g
2¼ lb	1 kg
3 lb	1.4 kg
4 lb	1.8 kg

VOLUME EQUIVALENTS

These are not exact equivalents for American cups and spoons, but have been rounded up or down slightly to make measuring easier.

American	Metric	Imperial
¼ t	1.2 ml	
½ t	2.5 ml	
1 t	5.0 ml	
½ T (1.5 t)	7.5 ml	
1 T (3 t)	15 ml	
¼ cup (4 T)	60 ml	2 fl oz
⅓ cup (5 T)	75 ml	2½ fl oz
½ cup (8 T)	125 ml	4 fl oz
⅔ cup (10 T)	150 ml	5 fl oz
¾ cup (12 T)	175 ml	6 fl oz
1 cup (16 T)	250 ml	8 fl oz
1¼ cups	300 ml	10 fl oz (½ pt)
1½ cups	350 ml	12 fl oz
2 cups (1 pint)	500 ml	16 fl oz
2½ cups	625 ml	20 fl oz (1 pint)
1 quart	1 liter	32 fl oz

OVEN TEMPERATURE EQUIVALENTS

Oven Mark	F	C	Gas
Very cool	250-275	130-140	½-1
Cool	300	150	2
Warm	325	170	3
Moderate	350	180	4
Moderately hot	375	190	5
	400	200	6
Hot	425	220	7
	450	230	8
Very hot	475	250	9

INDEX

(Page numbers in italic denote photographs.)

⊳⊣⊷⊶O⊷⊶⊢⊲

The text of this book is composed in Cheltenham

Printed and bound in Italy by Arnoldo Mondadori Editore SpA

⊳⊣⊷⊶O⊷⊶⊢⊲